QUESTIONS & ANSWERS:
Wills, Trusts & Estates

**Multiple Choice and Short Answer
Questions and Answers**

By

Thomas M. Featherston, Jr.
Mills Cox Professor of Law
Baylor University Law School

LexisNexis™

ISBN #: 0820556726

Editorial Offices
744 Broad Street, Newark, NJ 07102 (973) 820-2000
201 Mission St., San Francisco, CA 94105-1831 (415) 908-3200
701 East Water Street, Charlottesville, VA 22902-7587 (804) 972-7600

(Pub.3186)

DEDICATION

To my wife, Sherry, and daughters, Amy and Carrie.

ABOUT THE AUTHOR

Thomas M. Featherston, Jr. is the Mills Cox Professor of Law at Baylor Law School in Waco, Texas. He earned his J.D. with highest honors from Baylor Law School in 1972. After graduation, he entered private practice in Houston from 1972 through 1982. He is Board Certified in Estate Planning and Probate Law by the Texas Board of Legal Specialization (originally certified in 1979). Professor Featherston joined the Baylor Law School faculty in 1982, and in 1990, he was appointed to the Mills Cox Chair.

Professor Featherston was elected as an Academic Fellow of the American College of Trust and Estate Counsel in 1991 and a Fellow of the American Bar Foundation in 1993. He is active in both the State Bar of Texas and the American Bar Association, having previously served as past chair of the Real Estate, Probate, and Trust Law Section of the State Bar of Texas and currently serving on the governing council of the Real Estate, Probate, and Trust Law Section of the American Bar Association. He is also the Trusts and Estates Editor for Probate and Property, an ABA publication, and a co-author of *West's Texas Practice Guide - Probate* and *Drafting for Tax and Administration Issues*, an ABA publication.

Professor Featherston is a frequent author and lecturer in the areas of trusts, estates, marital property, fiduciary administration, and other related topics, the subjects that he teaches at Baylor Law School.

PREFACE

The law governing Wills, Trusts, and Estates in the United States finds its origins primarily in the common law of England. Today, it is increasingly based on statutory law. It is also largely "state law" oriented. Each state has its own set of rules, procedures, statutes, and case law. While there are many common denominators, the law can, and frequently will, differ from state to state. Some of these differences are significant.

To address this reality, most of the problems in this book are to be solved using the law of the hypothetical state of X. It is assumed that X has adopted both the Uniform Probate Code (1990, with 1993, 1997, and 2002 amendments) and the Uniform Trust Code (2000, with 2001 amendments). Throughout the book, the Uniform Probate Code and the Uniform Trust Code are abbreviated "UPC" and "UTC," respectively. Occasionally, some questions will instruct the student to assume that a particular provision of one of the uniform acts is not part of the law of X or that another relevant statute is to be interpreted a certain way.

If neither the Uniform Probate Code nor the Uniform Trust Code provides the answer, it is assumed that X's courts have adopted a generally accepted principle of the law of Wills, Trusts, and Estates. These generally-accepted principles may be the positions taken in a relevant Restatement of the Law published by the American Law Institute or explained in a recognized hornbook or treatise written by a leading authority such as Thomas E. Atkinson, George T. Bogert, William M. McGovern, Jr., or Sheldon F. Kurtz.

Also, in recognition of the differences in states' laws, most answers will also explain how the result may differ in a state that does not follow the position taken by the Uniform Probate Code, the Uniform Trust Code, or the "majority" case law rule. Regardless of the state law that the student has learned in class, the key issues are explained, and it is hoped that the relevant answer is made clear for each question.

A primary purpose of this book is to test the student's understanding of this area of the law. This book supplements the student's casebook and includes questions and answers in twelve main subject areas that correspond to basic topics covered in a typical Wills, Trusts, and Estates course. Unfortunately, space does not allow for the coverage of every topic. For example, the administration of trusts and estates is not addressed as its own topic. However, administration issues are interspersed throughout the entire book.

When answering most questions, it is suggested that the student (i) identify the type of disposition in question (testamentary, inter vivos, nonprobate, etc.); (ii) identify the parties involved (transferor, transferees, creditors, assignees, etc.); (iii) determine the effective date of the disposition (date of delivery, date of death, date of possession, etc.); (iv) understand the issue presented (who gets what, when, and how); and (v) apply to the facts the appropriate substantive principle (the relevant statute or case law precedent).

The author wishes to express appreciation for the patience and understanding of the author's wife, Sherry, and the invaluable assistance and hard work of Jami Symank and two Baylor Law students, Cheryl Slack and Erin Huber.

Professor Thomas M. Featherston, Jr.
Baylor Law School
Waco, Texas
November 2003

TABLE OF CONTENTS

Page

QUESTIONS

1. O, an unmarried resident of the state of X, died recently in X. O was survived by several members of O's family residing in several different states. Immediately prior to O's death, O owned fee simple title to various items of tangible personal property (such as household furnishings, jewelry, clothing, and other personal effects, all located in a rented apartment in the state of X), an automobile registered and located in the state of X, a checking account at a local branch of a national bank, shares of stock in a corporation incorporated in the state of Y, and other items of tangible personal property located in O's parents' house in the state of Z.

    Which answer best describes the law to apply in determining the proper succession to the described assets?

    (A) Federal law will determine who succeeds to the ownership of the described personal property.

    (B) The law of X determines the succession to the tangible personal property located in X; federal law determines the succession of the bank account; the law of Y governs the succession of the shares of stock; and the law of Z governs the succession of the tangible personal property located in Z.

    (C) The law of X governs not only the succession of the tangible personal property located in X but also the checking account; the law of Y will govern the succession of the shares of stock; and the law of Z will govern the succession of the tangible personal property located in that state.

    (D) The law of X will determine who succeeds to the ownership of the described personal property.

2. Refer to Question 1 and assume O owned the fee simple title to three tracts of lands, one tract located in each of the states of X, Y, and Z.

    Which answer best describes the law that will govern the proper succession to the tracts of land?

    (A) The law of X governs the succession of all three tracts.

    (B) The law of X governs the succession of the land in X; the law of Y will govern the succession of the land in Y; and the law of Z will govern the succession of the land in Z.

(C) Federal law governs the succession of the three tracts to the extent of any inconsistencies existing among the laws of X, Y, and Z.

(D) Federal law governs the succession of all three tracts of land because O and the heirs resided in different states.

3. O, an unmarried resident of the state of X, died while vacationing in the state of Y. In addition to the tangible personal property in O's physical possession at the time of O's death, O owned real and personal property located in the state of X, but O's more valuable assets were real and personal property located in the state of Z. O was survived by several members of O's family who all reside in the state of X.

Which answer best describes which states' courts have subject matter jurisdiction over the decedent's property?

(A) X has exclusive jurisdiction over the assets within its boundaries; Y has exclusive jurisdiction over the assets within its boundaries; and Z has exclusive jurisdiction over the assets within its boundaries.

(B) X and Z have exclusive jurisdiction over the real property located within their respective boundaries, but X has exclusive jurisdiction over all personal property wherever located.

(C) Each state has jurisdiction over the assets located within its boundaries, but X also has jurisdiction over the personal property located in Y and Z.

(D) Each state has jurisdiction over the assets located within its boundaries, but X also has jurisdiction over all assets located in Y and Z.

4. Refer to Question 3. Which answer best describes which states' laws a court should apply in determining whether the decedent died testate or intestate?

(A) The law of X.

(B) X's law for the property located in X; Y's law for the property located in Y; and Z's law for the property located in Z.

(C) The law of X for all the assets except for the real property located in Z.

(D) The law of X for all the assets except for the real and personal property located in Z.

5. Refer to Question 3 and assume the amount of property (and/or its value) in each state justifies the trouble and expense of a formal administration. Describe the states where formal administration of the decedent's estate would be proper.

ANSWER:

6. O, an unmarried resident of the state of X, died recently. Immediately prior to O's death, O owned fee simple title to real and personal property located in the state of X. In addition to those assets, O owned a life estate in Blackacre, a tract of land located in X; A owned the remainder interest. O also owned a remainder interest in Whiteacre, another tract of land located in X; B owned the life estate. A and B are not related to O, and both A and B survived O. O died intestate, and, as O's sole heir at law, C inherits O's entire probate estate.

    Which answer best describes the interests, if any, C is likely to acquire in Blackacre and Whiteacre?

    (A) C inherits fee simple title to Blackacre but acquires no interest in Whiteacre.

    (B) C inherits the remainder interest in Whiteacre but acquires no interest in Blackacre.

    (C) C acquires a life estate in Blackacre and the remainder interest in Whiteacre.

    (D) C acquires no interest in either Blackacre or Whiteacre.

7. Refer to Question 6, but assume that both A and B died intestate shortly before O.

    Which answer best describes the interest, if any, C is most likely to acquire in Whiteacre and Blackacre?

    (A) C inherits the fee simple title to both tracts.

    (B) C inherits the fee simple title to Blackacre but acquires no interest in Whiteacre.

    (C) C inherits the fee simple title to Whiteacre but acquires no interest in Blackacre.

    (D) C inherits no interest in either Whiteacre or Blackacre.

8. Refer to Question 6 and assume O also owned (i) a savings account entitled "O payable on O's death to D" and (ii) an insurance policy on O's life payable at O's death to E. Both D and E survived O.

    What interest, if any, is C most likely to acquire in the savings account and the life insurance policy?

ANSWER:

9. Refer to Question 8, but assume that D and E died shortly before O. D and E were not related to O.

Which answer best describes the interest, if any, C is most likely to acquire in the savings account and the life insurance policy?

(A) C inherits ownership of the account, the policy, and its proceeds.

(B) C inherits ownership of the account but no interest in the policy or its proceeds.

(C) C inherits ownership of the policy and its proceeds but no interest in the account.

(D) C inherits no interest in the policy, its proceeds, or the account.

10. Refer to Questions 6 and 8. How would your answers differ if O had died with a valid will that had been admitted to probate leaving "all my property" to F?

(A) My answers would not change.

(B) F inherits the remainder interest in Whiteacre but acquires no interest in Blackacre, the account, or the policy.

(C) F inherits the account but acquires no interest in Blackacre, Whiteacre, or the policy.

(D) F inherits the proceeds of the policy but acquires no interest in Whiteacre, Blackacre, or the account.

11. Refer to Questions 7 and 9. How would your answers differ if O had died with a valid will that had been admitted to probate leaving "all my property" to F?

(A) My answers would not change.

(B) F inherits Whiteacre but acquires no interest in Blackacre, the account, or the policy.

(C) F inherits Whiteacre, the account, and the policy but no interest in Blackacre.

(D) F inherits the account and the policy but acquires no interest in Whiteacre or Blackacre.

12. H and W were married for over 10 years. Both H and W were residents of the state of X. During the marriage, H acquired real and personal property located in X; all assets were titled in H's name. H recently died. H's valid will has been admitted to probate, and the will leaves all of H's property to C, H's adult child by a prior marriage. C is an independent adult residing in the state of Y.

Assuming all debts and taxes have been satisfied, describe W's interest in each of the described assets.

ANSWER:

Note: _Except where specifically indicated, answer the remaining questions ignoring a surviving spouse's homestead, exempt property, and family allowance rights and assuming X is a non-community property state that has abolished the common law concepts of dower and curtesy._

13. Refer to Question 12 and assume that, at the time of death, H was a participant in a pension plan provided by H's employer. H's employer also provided each employee with a group life insurance policy as part of its employee benefit package. The employer's records indicate that H had not signed the appropriate forms necessary to designate the beneficiaries of the plan and policy in the event of H's death. Which answer best describes the most likely disposition of the death benefits payable by reason of the pension plan and life insurance policy?

    (A) The death benefits pass as part of the probate estate.

    (B) The death benefits pass nonprobate to W.

    (C) The insurance proceeds pass as part of the probate estate, and the plan benefits pass nonprobate to W.

    (D) The plan benefits pass as part of the probate estate, and the insurance proceeds pass nonprobate to W.

14. Refer to Question 12, but assume H's will leaves Greenacre to W and the "rest, residue, and remainder of my property" to C.

    Assuming all debts and taxes have been satisfied, which answer best describes the most likely disposition of the described assets?

    (A) Greenacre passes to W, and the remaining assets pass to C.

    (B) Greenacre passes to W, and the remaining assets are shared equally by W and C.

    (C) Greenacre passes to W, and the remaining assets pass 30% to W and 70% to C.

    (D) The value of Greenacre is deducted from W's share of O's estate.

15. Refer to Question 12, but assume H's will leaves all of H's property to W. Assuming all debts have been satisfied, which answer best describes the interest of W in the described assets?

    (A) W succeeds to the entire estate.

    (B) C is entitled to an intestate share of the estate, and W owns the balance.

    (C) An amount necessary for C's support during formal administration may be set aside for C, and W owns the balance.

    (D) An amount necessary for C's support for the remainder of C's lifetime is set aside for C, and W owns the balance, if any.

16. Refer to Question 15, but assume that C is a minor at the time of O's death.

    Assuming all debts and taxes have been satisfied, what is the most likely disposition of the described assets?

ANSWER:

17. Refer to Question 12, but assume H's will leaves Greenacre to C and the "rest, residue, and remainder of my property" to W. Assuming all debts and taxes have been satisfied, which answer best describes the most likely disposition of the described assets?

   (A) Greenacre passes to C, and W owns to the balance.

   (B) Greenacre is shared equally by C and W, and W owns to the balance.

   (C) W must elect to take either her elective share or only what is devised to her in the will.

   (D) C must elect to take C's intestate share or Greenacre.

18. H and W were married and have always resided in the state of X. H died recently. During the marriage, H acquired real and personal property located in X; all assets were titled in H's name. H's original will left all of H's property equally to W and C, H's adult child by prior marriage. However, H revoked the described will shortly before H died and then validly executed a new will leaving "all of my property" to P, H's girlfriend. Assuming all debts and taxes have been satisfied, which answer best describes the most likely disposition of the described assets?

   (A) P succeeds to the assets.

   (B) W takes her elective share, C takes an intestate share, and P inherits the balance.

   (C) W takes her elective share, and P inherits the balance.

   (D) C takes an intestate share, and P inherits the balance.

19. H and W were divorced last year after 10 years of marriage. Both H and W resided in the state of X. H died intestate recently and was survived by H's parents, M and F. Two of the more significant assets existing at the time of H's death were two savings accounts. The first account's signature card at the bank indicates that it is a "joint account with survivorship rights" in the names of H and W. The second account's signature card indicates the account is "payable on death" to W. Apparently, H forgot to change the deposit agreements with the bank after the bitter divorce because H was awarded ownership of both accounts as part of the divorce settlement and did not have an obligation to leave W's name on the accounts. Which answer best describes the most likely disposition of the accounts?

   (A) Both accounts pass nonprobate to W

   (B) The joint account passes to M and F, and the POD account passes nonprobate to W.

   (C) The POD account passes to M and F, and the joint account passes nonprobate to W.

   (D) Both accounts pass to M and F.

20. Refer to Question 19 and assume that there were also an insurance policy on O's life and a pension plan provided by H's employer. The policy was owned by H and still made payable at H's death to W. The death benefit of the pension plan was also still payable to W. Apparently, H forgot to change the beneficiary designations after the bitter divorce because H was awarded the policy and plan as part of the divorce settlement and was not obligated to designate W as the beneficiary of either the policy or plan. What is the most likely disposition of the death benefits?

ANSWER:

21. O, an unmarried resident in the state of X, died recently without a will. O had four children born of O's only marriage, which ended in divorce. The children were C1, C2, C3, and C4. C2 was married to S2, and they had one child, G2; C3 was married to S3, and they had one child, G3; and C4 was married to S4, and they had one child, G4. C1 died one day prior to O; C2 died at the same time as O; C3 died one day after O; and C4 died one week after O. Each child had a valid, probated will leaving his or her property to his or her spouse. O and C2 acquired Whiteacre at a time when neither O nor C2 was married. Whiteacre had been devised to O and C2 years ago in the will of O's father, which does not indicate whether O and C2 acquired title as "joint tenants" or as "tenants in common." Who is most likely to succeed to the ownership of Whiteacre by reason of the deaths of both O and C2?

     (A) S2.

     (B) G2, G3, and S4.

     (C) One-half to S2 and one-half to G2, G3, and S4.

     (D) One-half to G2 and one-half to G2, G3, and S4.

22. Refer to Question 21 and assume that O's father had also specifically devised Brownacre to O for life, remainder to C2. The residuary estate of O's father was devised in the will to a charity. Which answer best describes who is most likely to succeed to the ownership of Brownacre by reason of the deaths of both O and C2?

     (A) S2.

     (B) G2.

     (C) G2, G3, and S4.

     (D) The charity.

23.   Refer to Question 22, but assume that O's father specifically devised Brownacre to O provided that, if O died without leaving children, Brownacre passes to the charity.

Which answer best describes who is most likely to succeed to Brownacre by reason of the deaths of O and his children?

(A) The charity.

(B) S2, S3, and S4.

(C) G2, G3, and S4.

(D) G2, G3, and G4.

24.   Refer to Question 23. How would your answer differ if all of O's children had died before O.

ANSWER:

25.   O, an unmarried resident of the state of X, died recently. O did not have any children or siblings. O was survived by O's now divorced parents, H and W. H is currently married to W2, and W is currently married to H2. Additionally, the parents of H, W, W2, and H2, as well as siblings of H, W, W2, and H2, plus a number of descendants of those siblings, survived O. O executed a will just prior to O's death that leaves all of O's property to F, a friend. F has filed the will for probate.

Which answer best describes the members of O's family that have standing to contest the will?

(A) H, W, W2, and H2, their parents, and the descendants of their parents.

(B) H, W, their parents, and the descendants of their parents.

(C) H, W, and their parents.

(D) H and W.

26.   O, an unmarried resident of the state of X, died recently. O did not have any children and was survived by O's divorced parents, H and W, as well as S1 and S2, two other children born to H and W, and two other siblings, S3, who is H's child from a prior marriage, and S4, who is W's child from a subsequent marriage to H2. O executed a will that leaves all of O's property to F, a friend. F has filed the will for probate.

Which answer best describes the members of O's family that have standing to contest the will?

(A) S1, S2, S3, and S4, as well as H and W.

(B) S1 and S2, as well as H and W.

(C) H and W.

(D) H or W, depending on who was awarded custody of O at the time of the divorce.

27.   Refer to Question 26. How would your answer differ if, following the divorce of O's parents, O had been adopted by W's second husband, H2, who did not adopt S1 and S2?

(A) My answer would not change.

(B) Only W would have standing.

(C) H, W, and H2 would have standing.

(D) W and H2 would have standing.

28. Refer to Question 27, but assume (i) H died intestate before O and (ii) H never remarried. Which answer best describes the identity of H's heirs?

(A) O, S1, S2, and S3.

(B) O, S1, and S2.

(C) S1, S2, and S3.

(D) S1 and S2.

29. Refer to Question 27, but assume (i) H2 had two children from a prior marriage, S5 and S6, and (ii) H2 died intestate before O. Which children are heirs of H2?

ANSWER:

30. Refer to Question 29 and assume S5 died intestate after H2's death but before O's death. Which answer best describes which siblings of S5 are heirs of S5?

(A) S6.

(B) S6, S4, and O.

(C) S6 and S4.

(D) None of the siblings are heirs.

31. O, an unmarried resident of the state of X, died recently. O did not have any children. O's divorced parents, H and W, did not survive O. O was survived by one sibling, S1, who was also born to H and W. O was also survived by two other siblings: S2, who is H's child from a prior marriage, and S3, who is W's child from a subsequent marriage following H's death. W's second husband, H2, had a child from a prior marriage, S4. O executed a will that leaves all of O's property to F, a friend. F has filed the will for probate. Which answer best describes the members of O's family that have standing to contest the will?

(A) S1, S2, S3, and S4.

(B) S1, S2, and S3.

(C) S1 and S2.

(D) S1.

32. O, an unmarried resident of the state of X, died recently. O was not survived by O's parents. O was survived by a sibling, S. Additionally, O was also survived by a child from O's first marriage, C1; another child born to O during O's second marriage; C2; and a child born to O's second spouse during a prior marriage of that spouse, C3. C1, C2, and C3 are minors. O executed a will that leaves all of O's property to F, a friend. F has filed the will for probate.

Which answer best describes the members of O's family that have standing to contest the will?

(A) S, C1, C2, and C3.

(B) S, C1, and C2.

(C) C1, C2, and C3.

(D) C1 and C2.

33. Refer to Question 32. How would your answer differ if, in addition to C1 and C2, O had fathered a child born out of wedlock prior to even meeting O's first wife? This child is C4, who is now an adult.

ANSWER:

34. O, an unmarried resident in the state of X, died recently without a will. O had four children born during O's two marriages, both of which ended in divorce while all four children were minors. The first spouse was awarded custody of the two older children. The second spouse was awarded custody of the two younger children. The children were C1, C2, C3, and C4. C1 died one day prior to O; C2 died at the same time as O; C3 died one day after O; and C4 died one week after O. The children never married and did not have any children of their own.

Which answer best describes the identity of O's heirs?

(A) C1, C2, C3, and C4.

(B) C2, C3, and C4.

(C) C3 and C4.

(D) C4.

35.   Refer to Question 34, but assume that C2 was married to S2, and they had one child, G2; C3 was married to S3, and they had one child, G3; and C4 was married to S4, and they had one child, G4. Each of C2, C3, and C4 had a valid, probated will leaving his or her property to his or her spouse. Following the payment of all debts and taxes, which answer best describes those who will actually take possession of O's estate following formal administration?

(A) S2, S3, and S4, equally.

(B) G2, S3, and S4, equally.

(C) G2, G3, and S4, equally.

(D) G2, G3, and G4, equally.

36.   Refer to Question 35. How would your answer differ if C2's wife was pregnant at the time of the deaths of both O and C2? This child, G5, was born six months after O's death. In addition, before O's death, C3 had adopted G6, a child of S3 by a prior marriage.

(A) G5 would share equally with G2 one-third of the estate, but G6 is excluded.

(B) G6 would share equally with G3 one-third of the estate, but G5 is excluded.

(C) G5 would share equally with G2 one-third of the estate, and G6 would share equally with G3 one-third of the estate.

(D) G5 would share equally with G2 one-third of the estate, and G6 would share with G3 one-third of the estate, but G3 would receive twice as much of that one-third as G6.

37.   Refer to Question 36 but assume that C1, C2, C3, and C4 all died before O. Who will take possession of O's estate following formal administration?
ANSWER:

38.   Refer to Question 37, but assume that G4 also died before O, and G4 was survived by G4's child, GG. Which answer best describes who will take possession of O's estate following formal administration?

(A) O's estate would be distributed equally to G2, G5, G3, and G6.

(B) O's estate would be distributed 4/9 to G2 and G5; 4/9 to G3 and G6; and 1/9 to GG.

(C) O's estate would be distributed 1/3 to G2 and G5; 1/3 to G3 and G6; and 1/3 to GG.

(D) O's estate would be distributed 1/5 to each of G2, G5, G3, G6 and GG.

39.   O, an unmarried resident of X, died recently. O's only living relatives at the time of O's death were A, the first cousin of O's mother, and B, a child of a great uncle of O's father. Which answer best describes the identity of O's heirs at law?

   (A) A and B.

   (B) A.

   (C) B.

   (D) State of X.

40.   Refer to Question 39 and assume that, in addition to A and B, O was survived by C, the child of O's deceased first cousin. Which answer best describes who succeeds to O's probate estate?

   (A) State of X.

   (B) State of X and C.

   (C) C.

   (D) B and C.

41.   Refer to Question 39. How would your answer differ if C were a citizen of a foreign country residing in that country?

ANSWER:

42. O, an unmarried resident in the state of X, died recently without a will. O had two children born of O's only marriage, which ended when O's spouse died years ago. The children are C1 and C2, and they both survived until the termination of the formal administration of O's estate. The children have never married and do not have any children. Prior to O's death, O conveyed Blackacre to C2. What effect does the conveyance have on C2's share of O's probate estate?

ANSWER:

43. O, an unmarried resident in the state of X, died recently without a will. O had four children born of O's only marriage, which ended when O's spouse died years ago. The children were C1, C2, C3, and C4. C1 died one day prior to O; C2 died at the same time as O; C3 died one day after O; and C4 died one week after O. The children never married, and they did not have any children of their own. Which answer best describes the identity of O's heirs?

(A) C1, C2, C3, and C4.

(B) C2, C3, and C4.

(C) C3 and C4.

(D) C4.

44. Refer to Question 43, but assume that C2 was married to S2, and they had one child, G2; C3 was married to S3, and they had one child, G3; and C4 was married to S4, and they had one child, G4. Each child had a valid, probated will leaving his or her property to his or her spouse. Following the payment of all debts and taxes, which answer best describes those who will actually take possession of O's estate following formal administration?

(A) S2, S3, and S4, equally.

(B) G2, S3, and S4, equally.

(C) G2, G3, and S4, equally.

(D) G2, G3, and G4, equally.

45.   Refer to Question 44 and assume that, prior to O's death, O had conveyed Blackacre to C4. Which answer best describes the effect the conveyance would have on S4's share in O's probate estate?

   (A) S4's share of the estate would not be affected.

   (B) S4's share of the estate would be reduced by the value of Blackacre.

   (C) S4 would be barred from sharing in the estate.

   (D) S4 would have to reimburse O's estate for two-thirds of the value of Blackacre.

46.   Refer to Question 44 and assume that, prior to the death of O, O had conveyed Blackacre to G4. Which answer best describes who succeeds to O's estate after the completion of formal administration?

   (A) S2, S3, and S4, equally.

   (B) G2, S3, and S4, equally.

   (C) G2, G3, and S4, equally.

   (D) G2, G3, and G4, equally.

47.   Refer to Question 45 but assume that C4 died before O. Which answer best describes the effect the conveyance will have on G4's share of the estate?

   (A) G4's interest in the estate would not be affected.

   (B) G4's share of the estate would be reduced by the value of Blackacre.

   (C) G4 would be barred from sharing in the estate.

   (D) G4 would have to reimburse O's estate for two-thirds of the value of Blackacre.

48.   Refer to Question 44, but assume C4 also died before O. Additionally, prior to the deaths of both O and C4, O conveyed Blackacre to G4, not C4. What effect does the conveyance have on G4's share of the estate?
ANSWER:

49.   Refer to Question 44. How would your answer differ if, prior to O's death, C3 assigned C3's "interest in O's estate" to an unrelated third party?

   (A) My answer would not change; the assignment has no legal effect on the distribution of O's estate.

   (B) The interest in O's estate that would have passed to G3 had it not been for the assignment passes to the third party assignee.

(C) The interest in O's estate that would have passed to G3 had it not been for the assignment passes to the third party assignee if the third party assignee paid good and valuable consideration for the assignment.

(D) The third party has a claim against O's estate as a creditor if the third party assignee paid good and valuable consideration for the assignment.

50. Refer to Question 44. How would your answer differ if, following O's death, but prior to C4's death, C4 assigned C4's "interest in O's estate" to an unrelated third party?

(A) My answer would not change; the assignment has no legal effect on the distribution of O's estate.

(B) The interest in O's estate that would have passed to S4 had it not been for the assignment passes to the third party assignee.

(C) The interest in O's estate that would have passed to S4 had it not been for the assignment passes to the third party assignee if the third party assignee paid good and valuable consideration for the assignment.

(D) The third party assignee has a claim against O's estate as a creditor if the third party assignee paid good and valuable consideration for the assignment.

51. Refer to Question 50. What effect would the assignment have if C4's assignment had occurred prior to O's death?

ANSWER:

52. Refer to Question 44. How would your answer differ if a creditor of C3 had a judgment lien against C3 at the time of O's death?

(A) My answer would not change; the lien cannot attach to any part of O's estate.

(B) The creditor can attach the one-third interest that would have passed to G3.

(C) The creditor can attach the one-third interest that would have passed to G3, if the original debt was tortious in nature.

(D) The creditor has a claim only against O's estate.

53. Refer to Question 52. How would your answer differ if C3 would not have died until shortly before the termination of the formal administration of O's estate several months after O's death?

(A) The lien cannot attach to any part of O's estate several months after O's death.

(B) The creditor can attach C3's one-third interest.

    (C) The creditor can attach C3's one-third interest, if the original debt was tortious in nature.

    (D) The creditor has only a claim against O's estate.

54. Refer to Question 52. What would your answer be if C3 would have survived O by only one week?

    (A) The lien cannot attach to any part of O's estate.

    (B) The creditor can attach the one-third interest that would have passed to S3.

    (C) The creditor can attach the one-third interest that would have passed to S3, if the original debt was tortious in nature.

    (D) The creditor has only a claim against O's estate.

55. Refer to Question 44 and assume that, following O's death, a qualified disclaimer of C4's interest in O's estate was properly filed in the probate proceedings of O's estate, because a creditor of C4 had filed a large judgment lien against C4 prior to O's death. What is the legal effect of the disclaimer on C4's interest in O's probate estate?

ANSWER:

56. Refer to Question 55, but assume that (i) the judgment lien did not exist and (ii) the disclaimer was filed in order for C4's one-third interest in O's estate to pass to G4. Which answer best describes the federal transfer consequences, if any, of the disclaimer?

    (A) There are no transfer tax consequences.

    (B) If C4 filed the disclaimer, it would be considered a gift to G4 of C4's interest in O's estate. If the executor filed the disclaimer, C4's one-third interest in O's estate would be included in C4's gross estate for federal transfer tax purposes.

    (C) If C4 filed the disclaimer, there would be no transfer tax consequences. If the executor filed the disclaimer, C4's one-third interest in O's estate would be included in C4's gross estate for federal transfer tax purposes.

    (D) If C4 filed the disclaimer, it would be considered a gift to G4 of C4's one-third interest in O's estate. If the executor filed the disclaimer, there would be no transfer tax consequences.

57. Refer to Question 44 and assume that C4 had borrowed $12,000 from O and had not repaid the debt prior to O's death. What effect does the $12,000 debt have on C4's interest in O's estate?

ANSWER:

58. Refer to Question 44, but assume that C4 murdered O. Which answer best describes the effect of C4's crime?

    (A) The fact that C4 murdered O disqualifies C4 as an heir, and the one-third of the estate to which C4 would have been entitled passes to S4.

    (B) The fact that C4 murdered O disqualifies C4 as an heir, and the one-third of the estate to which C4 would have been entitled passes to G4.

    (C) The fact that C4 murdered O disqualifies C4 as an heir, and the one-third of the estate to which C4 would have been entitled passes to G2 and G3.

    (D) The only legal remedy of G2 and G3 is to impose a constructive trust on S4 to avoid unjust enrichment on the part of C4, G4, or S4.

59. Refer to Question 44 and assume that C3 and a family friend discovered O had died when C3 and the friend took breakfast to O as they had done every day for several months. C3 and the friend entered O's house through the back door directly into O's kitchen using a key O had given to C3. Upon entering the kitchen, C3 and the friend found an envelope with C3's name on it; they opened the envelope and discovered $10,000 in cash and an unrecorded deed signed by O whereby O conveyed O's house to C3. After opening the envelope, C3 and the friend discovered O had died the night before.

    Which answer best explains the likely disposition of the house and the $10,000?

    (A) Both the house and the $10,000 pass as part of O's probate estate.

    (B) Because O made a gift to C3 of the house and the $10,000, the house and the $10,000 were inherited by S3 at C3's death.

    (C) Because O made a gift to C3 of the $10,000, but not the house, the $10,000 was inherited by S3 when C3 died, and the house passed as part of O's probate estate.

    (D) Because O made a gift to C3 of the house, but not the $10,000, the house was inherited by S3 when C3 died, and the house passed as part of O's probate estate.

60. O, an unmarried resident of the state of X, died recently. O was survived by two adult children, C1 and C2. O never signed a will but verbally told a number of friends over an extended period of time that O wanted C1 to have O's home and its contents when O died. At all relevant times, O was a competent individual, and O's friends are willing to testify as to O's verbal statements. No document appearing to be a will was found after O's death. Which answer best explains the most likely disposition of O's home and its contents?

    (A) C1 inherits both the home and its contents.

    (B) C1 inherits the contents but not the home.

    (C) C1 inherits the home but not the contents.

    (D) C1 and C2 inherit both the home and the contents.

61.   Refer to question 60. How would your answer differ if, moments before O died, a still-competent O told O's doctor and two nurses that O really did want C1 to have O's home and its contents when O died?

    (A) My answer would not change.

    (B) C1 inherits both the home and its contents.

    (C) C1 inherits the contents but not the home.

    (D) C1 inherits the home but not the contents.

62.   Refer to Question 60. How would your answer differ if C1 can produce credible witnesses who will testify that O verbally told C1 that, if C1 would drop out of school, return home, and care for O in O's declining years, C1 would receive the home and its contents at O's death? C1 did drop out of school, returned home, and cared for O until O's death.

ANSWER:

63.   Refer to Question 60. How would your answer differ if C1 can produce a written agreement signed by C1 and O, whereby O promised to devise the home and its contents to C1, if C1 dropped out of school, moved in with O, and cared for O in O's declining years? C1 did drop out of school and cared for O until O's death.

    (A) My answer would not change.

    (B) The house and its contents passed to C1.

    (C) The contents, but not the house, passed to C1.

    (D) C1 would have a claim against O's estate.

64.   O, an unmarried resident of the state of X, died recently survived by two adult children, C1 and C2. In the presence of several friends, O typed a letter addressed to both C1 and C2, stating that at O's death the home and its contents were to pass to C1. O explained to the friends what he was doing and then signed the letter. At all relevant times, O was a competent individual, and O's friends are willing to testify as to O's verbal statements. C1 and C2 did not receive the letter until after O's death. Which answer best explains the most likely disposition of O's home and its contents?

(A) The house and contents pass to C1 and C2.

(B) The house and its contents would pass to C1.

(C) The house but not the contents would pass to C1.

(D) The contents but not the house would pass to C1.

65.   Refer to Question 64. How would your answer differ if the letter actually was delivered to C1 and C2 prior to O's death?

(A) My answer would not change.

(B) The house and its contents would pass to C1.

(C) The house but not the contents would pass to C1.

(D) The contents but not the house would pass to C1.

66.   Refer to Question 64. How would your answer differ if the letter described would have been entirely in O's handwriting and signed by O?

(A) My answer would not change.

(B) The home and its contents would pass to C1.

(C) The home but not the contents would pass to C1.

(D) The contents but not the home would pass to C1

67.   A and B are two competent, unmarried siblings who reside in the state of X. A and B inherited Blackacre as tenants in common when their parent, O, died. Following O's death, A and B executed a single written document in 1990 meeting the requirements of a valid will in the state of X. In this document, the first to die devises her interest in Blackacre to the survivor. In addition, the will devises Blackacre to their niece, C, upon the survivor's death. A has recently died survived by B, C, and D, who is C's mother and a sister of A and B. The family has discovered a validly executed will signed in 2000 by A that devises A's entire

estate, including Blackacre, to F, a friend. Which answer best describes the most likely disposition of Blackacre by reason of A's death?

(A) A's interest passes nonprobate to B.

(B) B succeeds to A's interest pursuant to the 1990 will.

(C) F succeeds to A's interest pursuant to the 2000 will.

(D) F succeeds to A's interest pursuant to the 2000 will, and B's only remedy is a breach of contract action against A's estate.

68.　　Refer to Question 67. What would your answer be if the 1990 will included a provision stating that A and B agreed never to revoke the 1990 will?

ANSWER:

69.　　Refer to Question 67. What would your answer be if the 1990 document were a written agreement signed and acknowledged only by A and B before a notary public providing that Blackacre would become the survivor's property upon the first of A or B to die?

(A) A's interest passes nonprobate to B.

(B) B succeeds to A's interest upon the probate of the 1990 document.

(C) F succeeds to A's interest pursuant to the 2000 will.

(D) F succeeds to A's interest pursuant to the 2000 will, and B's only remedy is a breach of contract action against A's estate.

70.　　Refer to Question 67 and assume that the 2000 will was not valid and the 1990 will has been admitted to probate. B is seeking legal advice. B now wishes to devise B's entire estate, including Blackacre, to G when B dies. What answer best describes the legal advice that should be given to B?

(A) You are free to devise Blackacre to anyone you choose.

(B) You can devise Blackacre to G, but C may sue you for breach of contract.

(C) You can devise Blackacre to G, but C may have a breach of contract action against your estate.

(D) You cannot devise Blackacre to G. C inherited a remainder interest in Blackacre at A's death that will become possessory at your death.

71. Refer to Question 70. How would your answer differ if the 1990 will contained a provision stating that A and B agreed not to revoke the will?

    (A) My answer would not change.

    (B) You can devise Blackacre to G, but C may sue you for breach of contract.

    (C) You can devise Blackacre to G, but C may have a breach of contract action against your estate.

    (D) You cannot devise Blackacre to G. C's remainder interest in Blackacre becomes a possessory fee interest when you die.

72. Refer to Question 71. Which answer best describes the legal advice that should be given to B if C had died one week after A's death? C never married and had no children; C's valid, probated will left C's estate to H.

    (A) You are free to devise Blackacre to anyone you choose.

    (B) You can devise Blackacre to G, but H may sue you for breach of contract.

    (C) You can devise Blackacre to G, but H may have a breach of contract action against your estate.

    (D) You cannot devise Blackacre to G. C's remainder interest in Blackacre was devised by C to H.

73. Refer to Question 72. How would your answer differ if C would have been survived by a child, J?

    (A) My answer would not change.

    (B) You cannot devise Blackacre to G. C inherited a remainder interest in Blackacre at A's death that was devised to H.

    (C) You can devise Blackacre to G, but J may sue you for breach of contract.

    (D) You can devise Blackacre to G, but J may have a breach of contract action against your estate.

74. Refer to Question 71. Which answer best describes the legal advice that should be given to B if B's intention is to devise Blackacre to G and the rest of B's estate equally to C and G?

    (A) You can do that!

    (B) You can do that, but C will still have a breach of contract action against your estate.

    (C) You can do that, and C will have to elect to pursue the breach of contract action against your estate or accept the benefits conferred by your will.

    (D) You can't do that.

75.   Refer to Question 71. How would your answer differ if A and B had inherited Blackacre as joint tenants rather than tenants in common?

ANSWER:

76.   Refer to Question 68. Additionally, assume A's 2000 will devised Blackacre to F and the rest of A's estate equally to F and B. What answer best describes the most likely disposition of Blackacre if A and B had inherited Blackacre as joint tenants rather than tenants in common?

   (A) A's interest in Blackacre would pass nonprobate to B.

   (B) A's interest in Blackacre passes nonprobate to B, but B cannot accept any benefits from A's estate unless B conveys A's one-half interest to F.

   (C) A's interest in Blackacre passes nonprobate to B, but B cannot accept any interest in A's estate unless B conveys all of Blackacre to F.

   (D) A's one-half interest in Blackacre passes to F.

77.   Refer to Question 76. What would your answer be if B would have died one week before A, and B's valid, probated 1995 will left all of B's estate to B's spouse, S? B was also survived by a child, B1.

   (A) Blackacre passes to F, and the balance of A's estate passes equally to F and S.

   (B) Blackacre passes to F, and the balance of A's estate passes equally to F and B1.

   (C) The entire estate, including Blackacre, passes to F.

   (D) C will seek specific performance of the original contract between A and B.

Note: Answer Questions 78-119 assuming that a party, who would like the court to exercise its "dispensing power" and excuse O's "non-compliance" with the statutory requirements of will execution or revocation, cannot meet the burden of proof required in UPC § 2-503 (or a "substantial compliance" rule in a jurisdiction that has not adopted the Uniform Probate Code). These so-called "harmless error" statutes generally permit a court to admit a will to probate that was not executed with statutory formalities if the proponent can establish by clear and convincing evidence that the testator intended the document to be a will.

78.   O, an unmarried resident of the state of X, died recently, survived by an adult child, A. A resides in the state of Y. O's apparently valid will (i.e., a document in writing signed by O in the presence of three witnesses) leaves all of O's estate to O's live-in caretaker, F. O signed the will shortly after O's medical records indicate that O had been diagnosed with Alzheimer's disease. Which answer best explains whether the document will be admitted to probate?

    (A) The court will deny the will's probate due to the diagnosis of Alzheimer's.

    (B) The court will admit the will to probate unless A proves that O lacked the mental capacity to execute a will.

    (C) The court will admit the will to probate if F can prove that O had the capacity to execute a will, notwithstanding the Alzheimer diagnosis.

    (D) The court will admit the will to probate, notwithstanding the diagnosis of Alzheimer's, because a court had not determined that, during O's lifetime, the Alzheimer's had rendered O incapacitated.

79.   Refer to Question 78. What would your answer be if, shortly after the execution of the will, due to the Alzheimer's, A had been appointed the guardian (conservator) of O?

    (A) The court will deny the will's probate due to the finding of incapacity in the guardianship proceeding.

    (B) The court will admit the will to probate unless A proves that O lacked the mental capacity to execute a will.

    (C) The court will admit the will to probate if F can prove that O had the capacity to execute a will, notwithstanding the guardianship.

    (D) The court will admit the will to probate, notwithstanding the guardianship.

80.   Refer to Question 79. What would your answer be if the will had been executed after A had been appointed the guardian (conservator) for O?

   (A) The court will deny the will's probate due to the guardianship.

   (B) The court will admit the will to probate unless A proves that O lacked the mental capacity to execute a will.

   (C) The court will admit the will to probate if F can prove that O had the capacity to execute a will, notwithstanding the guardianship.

   (D) The court will admit the will to probate, notwithstanding the guardianship.

81.   Refer to Question 79. What would your answer be if one of the factors that motivated A to proceed with the guardianship for O was A's concern about an improper relationship between O and F?

   (A) If O had testamentary capacity, evidence of an improper relationship between O and F is irrelevant.

   (B) Evidence of the improper relationship can only be used in the determination of O's testamentary capacity.

   (C) Even if O had testamentary capacity, the will is invalid if A can prove F improperly influenced O during the execution of the will.

   (D) Even if O had testamentary capacity, the will is still valid if F can prove that F did not improperly influence O during the execution of the will.

82.   Refer to Question 78 but assume O had testamentary capacity, notwithstanding the Alzheimer's. What would your answer be if O had been physically too weak to sign O's full name on the will and had written only O's first name only rather than O's first and last names in the place provided in the will for the testator's full signature?

ANSWER:

83.   Refer to Question 78, but assume O had testamentary capacity, notwithstanding the Alzheimer's. What would your answer be if O had been physically too weak to sign even O's first name and had just been able to place an "X" in the place provided in the will for the testator's signature?

   (A) Because O did not sign O's full name, the will cannot be admitted to probate.

   (B) Even though O did not sign O's full name, the will can be admitted to probate.

   (C) Even though O did not sign O's full name, the will may be admitted to probate.

   (D) Because O did not sign even part of O's name, the will cannot be admitted to probate.

84.   Refer to question 78, but assume O had testamentary capacity, notwithstanding the Alzheimer's. What would your answer be if O had been physically too weak to sign the will in any way and asked one of the witnesses to sign the will on O's behalf? The witness signed O's name in the place provided in the will for the testator's signature while O was in the same room, but not in a position to actually see the witness sign the will.

(A)   Because O did not sign the will, the will cannot be admitted to probate.

(B)   Even though O did not sign the will, the will can be admitted to probate.

(C)   Even though O did not sign O's full name, the will may be admitted to probate.

(D)   I need to research the question.

85.   Refer to question 78, but assume O had testamentary capacity, notwithstanding the Alzheimer's. What would your answer be if the witnesses did not know the document they signed was O's will at the time they signed the will?

ANSWER:

86.   Refer to Question 78, but assume O had testamentary capacity, notwithstanding the Alzheimer's. How would your answer differ if the witnesses were not actually present when O signed the will?

(A)   Because the witnesses did not see O sign the will, the will cannot be admitted to probate.

(B)   Even if the witnesses did not see O sign the will, the will can be admitted to probate.

(C)   Even if the witnesses did not see O sign the will, the will may be admitted to probate.

(D)   I need to research the question.

87.   Refer to Question 78, but assume O had testamentary capacity, notwithstanding the Alzheimer's. How would your answer differ if each witness signed the will but not while the other two witnesses were present?

(A)   Because all witnesses did not see the others sign the will, the will cannot be admitted to probate.

(B)   Even if the witnesses did not observe the other witnesses sign the will, the will can be admitted to probate.

(C)   Even if the witnesses did not observe the other witnesses sign the will, the will may be admitted to probate.

(D)   I need to research the question.

88.   Refer to Question 78, but assume O had testamentary capacity, notwithstanding the Alzheimer's. How would your answer differ if the witnesses observed a bedridden O sign the will before the witnesses signed the will on a table with their backs to O so that O was unable to observe them sign the will?

(A) Because O did not see the witnesses sign the will, the will cannot be admitted to probate.

(B) Even though O could not see the witnesses sign the will, the will can be admitted to probate.

(C) Even though O could not see the witnesses sign the will, the will may be admitted to probate.

(D) I need to research the question.

89.   Refer to Question 78, but assume O had testamentary capacity, notwithstanding the Alzheimer's. How would your answer differ if the witnesses did not sign the will until shortly after O's death?

ANSWER:

90.   Refer to Question 78, but assume O had testamentary capacity, notwithstanding the Alzheimer's. How would your answer differ if there had been only two witnesses rather than three?

(A) Because there were only two witnesses, the will cannot be admitted to probate.

(B) Because there were at least two witnesses, the will can be admitted to probate.

(C) Because there were at least two witnesses, the will may be admitted to probate.

(D) I need to research the question.

91.   Refer to Question 78, but assume O had testamentary capacity, notwithstanding the Alzheimer's. How would your answer differ if the will form used by a non-lawyer friend of O who typed the will provided for O to sign the will only in a blank space in the first sentence of the will (i.e., "I, _____, hereby declare this document to be my last will")? The witnesses signed at the end of the document.

(A) Because a will must be signed at its end by the testator, the will cannot be admitted to probate.

(B) Even if the testator did not sign at the end of the will, the will can be admitted to probate.

(C) Even if the testator did not sign at the end of the will, the will may be admitted to probate.

(D) I need to research the question.

92.   O, an unmarried resident of the state of X, died recently, survived by two adult children, C1 and C2, and C1's child, G. In 1990, O, being disappointed in C2, executed a valid attested will prepared by O's lawyer that left O's estate to C1. Shortly before O's death, a fully-competent O e-mailed the lawyer. In the e-mail, O explained that O was now extremely disappointed in both C1 and C2 and that O wanted all of O's property to pass to G when O died. O then instructed the lawyer to "formalize" O's wishes. The lawyer prepared a new will for O leaving all of O's estate to G, but O died before O had an opportunity to execute the new will. Who is most likely to succeed to O's estate under the circumstances?

ANSWER:

93.   Refer to Question 92. What would your answer be if the message to the lawyer was in a type-written letter dated by O, signed by O, and mailed by O to the lawyer?

(A) C1 and C2.

(B) C1

(C) G

(D) C2 and G.

94.   Refer to Question 92. What would your answer be if the message to the lawyer would have been in a handwritten note written by O, dated by O, and signed by O and then mailed to the lawyer?

(A) C1 and C2.

(B) C1.

(C) G.

(D) C2 and G.

95.   Refer to Question 92. What would your answer be if following O's death, a one-page type-written document, dated shortly before O's death and signed by O, was found in O's safe-deposit box, along with the original of the 1990 will? The document simply stated: "At my death I leave all my property to G."

(A) C1 and C2.

(B) C1.

(C) G.

(D) C2 and G.

96.   Refer to Question 95. What would your answer be if the document found in the safe deposit box would have been entirely in O's handwriting, dated by O, and signed by O, all shortly before O's death?

ANSWER:

97.   Refer to Question 96. What would your answer be if the handwritten document signed by O had been written by O on hotel stationery? The date was filled in by O at the top of the page immediately below the name and address of the hotel, where the preprinted form provided "_____ ___, 20__." O filled in the month and day and the last two digits of the year.

(A) C1 and C2.

(B) C1.

(C) G.

(D) C2 and G.

98.   Refer to Question 92. What would your answer be if there is no evidence of O's intent to revoke the 1990 will other than the fact that the 1990 will was discovered after O's death in O's safe-deposit box with an "X" marked across the signature of O?

(A) C1 and C2.

(B) C1.

(C) G.

(D) C2 and G.

99.   Refer to Question 92. What would your answer be if, rather than sending the email, O had telephoned the lawyer explaining that O wanted all of O's property to go to G when O died and instructed the lawyer to (i) retrieve the 1990 will from the firm's vault and destroy it and (ii) draft a new will leaving all of O's property to G? The lawyer immediately destroyed the 1990 will and later prepared the new will, but O did not sign it before O died.

(A) C1 and C2.

(B) C1.

    (C) G.

    (D) C2 and G.

100. Refer to Question 92. What would your answer be if O had validly executed the new will leaving all of O's property to G and had physically destroyed the 1990 will? However, shortly prior to her death, distraught over the news that G, a U.S. Marine, had been killed in action fighting the war on terrorism, O destroyed the will in favor of G; unfortunately, O died prior to receiving the news that G had not died, but had been taken prisoner and had just been rescued.

ANSWER:

101. O, an unmarried resident of the state of X, died recently, survived by one adult child, C, and several cousins. In 1990, because O was estranged from C, O validly executed a typewritten, witnessed will leaving all of O's estate to a friend, A. In 2000, O validly executed a new typewritten, witnessed will expressly revoking all prior wills and leaving all of O's property to another friend, B. Before O's death, while O was angry with B, and while several friends were present, a competent O intentionally destroyed the 2000 will by tossing it in a fire in the fireplace and told the friends that O wanted the estate to pass to A when O died. The 1990 will is still located in O's safe deposit box. O had never reconciled with C. Which answer best describes who is most likely to succeed to O's estate?

    (A) C.

    (B) A.

    (C) B.

    (D) The cousins.

102. Refer to Question 101. Who is likely to succeed to O's estate if the 2000 will had not expressly revoked all earlier wills and had simply left all of O's estate to B?

    (A) C.

    (B) A.

    (C) B.

    (D) The cousins.

103. Refer to Question 102. Who is likely to succeed to O's estate if the 2000 document had not been a typewritten attested will, but a document entirely in O's handwriting and signed by O?

    (A) C.

    (B) A.

    (C) B

    (D) The cousins.

104. Refer to Question 101, but assume that the 2000 will was never signed by O and it was the unsigned 2000 will that was tossed into the fire by O. Additionally, the original 1990 will was not in the safe deposit box after O died and has not been found. O's lawyer will testify that, after the 1990 will had been executed, O took the original and explained that O was going to place the original in O's safe deposit box. Which answer best describes who is most likely to succeed to O's estate?

    (A) C.

    (B) A.

    (C) B.

    (D) The cousins.

105. Refer to Question 101. Who is likely to succeed to O's estate if, after the 1990 will had been executed, O had left the original 1990 will with the lawyer, and the lawyer destroyed the 1990 will in 2001 when the lawyer was cleaning out the lawyer's file room? The lawyer will testify that the lawyer thought retention of the original was unnecessary because the 1990 will had been revoked when the 2000 will was executed by O.

ANSWER:

106. Refer to Question 101. Who is likely to succeed to O's estate if a competent, but bedridden, O had not personally destroyed the 2000 will, but had asked O's nurse to destroy the will? The nurse found the 2000 will in a desk in O's study, returned to the bedroom, and while O was watching, tossed the 2000 will into the fire.

    (A) C.

    (B) A.

    (C) B.

    (D) The cousins.

107. O, an unmarried resident of the state of X, died recently. O was survived by O's two children, C1 and C2, and C1's child, G. Shortly before O died, angry with both children, a competent O phoned O's lawyer to prepare a will leaving all of O's property to G. The lawyer prepared the will and phoned O to advise that the will was ready for execution. Dependent on C1 for transportation, O asked C1 to take O to the lawyer's office in order to take care of "a few matters." Unknown to O, C1 had overheard O's telephone conversation with the lawyer and continued to postpone the trip to the lawyer's office. O died without ever executing the will. There were no earlier wills. What is the most likely disposition of O's estate?

ANSWER:

108. O, an unmarried resident of the state of X, died recently survived by one child, C, and C's two children G1 and G2. Shortly before O died, while C was out of town, G1, using physical threats, forced a competent, but bedridden, O to sign a typewritten will that G1 had prepared. Two of G1's friends were present and served as the witnesses. The will purports to devise O's estate to G1 and G2. O died. One of the witnesses has had a change of heart and is willing to testify as to what occurred. Which answer best explains the most likely disposition of O's estate?

    (A) The will can be admitted to probate; G1 and G2 take.

    (B) The will cannot be admitted to probate; C takes.

    (C) The will can be admitted to probate, but C may take the entire estate anyway.

    (D) The will can be admitted to probate, but C may take G1's half of the estate.

109. O, an unmarried resident of the state of X, died recently, survived by O's two children, C1 and C2, and C2's child, G. O had validly executed a will leaving all of O's property to G at a time when O was angry with both children. Shortly prior to O's death, having been threatened with physical harm by C1, a competent, but bedridden, O directed a nurse to retrieve the will from the study. The nurse brought the will to O, and O tore the will into many pieces. Unknown to C1, the nurse had overheard C1's physical threats.

    Which answer best explains the most likely disposition of O's estate?

    (A) The will can be admitted to probate; G takes.

    (B) The will cannot be admitted to probate; C1 and C2 take.

    (C) The will cannot be admitted to probate, but G may take the entire estate.

    (D) The will cannot be admitted to probate, but G may take C1's half of the estate.

110. O, an unmarried resident of the state of X, died recently, survived by a child, C, and C's two children, G1 and G2. O had validly executed a will whereby O left O's entire estate to G1 and G2. Shortly prior to O's death, a competent, but bedridden, O directed O's nurse to retrieve the will from O's desk located in O's study so that O could destroy the will. Unknown to O, G1 overheard O's instructions to the nurse and took the will before the nurse could retrieve it. O died shortly thereafter without destroying the will. Which answer best explains the most likely disposition of O's estate?

   (A) The will can be admitted to probate; G1 and G2 take.

   (B) The will cannot be admitted to probate; C takes.

   (C) The will can be admitted to probate, but C may take.

   (D) The will can be admitted to probate but C may G1's half of the estate.

111. O, an unmarried resident of the state of X, died. O was survived by O's children, C1 and C2, and O's grandchildren, G1 and G2. O had validly executed a typewritten witnessed will leaving all of O's property to G1 and G2. Near the time O was diagnosed with Alzheimer's, O, in the presence of two family friends, destroyed the will, explaining to the friends that O had reconciled with C1 and C2. Explain the most likely disposition of O's estate.

ANSWER:

112. Refer to Question 111 and assume that O had testamentary capacity and that O had not destroyed the old will but had, in O's own handwriting, written the following note: "I hereby revoke all prior wills and leave all my property to C1." O signed the note while two family friends watched. Which answer best explains who is likely to succeed to O's estate?

   (A) G1 and G2.

   (B) C1 and C2.

   (C) C1 and G2.

   (D) C1.

113. Refer to Question 112. What would your answer be if the note written and signed by O would have simply said: "I revoke all of my prior wills"?

   (A) G1 and G2.

   (B) C1 and C2.

   (C) C1 and G2.

   (D) C1.

114. O, a married resident of the state of X, died recently. O was survived by O's spouse, S, and O's parents, M and F; O never had any children. O's will was validly executed prior to O's marriage to S; O never changed the will. It devises O's entire estate to M and F. What is the most likely disposition of O's estate?

ANSWER:

115. Refer to Question 114. What would your answer be if the will had been executed during the marriage of O and S?

(A) The will can be admitted to probate; the entire estate passes to M and F.

(B) The will cannot be admitted to probate; the entire estate passes to W.

(C) The will can be admitted to probate; S will be entitled to S's marital share, if any, and M and F will succeed to everything else.

(D) The will cannot be admitted to probate; the estate will be shared by S, M, and F.

116. O, an unmarried resident of the state of X, died recently. O was survived by O's parents, M and F. O was divorced from O's spouse, S, two years prior to O's death. After the divorce, O did not change the will that O had executed while married to S and that left all of O's property to S. What is the most likely disposition of O's estate?

ANSWER:

117. O, an unmarried resident of the state of X, died recently. O was survived by O's spouse, S, and their two minor children, C1 and C2. O's will, which O executed after O married S but before the births of C1 and C2, leaves all of O's property to S. Which answer best describes the most likely disposition of O's estate?

(A) The will can be admitted to probate; the entire estate passes to S.

(B) The will cannot be admitted to probate; the entire estate passes to C1 and C2.

(C) The will cannot be admitted to probate; S, C1, and C2 share the estate.

(D) The will can be admitted to probate, but C1 and C2 will be entitled to an intestate share of the estate, and the balance of the entire estate passes to S.

118. Refer to Question 117. How would your answer differ if the will had been executed following the births of C1 and C2?

    (A) The will can be admitted to probate; the entire estate passes to S.

    (B) The will cannot be admitted to probate; the entire estate passes to C1 and C2.

    (C) The will cannot be admitted to probate; S, C1, and C2 share the estate.

    (D) The will can be admitted to probate, but C1 and C2 will be entitled to an intestate share of the estate, and the balance of the estate passes to S.

119. O, an unmarried resident of the state of X, died recently. O was survived by O's spouse, S, and their two minor children, C1 and C2. O's will, which O executed after O married S but before the births of C1 and C2, leaves all of O's property to S. It was also executed before the birth of C3, a child born of an extramarital affair of O and P; C3 also survived O. Which answer best describes the most likely disposition of O's estate?

    (A) The will can be admitted to probate; the entire estate passes to S.

    (B) The will cannot be admitted to probate; the entire estate passes to C1, C2, and C3.

    (C) The will can be admitted to probate, but C1, C2, and C3 will be entitled to an intestate share of the estate, and the balance of the entire estate passes to S.

    (D) The will can be admitted to probate, but C3 will be entitled to an intestate share of the estate, and the balance of the entire estate passes to S.

120. O, an unmarried resident of the state of X, died recently. O was survived by an adult child, C, who resided in the state of Y. O's valid, probated will leaves to C all of O's property, including tangible and intangible personal property and several tracts of unimproved real estate located in X. After O's death, the personal representative determined that the fair market value of O's estate was $100,000. It was also determined that O owed unsecured contractual creditors $25,000 and tort creditors $50,000; the expenses of O's last illness were $25,000. Which answer best explains how O's assets will be distributed?

    (A) All of the assets will be sold to pay the creditors.

    (B) Only the personal property can be sold to pay the creditors on a pro rata basis.

    (C) All of the assets will be sold to pay the tort creditors and the last illness expenses.

    (D) Only the personal property can be sold in order to pay the tort creditors and the last illness expenses on a pro rata basis.

121. Refer to Question 120. How would your answer differ if C would have been a minor at the time of O's death?

ANSWER:

122. Refer to Question 120. How would your answer differ if O had also been survived by S, O's second spouse who was not a parent of C, and that the real estate owned by O consisted only of the home?

    (A) The home will likely be sold to pay the creditors.

    (B) The home will not be sold to pay the debts, and C will inherit the house.

    (C) The home would not be sold to pay the debts, and S would inherit the home.

    (D) The home will not be sold to pay the debts, and will be owned by C, but S will have a right to live there.

123. O, an unmarried resident of the state of X, died recently. O was survived by two children, S and D. O's valid will has been admitted to probate; it simply states: "I devise my home to S and the rest, residue, and remainder of my estate to D." At the time of O's death, the significant assets of the estate consisted of the home (fair market value of $100,000) and shares of a New York Stock Exchange company (fair market value of $100,000). The only debt or expense of O's estate is a note signed by O and secured by the home; the outstanding bal-

ance of the debt at the time of death was $50,000. The will does not direct how the decedent's debts are to be paid. Which answer best explains the most likely disposition of O's estate?

(A) S receives the home, subject to the outstanding indebtedness, and D receives all of the shares of stock.

(B) S receives the home, free of any indebtedness, and D receives only the shares of stock remaining after enough shares are sold to pay the debt.

(C) One-half of the debt should be paid by S, or out of the sales proceeds of the house, and the other one-half of the debt should be paid out of the sales proceeds of part of the stock.

(D) The answer depends on the decisions the creditor makes after O's death.

124. Refer to Question 123. How would your answer differ if the $50,000 debt was not a note secured by the home but an unsecured debt of $50,000 owing by O at the time of O's death?

(A) S receives the home, free of any indebtedness, and D receives only the stock remaining after the debt is paid.

(B) D would receive the stock, and the home would be sold in order to pay the debt with S receiving the balance of the proceeds of the sale after the debt is paid.

(C) One-half of the debt should be paid by S, or out of the sales proceeds of the house, and the other one-half of the debt should be paid by D, or out of the sales proceeds of part of the stock.

(D) The answer depends on the intention of the creditor after O's death.

125. O, an unmarried resident of the state of X, died recently. O was survived by three adult children, A, B, and C. At the time of O's death, O's estate consisted of O's home and the home's contents (fair market value of $100,000), stocks and bonds (fair market value $100,000), and $100,000 cash. At the time of O's death, there were outstanding unsecured debts of $100,000. O's valid will has been admitted to probate, and the will devises the home and its contents to A, $100,000 to B, and the rest, residue, and remainder of O's estate to C. Which of the described assets should be used by the executor to satisfy the debts?

ANSWER:

126. Refer to Question 125, but assume the will devises $100,000 to B, the stocks and bonds to C, and the rest, residue, and remainder of O's estate to A. Which answer best describes the assets the executor should use to satisfy the debts?

(A) The house and its contents.

(B) Cash.

(C) The stocks and bonds.

(D) One-third of the home and its contents, one-third of the cash, and one-third of the stocks and bonds.

127. Refer to Question 125, but assume the will devises $100,000 to B and the rest, residue, and remainder of O's estate to A and C. Which answer best describes the assets the executor should use to satisfy the debts?

(A) Cash.

(B) One-half of the house and its contents and one-half of the stocks and bonds.

(C) The home and its contents.

(D) The stocks and bonds.

128. O, an unmarried resident of the state of X, died recently. O was survived by three adult children, A, B, and C. A's valid, probated will, dated 1990, devises all of O's Exxon stock to A, Blackacre to B, and the rest, residue, and remainder of O's estate to C. Following the execution of the will, O sold Blackacre and immediately used the sales proceeds to purchase Whiteacre. O originally resided on Blackacre but later moved into a house on Whiteacre. When Exxon and Mobil later merged, O's Exxon stock was exchanged for shares of stock in ExxonMobil. At the time of O's death, the significant assets of O were Whiteacre, the ExxonMobil stock, and just enough cash to pay O's debts and the administration expenses. Which answer best describes the disposition of the ExxonMobil stock and Whiteacre?

(A) The ExxonMobil stock passes to A, and Whiteacre passes to B.

(B) The ExxonMobil stock passes to A, and Whiteacre passes to C.

(C) The ExxonMobil stock passes to C, and Whiteacre to passes B.

(D) The ExxonMobil stock and Whiteacre pass to C.

129. O, an unmarried resident of the state of X, died recently. O was survived by O's three adult children, A, B, and C. O's valid will has been admitted to probate, and the will devises O's Cadillac to A, $100,000 to B, and the rest, residue, and remainder of O's estate to C. At the time O executed the will, O's significant assets consisted of the Cadillac (fair market value of $50,000), cash ($100,000), stocks and bonds (fair market value of $100,000), and a home (fair market value of $100,000). Immediately prior to O's death, the Cadillac had a fair market value of $25,000; there was no cash remaining, the stocks and bonds had declined in value to only $10,000, and the home had declined in value to $65,000. O died in a one-car automobile accident while driving the Cadillac, and O's insurance company has recently paid O's executor $25,000 in order to "total" the car ($24,000 for replacement value, $1,000

salvage value). The debts, all unsecured, and administration expenses totaled $50,000. Explain the likely disposition of the remaining assets of O's estate.

ANSWER:

130. O, a resident of the state of X, died recently. O was survived by O's three adult children, A, B, and C. O's valid will has been admitted to probate, and the will directs that $10,000 is to be paid to A and the rest, residue, and remainder of O's estate is to pass equally to B and C. After the execution of the will and six months prior to O's death, O made a gift of $10,000 to A and another gift of $10,000 to B. At the time of O's death, O's estate consisted primarily of cash with a total value of $100,000 after the debts were paid. Which answer best describes the most likely disposition of the remaining assets of O's estate?

   (A) $10,000 to A, $45,000 to B, and $45,000 to C.

   (B) $50,000 to B and $50,000 to C.

   (C) $10,000 to A, $40,000 to B, and $50,000 to C.

   (D) $45,000 to B and $55,000 to C.

131. Refer to Question 130, but assume that the $10,000 "given" to B was actually a loan by O that had not been repaid by B prior to O's death and that O's estate is insolvent (i.e., O's debts exceed the described assets by $10,000). Which answer best describes the effect the outstanding loan will have on the distribution of O's estate?

   (A) It has no effect; O's death extinguished the debt.

   (B) B must repay the entire debt.

   (C) B must repay one-half of the debt.

   (D) B must pay A $10,000.

132. Refer to Question 131, but assume that, at the time of O's death, O's estate was solvent (i.e., the value of the non-exempt liquid assets exceed the debts by more than $10,000). Which answer best describes the effect the outstanding loan will have on the administration of O's estate?

   (A) It has no effect; O's death extinguished the debt.

   (B) B must repay the entire debt.

   (C) B must repay one-half of the debt.

   (D) Although B does not have to repay the debt, B's share of the estate will be reduced by one-half of the amount of the debt.

133. Refer to Question 131, but assume that the loan from O to B occurred more than 10 years prior to O's death. What effect would the outstanding loan have on the administration of O's estate?

(A) It has no effect.

(B) B must repay the entire debt.

(C) B must repay one-half of the entire debt.

(D) Although B does not have to repay the debt, B's share of the estate will be reduced by one-half of the amount of the debt.

134. Refer to Question 132, but assume that the loan from O to B occurred more than 10 years prior to O's death. Which answer best explains the effect the loan will have on the administration of O's estate?

(A) It has no effect.

(B) B must repay the entire debt.

(C) B must repay one-half of the entire debt.

(D) Although B does not have to repay the debt, B's share of the estate will be reduced by one-half of the amount of the debt.

135. O, an unmarried resident of the state of X, died recently. At the time O executed O's will, O had three adult children, A, B, and C. O's valid will has been admitted to probate, and the will devises Blackacre to A, Whiteacre to B, and the rest, residue and remainder of O's estate to C. A predeceased O. B died one day after O. C died one week after O. O was also survived by several cousins. Each child of O had a valid, probated will that devised that child's estate to that child's spouse. O's children never had any children. What is the most likely disposition of O's estate following formal administration?

ANSWER:

136. Refer to Question 135, but assume that A was also survived by a child, A1, that B was also survived by a child, B1, and that C was also survived by a child, C1. A1, B1, and C1 are adults. Which answer best describes the most likely disposition of O's estate following formal administration?

(A) Blackacre passes to A's spouse and A1; Whiteacre passes to B's spouse and B1; and the rest, residue, and remainder passes to C's spouse.

(B) Blackacre passes to A1; Whiteacre passes to B1; the rest, residue, and remainder passes to C1.

(C) Blackacre passes to A1; Whiteacre passes to B's spouse; the rest, residue, and remainder passes to C's spouse.

(D) Blackacre passes to A1; Whiteacre passes to B1; the rest, residue, and remainder passes to C's spouse.

137. Refer to Question 135, but assume that A, B, and C all died before O died. The children's spouses survived O. Which answer best describes the most likely disposition of O's estate following formal administration?

(A) Blackacre passes to A's spouse; Whiteacre passes to B's spouse; the rest, residue, and remainder passes to C's spouse.

(B) Blackacre passes to A's spouse; Whiteacre passes to B's spouse; the rest, residue, and remainder to the cousins.

(C) Blackacre and Whiteacre pass to the cousins; the rest, residue, and remainder passes to C's spouse.

(D) The entire estate passes to the cousins.

138. O, an unmarried resident of the state of X, died recently. O was survived by O's adult daughter, D. At the time O executed O's will, O had a close friend, F, who had three children, A, B, and C. O's valid will has been admitted to probate and devises Blackacre to A, Whiteacre to B, and the rest, residue, and remainder of the estate to C. A, B, and C predeceased O. The will of each child of F devises that child's estate to that child's surviving spouse. Each of A, B, and C had a child. What is the most likely disposition of O's estate following formal administration?

ANSWER:

139. O, an unmarried resident of the state of X, died recently. O was survived by a child, D. Another child of O, S, died several years before O died; S was survived by S's children, A, B, and C. O's valid will has been admitted to probate and simply says: "I devise all of my property equally to A, B, and C." A died one day before O died; A was survived by A's spouse, who is the sole beneficiary of A's will, and A's child, A1. B died one day after O died; B was survived by B's spouse, who is the beneficiary of B's will, and B's child, B1. C survived O. Which answer best explains the most likely disposition of O's estate following the formal administration of O's estate?

(A) The entire estate passes to C.

(B) One-third passes to A's spouse; one-third passes to B's spouse; and one-third passes to C.

(C) One-third passes to A1; one-third passes to B1; and one-third passes to C.

(D) Two-thirds pass to C and D; and one-third passes to C.

140. Refer to Question 139, but assume A and B were not survived by any children. Which answer best describes the most likely disposition of O's estate?

(A) The entire estate passes to C.

(B) One-third passes to A's spouse; one-third passes to B's spouse; and one-third passes to C.

(C) One-third passes to B's spouse, and two-thirds pass to C.

(D) One-third passes to C, and two-thirds pass to D and C.

141. Refer to Question 139. How would your answer differ if S would have had another child after the execution of the will and before S died? This child, E, survived O.

(A) My answer would not change.

(B) E and C would share one-third of the estate.

(C) E and C would share one-half of the estate.

(D) A1, B1, C, and E would share the estate equally.

142. Refer to Question 139, but assume O's will simply stated: "I devise all of my property to my grandchildren." Which answer best describes the most likely disposition of O's estate following formal administration?

(A) One-third passes to A1; one-third passes to B1; and one-third passes to C.

(B) One-third passes to A1; one-third passes to B's spouse; and one-third passes to C.

(C) The entire estate passes to C.

(D) Two-thirds pass to D, and one-third passes to C.

143. Refer to Question 139, but assume that O's will states: "I devise all of my property to my grandchildren who survive me." What is the most likely disposition of the estate following formal administration?

ANSWER:

144. Refer to Question 142. How would your answer differ if S would have had another child, E, before S died, and E had survived O?

(A) My answer would not change.

(B) E and C would share one-third of the estate.

(C) E and C would share one-half of the estate.

(D) A1, B1, C, and E would share the estate equally.

145. Refer to Question 142, but assume A and B were not survived by any children. Which answer would best describe the most likely disposition of O's estate following formal administration?

(A) The entire estate passes to C.

(B) Two-thirds pass to D, and one-third passes to C.

(C) One-half passes to D, and one-half passes to C.

(D) One-third passes to A's spouse; one-third passes to B's spouse; and one-third passes to C.

146. Refer to Question 139, but assume A, B, and C were actually the stepchildren of S (the children of S's spouse by a prior marriage). S never adopted A, B, and C. Which answer best describes the most likely disposition of O's estate following formal administration?

(A) The entire estate passes to D.

(B) Two-thirds pass to D, and one-third passes to C.

(C) One-third passes to A1; one-third passes to B1; and one-third passes to C.

(D) The entire estate passes to C.

147. Refer to Question 142, but assume A, B, and C were actually the stepchildren of S, the children of S's spouse by prior marriage who S did not adopt. Which answer best describes the most likely disposition of O's estate following formal administration?

ANSWER:

148. Refer to question 139 and assume C, who was married to C's spouse and also the father of two children, C1 and C2, filed a valid disclaimer in the probate proceedings of O's estate. Which answer best describes the effect the disclaimer would have on the disposition of O's estate following formal administration?

(A) C's one-third interest would pass to C's spouse.

(B) C's one-third interest would pass to C1 and C2.

(C) C's one-third interest would pass to A1 and B1.

(D) C's one-third interest would pass to D.

149. Refer to Question 146 and assume C, who was married to C's spouse and also the father of two children, C1 and C2, filed a valid disclaimer in the probate proceedings of O's estate. Which answer best describes the effect the disclaimer would have on the disposition of O's estate following formal administration?

    (A) The entire estate would pass to D.

    (B) Two-thirds of the estate would pass to D, and one-third passes to C's spouse.

    (C) Two-thirds of the estate would pass to D, and one-third passes to C1 and C2.

    (D) The entire estate would pass to C1 and C2.

150. O, an unmarried resident of the state of X, died. O was survived by O's only child, C, a resident of the state of Y, and C's only child, G, also a resident of the state of Y. O's valid will has been admitted to probate and devises Blackacre to G and the rest, residue, and remainder of O's estate to a charity. Due to G's serious financial difficulties, G filed a valid disclaimer in the probate proceedings of O's estate. G did not have any children. What is likely disposition of Blackacre following the formal administration of O's estate?

    ANSWER:

151. O, an unmarried resident of the state of X, died recently. O was survived by O's only child, D. A, B, and C were friends of O. O's valid will has been admitted to probate, and the will provides that: (i) the stock certificates located in O's safe deposit box are devised to A, (ii) the jewelry listed on O's homeowner's insurance policy is devised to B, (iii) any other personal property is to be distributed by the executor pursuant to the instructions the testator intends to leave in a memo that will be attached to the will, and (iv) and the rest, residue, and remainder of O's estate is devised to D. A memo was attached to the will at the time O died. The memo was dated several months after the execution of the will and indicated that certain described items of tangible personal property were to be delivered to C by the executor. This memo was typewritten and signed by O. Which answer best describes the most likely disposition of the stock certificates located in the safe deposit box, the jewelry listed on the insurance policy, and the items of personal property described in the memo following the formal administration of O's estate?

    (A) The stock, jewelry, and personal property pass to D.

    (B) The stock passes to A; the jewelry passes to B; and the personal property passes to C.

    (C) The stock passes to A; the jewelry passes to B; and the personal property passes to D.

    (D) The stock passes to A, and the jewelry and personal property pass to D.

152. O, an unmarried resident of the state of X, died recently. O was survived by O's child, C, and C's child, G. O's valid will has been admitted to probate. O's will devises Blackacre to F, a friend of O, and the rest, residue, and remainder of O's estate to a charity. However, other friends of both F and O will testify that O and F had orally agreed, prior to O's execution of the will, that F would manage Blackacre for C during C's lifetime, paying C any income generated; at C's death, F would convey Blackacre to G. What is the most likely disposition of Blackacre following formal administration of O's estate?

ANSWER:

153. Refer to Question 152, but assume that the agreement between O and F had been memorialized in a written agreement signed by both F and O at the time the will was signed. What is the most likely disposition of Blackacre following the formal administration of O's estate?

   (A) An express trust has been created with F, as trustee, and C and G, as the beneficiaries.

   (B) F acquired fee simple title to Blackacre because the terms of the agreement are not in the will.

   (C) C, as O's sole heir, or the charity will have the court impose a resulting trust on F in favor of C because O's attempt to create an express trust failed.

   (D) The court will impose a constructive trust on F in favor of C and/or G in order to avoid unjustly enriching F.

154. Refer to Question 152, but assume O's will had devised Blackacre to "F as trustee." Which answer best describes the most likely disposition of Blackacre following formal administration of O's estate?

   (A) An express trust has been created with F, as trustee, and C and G, as the beneficiaries.

   (B) The charity will acquire fee simple title to Blackacre because the terms of the agreement are not in the will.

   (C) C, as O's sole heir, will have the court impose a resulting trust on F in favor of C because O's attempt to create an express trust failed.

   (D) The court will impose a constructive trust on F in favor of C and/or G in order to avoid unjustly enriching F and/or the charity.

155. Refer to Question 152, but assume that O's will devises Blackacre to "F in trust for C and G." What is the most likely disposition of Blackacre following formal administration of O's estate?

ANSWER:

156. Refer to Question 152 and assume that O's will had devised Blackacre to "F as trustee" but there is no evidence of (i) any agreement existing between O and A prior to O's death related to the disposition of Blackacre or (ii) what O intended F to do with the property. Which answer best describes the most likely disposition of Blackacre following O's death?

(A) An express trust has been created with F, as trustee, and the charity, as the beneficiary.

(B) The charity acquired fee simple title to Blackacre.

(C) C, as O's sole heir, will have the court impose a resulting trust on Blackacre in favor of C.

(D) F acquired fee simple title to Blackacre.

157. Refer to Question 156, but assume that O's will had devised Blackacre to "F in trust for C and G." Which answer best describes the most likely disposition of Blackacre following formal administration of O's estate?

(A) An express trust has been created with F, as trustee, and C and G, as the beneficiaries.

(B) The charity acquired fee simple title to Blackacre.

(C) C, as O's sole heir, will have the court impose a resulting trust on Blackacre in favor of C.

(D) C and G acquired fee simple title.

158. Refer to Question 152, but assume that C died one day prior to O. C was survived by a spouse, S, as well as G and one other child of C, G2. C's valid will has been admitted to probate and devises all of C's property to S. Which answer best describes the most likely disposition of Blackacre following formal administration of O's estate?

(A) An express trust has been created with F, as trustee, and G, as beneficiary.

(B) F acquired fee simple title to Blackacre because the terms of the agreement are impossible to complete.

(C) G and G2, as O's heirs, will have the court impose a resulting trust on F in favor of G and G2 because O's attempt to create an express trust failed.

(D) G will have the court impose a constructive trust on F in favor of G in order to avoid unjustly enriching F.

159. Refer to Question 158, but assume G, rather than C, died one day prior to O. G was survived by G's spouse, GS, and one child, GG. G's valid will has been admitted to probate and devises all of G's property to GS. What is the most likely disposition of Blackacre following formal administration of O's estate?

ANSWER:

160. Refer to Question 152, but assume F died one day prior to O. F was survived by F's spouse, S, and one child, F1. F's valid will has been admitted to probate and devises all of F's property to S. What is the most likely disposition of Blackacre following the termination of O's estate?

    (A) C and G will have the court impose a constructive trust on F's spouse to avoid unjust enrichment.

    (B) C and G will have the court impose a constructive trust on F's child to avoid unjust enrichment.

    (C) C will have the court impose a resulting trust on the charity because the attempt to create an express trust failed.

    (D) The charity acquired Blackacre.

161. Refer to Question 152, but assume both C and G died one day prior to O. C was survived by C's spouse, S, and C's valid will has been admitted to probate and devises all of C's property to S. G was survived by G's spouse, GS, and one child, GG; G's valid will has been admitted to probate and devises all of G's property to GS. Which answer best describes the most likely disposition of Blackacre following formal administration of O's estate?

    (A) GS will have the court impose a constructive trust on F to avoid unjust enrichment.

    (B) GG will have the court impose a constructive trust on F to avoid unjust enrichment.

    (C) The charity will have the court impose a constructive trust on F to avoid unjust enrichment.

    (D) F retains the fee simple title.

162. Refer to Question 152. F has informed you that F acknowledges that F and O had the oral agreement but that F does not want to assume the responsibility of managing Blackacre for C and G. Which answer best describes the legal advice that should be given to F under these circumstances?

    (A) You can disclaim, and the title will vest in the charity.

    (B) You can disclaim and the title will vest in C.

    (C) You can accept the legal title to Blackacre, and then simply convey Blackacre to C and G.

    (D) You can disclaim, and the court will appoint a successor trustee to manage the express trust.

163. Refer to Question 152, but assume that the property subject to the oral agreement and devised to F in O's will was not Blackacre, but was shares of common stock in a publicly held corporation. What is the most likely disposition of the shares of stock?

ANSWER:

Note: For Questions 164-190, except where specifically indicated, assume that the applicable statute of frauds requires a writing for the creation of an enforceable trust of real property.

164. O, an unmarried resident of the state of X, conveyed Blackacre to a cousin, F. After the conveyance, O told G that, at the time of the conveyance, O and F had orally agreed that F would manage Blackacre until O's death; at that time, F would convey Blackacre to O's grandchild, G. G is the only child of C, who is O's only child. G also says that O told G that F had also agreed to pay to O any income generated by Blackacre during O's lifetime. The deed was duly recorded; no income had been generated since the conveyance, and O has recently died intestate. Record legal title is in F's name; F has paid all property taxes. F denies that F had any agreement with O concerning what F was to do with the property. Which answer best describes the most likely disposition of Blackacre following O's death?

    (A) G can have the court enforce the terms of the oral express trust.

    (B) F retains Blackacre because the oral express trust is unenforceable.

    (C) C will have the court impose a resulting trust on F in favor of C because O's attempt to create an express trust failed.

    (D) G will have the court impose a constructive trust on F in favor of G because F breached the oral agreement.

165. Refer to Question 164, but assume F admits that F and O had the oral agreement but says F will not abide by the agreement because it was not in writing. Which answer best describes the most likely disposition of Blackacre following O's death?

    (A) G can have the court enforce the terms of the oral express trust.

    (B) F retains Blackacre because the oral express trust is unenforceable.

    (C) C will have the court impose a resulting trust on F in favor of C because O's attempt to create an express trust failed.

    (D) G will have the court impose a constructive trust on F in favor of G because F breached the oral agreement.

166. Refer to Question 164, but assume that F was also O's accountant. Which answer best describes the most likely disposition of Blackacre following O's death?

    (A) G will ask the court to enforce the terms of the oral express trust.

    (B) F retains Blackacre because the oral express trust is unenforceable.

(C) G will have the court impose a constructive trust on F in favor of C because O's attempt to create an express trust failed.

(D) C will have the court impose a constructive trust on F in favor of C.

167. Refer to Question 164, but assume that other friends were present at the time of the original transaction. What is the most likely disposition of Blackacre by reason of O's death?

ANSWER:

168. Refer to Question 164, but assume that other friends were present at the time of the original transaction. Also assume that the property transferred by O to F pursuant to the oral agreement was not Blackacre, but was shares of common stock in a publicly held corporation. Which answer best describes the most likely disposition of the shares of stock by reason of O's death?

(A) G will have the court impose a constructive trust on F in favor of G because F breached the oral agreement.

(B) G will have the court enforce the terms of the oral express trust.

(C) C will have the court impose a resulting trust on F in favor of C because O's attempt to create an express trust failed.

(D) F retains the stock because the oral express trust is unenforceable.

169. Refer to Question 164, but assume that other friends were present at the time of the original transaction and that the deed that O delivered to F was duly recorded and conveyed Blackacre to "F, as trustee." Which answer best describes the most likely disposition of Blackacre by reason of O's death?

(A) G will have the court enforce the terms of the oral express trust.

(B) G will have the court impose a constructive trust on F in favor of G because F breached the oral agreement.

(C) C will have the court impose a resulting trust on F in favor of C because O's attempt to create an express trust failed.

(D) F will retain Blackacre because the oral express trust is unenforceable.

170. Refer to Question 164, but assume that (i) G cannot produce any admissible evidence of the terms of an agreement between O and F concerning what F was to do with the property and (ii) the duly recorded deed conveyed Blackacre to "F, as trustee for G." Which answer best describes the most likely disposition of Blackacre by reason of O's death?

(A) Fee simple title is vested in C.

(B) Fee simple title is vested in G.

(C) F owns the legal interests, and G owns the equitable interests.

(D) F owns the legal title, and C owns the equitable interests.

171. Refer to Question 164, but assume that F acknowledges the oral agreement F had with O. However, a creditor of F has obtained a judgment against F and is seeking to satisfy the judgment by attaching Blackacre. Assuming the statute of frauds does not require a trust of real property to be in writing, what legal advice should be given to F?

ANSWER:

172. Refer to Question 164, but assume that F acknowledges the oral agreement F had with O. However, a creditor of F has obtained a judgment against F and is seeking to satisfy the judgment by attaching Blackacre. Assuming the statute of frauds requires a trust of real property to be in writing, what legal advice should be given to F?

ANSWER:

173. Refer to Question 164 but assume that a writing signed by O and F evidencing the creation of the trust and its terms has been discovered. However, a creditor of F has a judgment against F and is seeking to satisfy the judgment by attaching Blackacre. Which answer best describes the legal advice that should be given to F?

(A) You can convey Blackacre to G pursuant to your agreement with O notwithstanding the judgment against you.

(B) You can convey Blackacre to C pursuant to the agreement with O, but the creditor will have it set aside as a transfer in fraud of creditors.

(C) You can allow the creditor to attach Blackacre notwithstanding your agreement with O.

(D) The creditor can attach Blackacre regardless of what you decide to do.

174. O, an unmarried resident of the state of X, and F, a friend of O, entered into a written trust agreement signed by both O and F. Following the execution of the trust agreement, O conveyed Blackacre to F; record legal title is in F's name. The terms of the trust agreement direct F to manage Blackacre until O's death; at that time, F is to convey Blackacre to O's grandchild, G. Prior to O's death, any income generated was to be delivered to O but no income was generated. F has paid the property taxes. O died recently intestate, survived by O's only

child, C. G died one day before O, survived by G's spouse, S, and G's only child, GG. G's valid will has been admitted to probate and devises all of G's estate to S. Which answer best describes the most likely disposition of Blackacre by reason of O's death?

(A) C will ask the court to impose a resulting trust on F in favor of C.

(B) S will ask the court to enforce the express trust on F in favor of S.

(C) GG will ask the court to enforce the express trust on F in favor of GG.

(D) F retains fee simple title.

175. Refer to Question 174, but assume that the trust agreement between O and F had not been memorialized in a written document. However, there is sufficient evidence available to prove the existence and terms of the oral trust. If the statute of frauds does not require a trust of real property to be in writing, which answer best describes the most likely disposition of Blackacre by reason of O's death?

(A) C will ask the court to impose a resulting trust on F in favor of C.

(B) S will ask the court to enforce the express trust on F in favor of S.

(C) GG will ask the court to enforce the express trust on F in favor of GG.

(D) F retains fee simple title.

176. Refer to Question 174, but assume that the trust agreement between O and F had not been memorialized in a written document. However, there is sufficient evidence available to prove the existence and terms of the oral trust. If the statute of frauds does require a trust of real property to be in writing, what is the most likely disposition of Blackacre by reason of O's death?

ANSWER:

177. Refer to question 174, but assume, unknown to both O and F at the time of the written agreement and conveyance, G was already dead. Which answer best describes the most likely disposition of Blackacre by reason of O's death?

(A) C will ask the court to impose a resulting trust on F in favor of C.

(B) C will ask the court to impose a constructive trust on F in favor of C.

(C) GG will ask the court to impose a constructive trust.

(D) S will ask the court to impose a constructive trust.

178. Refer to question 175, but assume, unknown to both O and F at the time of the oral agreement and conveyance, G was already dead. What is the most likely disposition of Blackacre by reason of O's death?

    (A) C will ask the court to impose a resulting trust on F in favor of C.

    (B) C will ask the court to impose a constructive trust on F in favor of C.

    (C) GG will ask the court to impose a constructive trust.

    (D) S will ask the court to impose a constructive trust.

179. Refer to question 176, but assume, unknown to both O and F at the time of the oral agreement and assignment, G was already dead. Which answer best describes the most likely disposition of Blackacre by reason of O's death?

    (A) C will ask the court to impose a resulting trust on F in favor of C.

    (B) C will ask the court to impose a constructive trust on F in favor of C.

    (C) GG will ask the court to impose a constructive trust.

    (D) S will ask the court to impose a constructive trust.

180. Refer to Question 164, but assume that the terms of the oral agreement between O and F had been committed to writing in a separate written agreement signed by both O and F at the time the deed to Blackacre was conveyed by O to F. Which answer best describes the most likely disposition of Blackacre by reason of O's death?

    (A) G will ask the court to enforce the terms of the written express trust.

    (B) G will ask the court to impose a constructive trust on F in favor of G.

    (C) C will ask the court to impose a resulting trust on F in favor of C.

    (D) F retains fee simple title.

181. Refer to Question 180, but assume G died following the conveyance to F, but prior to O's death. G died intestate and was survived by G's parents, C and M. C and M are divorced. Which answer best describes the most likely disposition of Blackacre by reason of O's death?

    (A) C will ask the court to impose a resulting trust on F in favor of C.

    (B) C will ask the court to enforce the terms of the express trust.

    (C) C and M will ask the court to enforce the terms of the express trust.

    (D) F retains fee simple title.

182. Refer to Question 181, but assume that the terms of the written express trust directed F to deliver Blackacre at O's death to G only if G survived O. Which answer would most likely describe the disposition of Blackacre by reason of O's death?

    (A)   F retains fee simple title.

    (B)   C will ask the court to impose a resulting trust on F in favor of C.

    (C)   C will ask the court to enforce the terms of the express trust.

    (D)   C and M will ask the court to enforce the terms of the express trust.

183. Refer to Question 180, but assume that, prior to O's death, O asked F, in a letter addressed to F and signed by O, to convey Blackacre back to O, explaining that O was very disappointed in G and that O did not want G to have Blackacre when O died. F complied with O's request and conveyed Blackacre to O. O then sold Blackacre to X, a good faith purchaser. Is O's estate or F liable to G because of the described transactions?

ANSWER:

184. O, an unmarried resident of the state of X, died recently. O was survived by a child, C, and O's grandchild, G, a child of another child of O who predeceased O. O's valid will has been admitted to probate and devises 1,000 shares of the common stock of a publicly held corporation to C "with the request that C deliver the shares to G, if G graduates from college"; the rest, residue, and remainder of O's estate is devised to a charity. G was 18 at the time of O's death and had not yet graduated from high school. Which answer best explains the likely disposition of the shares of stock by reason of O's death?

    (A)   C is the trustee of an express trust for the benefit of G.

    (B)   G will ask the court to impose a constructive trust on C in favor of G to avoid unjust enrichment.

    (C)   The charity will ask the court to impose a resulting trust on C in favor of G because O's attempt to create a private express trust failed.

    (D)   C owns the stock.

185. Refer to Question 184, but assume that O's will devises the 1,000 shares to "C to be delivered to G when G graduates from college." Which answer best explains the likely disposition of the shares of stock by reason of O's death?

    (A)   C is the trustee of an express trust for the benefit of G.

    (B)   G will ask the court to impose a constructive trust on C in favor of G to avoid unjust enrichment.

(C) The charity will ask the court to impose a resulting trust on C in favor of G, because O's attempt to create a private express trust failed.

(D) C owns the stock.

186. Refer to Question 185, but assume G died after the will was executed by O but before O died. G had not yet graduated from high school. Which answer best explains the likely disposition of the shares of stock by reason of O's death?

(A) C is the trustee of an express trust for the benefit of G's heirs.

(B) The charity owns the stock.

(C) The charity will ask the court to impose a resulting trust on C in favor of the charity, because O's attempt to create an express trust failed.

(D) C owns the stock.

187. O, an unmarried resident of the state of X, died intestate recently. O was survived by child, C, and grandchild, G, the child of C. Prior to O's death, O told several friends that O was holding Blackacre as trustee for the benefit of G, and when G reached age 21, O was going to convey legal title to G. Record legal title then and now is in O's name. There is no written evidence of O's stated intent. When O died, G was age 18. C now claims Blackacre as O's heir. Assuming the statute of frauds does not require a trust of real property to be in writing, what is the most likely disposition of Blackacre by reason of O's death?

ANSWER:

188. Refer to Question 187, but assume that the property involved in the controversy is 1,000 shares of stock in a publicly held corporation. Which answer best explains the most likely disposition of the 1,000 shares of stock?

(A) The court should appoint a successor trustee of the express trust to manage the stock until G attains age 21.

(B) The trust is unenforceable; the stock passes to C.

(C) G will have the court impose a constructive trust on C to avoid unjust enrichment by C.

(D) The personal representative of O's estate should retain the stock until G attains age 21 and then deliver it to G.

189. Refer to Question 187, but assume a written memorandum stating O's intent and signed by O has been discovered. Record legal title to Blackacre remains in O's name. Which answer best describes the most likely disposition of Blackacre by reason of O's death?

(A) The court should appoint a successor trustee of the express trust to manage Blackacre until G attains age 21.

(B) The trust is unenforceable; Blackacre passes to C.

(C) G will have the court impose a constructive trust on C to avoid unjust enrichment by C.

(D) The personal representative of O's estate should retain Blackacre until G attains age 21 and then deliver Blackacre to G.

190. Refer to Question 189, but assume shortly prior to O's death O had conveyed Blackacre as a gift to O's friend F. F was unaware of the trust. O was insolvent at the time of O's death. Which answer best describes the legal advice you would give to G?

(A) That's life; there's nothing you can do.

(B) You should file suit against O's estate for breach of fiduciary duty.

(C) You should have the court impose a constructive trust on F because O breached a fiduciary duty.

(D) You should file suit against F for conspiring with O to breach a fiduciary duty.

191. O, an unmarried resident of the state of X, died recently. O was survived by O's adult child, C, and G, the adult child of C. Prior to O's death, in a written document signed by O, O declared that O was serving as the trustee of Blackacre and explained that O would manage Blackacre so long as O was willing and able to do so; if O would ever be unable or unwilling to continue to serve as trustee, O's friend, F, would serve as trustee until O's death. The document provides that F, as trustee, was to convey Blackacre to F at the time of O's death. Additionally, prior to O's death, O or F, whoever was serving as trustee, was to pay to O any income Blackacre generated. The terms of the written document also provide that the trust was irrevocable. O's valid will, executed the same day as the described written document, has been admitted to probate and devises all of O's estate to G. Record title to Blackacre stayed in O's name until O died. Which answer best describes the most likely disposition of Blackacre by reason of O's death?

    (A) Because the document was not executed with testamentary formalities, Blackacre passes to G.

    (B) Because the document was not executed with testamentary formalities, Blackacre passes to C.

    (C) Blackacre passes to F by reason of O's death.

    (D) F, as trustee, can convey legal title to F, individually.

192. Refer to Question 191, but assume that the terms of the described written document provide that the trust was revocable by O at any time prior to O's death. There is no evidence that O ever intended to revoke the trust. Which answer best describes the most likely disposition of Blackacre by reason of O's death?

    (A) Because the document was not executed with testamentary formalities, Blackacre passes to G.

    (B) Because Blackacre was not executed with testamentary formalities, Blackacre passes to C.

    (C) Blackacre passes to F by reason of O's death.

    (D) F, as trustee, can convey legal title to F, individually.

193. Refer to Question 192, but assume F died shortly before O with a valid will that has been admitted to probate and devises all of F's property to F's parents, M and D. Before F died, F had been managing Blackacre for O for several months due to O's poor health. F did not have any descendants who survived F. Which answer best explains the most likely disposition of Blackacre by reason of O's death?

(A) Blackacre passes to G.

(B) The trust fails; the court should impose a resulting trust in favor of C.

(C) The trust is still valid; the court should appoint a successor trustee to convey Blackacre to M and D.

(D) Blackacre passes to M and D.

194. O, an unmarried resident of the state of X, died recently. O was survived by two children, C1 and C2, as well as (i) a great grandchild, GG, the only child of C1's deceased child, G1, and (ii) G2, the only child of C2. O's valid will has been admitted to probate and devises all of O's estate to G2. Several years prior to O's death, O had executed a valid inter vivos declaration of trust, whereby O declared himself to be the trustee of Blackacre; F was named as the successor trustee. At that time, O was married to W. The document was duly recorded in the county where Blackacre is located. The terms of the written trust agreement provide that, for the remainder of O's life, O is to receive all of the trust's income; at O's death, all the income is to be paid to W; and at the death of the survivor of O and W, Blackacre is to be delivered to G1. The terms of the trust agreement also state that the trust is irrevocable. After the execution of the trust document, but before O died, O and W divorced, and G1 died, survived by G1's spouse, S, and G1's only child, GG. G1's valid will has been admitted to probate and devises all of his property to S. What is the most likely disposition of the trust estate by reason of O's death?

ANSWER:

195. Refer to Question 194. How would your answer differ if the trust agreement, by its own terms, was revocable, but there is no evidence that O ever intended to revoke the trust?

(A) My answer would not change.

(B) Because W was no longer O's spouse and G1 predeceased O, Blackacre should be delivered to G2.

(C) Because W was no longer O's spouse, Blackacre should be delivered to O's heirs at law.

(D) Because W was no longer O's spouse, Blackacre should be delivered to GG.

196. O, an unmarried resident of the state of X, died recently. O was survived by two children, C1 and C2, and two grandchildren, G1 and G2. Prior to O's death, O had properly executed a valid, enforceable inter vivos declaration of trust document, whereby O declared O to be the trustee of the trust. The terms of the trust provide that the income and principal could be used for O's health, education, maintenance, and support during the remainder of O's lifetime; at O's death, any real property is to be delivered to G1, and any personal property is to be delivered to G2. The terms of the trust provide that the trust was revocable. However,

there is no evidence that O ever intended to revoke the trust. The trust also provided that, if O was ever unable or unwilling to act, a local bank was named as the successor trustee. At the time the trust document was signed by O, O attached a ten-dollar bill to the trust document. No other assets were made subject to the trust during O's lifetime. Following the execution of the trust document, O validly executed a will, whereby O devised O's entire estate to the bank as trustee of the described inter vivos trust agreement. The significant assets of O's estate at the time of O's death were Blackacre (fair market value $100,000) and common stocks (fair market value $100,000). Neither the will nor the trust document addresses the payment of O's debts following O's death, but there were unsecured debts of $100,000 at O's death. What is the most likely disposition of Blackacre and the stocks by reason of O's death?

ANSWER:

197. Refer to Question 196, but assume that O was married to S at the time O executed the trust agreement and will and also at the time of O's death. Also, assume that, prior to O's death, O transferred to himself, as trustee of the trust, $100,000 cash still held in trust at O's death. Which answer best describes the legal advice you should give to S after S explains to you that S has been apparently disinherited by O?

(A) Don't worry, the trust agreement and will are void.

(B) You are entitled to your marital share of the $100,000, Blackacre, and the stocks.

(C) You are entitled to your marital share of Blackacre and the stocks.

(D) You are entitled to your marital share of Blackacre.

198. O created a valid, enforceable irrevocable express trust last year by a written agreement. The assets of the trust consist of real and personal property; title is in T's name. The trustee is T; the beneficiaries are C and G. C is entitled to all of the income for the rest of C's lifetime; at C's death, T is to deliver the trust estate to G. A creditor of O has recently obtained a judgment against O and is trying to attach the assets of the trust. Which answer best describes the legal advice you would give to T?

(A) The trust estate is not reachable by O's creditors.

(B) The trust estate is not reachable by O's creditors unless they are tort creditors.

(C) The trust estate may be reached by O's creditors.

(D) The trust estate is reachable by O's creditors.

199. Refer to Question 198, but assume that the trust agreement by its own terms was revocable by O; however, O has never evidenced any intention to revoke the trust. Which answer best describes the legal advice you would give to T?

(A) The trust estate is not reachable by O's creditors.

(B) The trust estate is not reachable by O's creditors unless they are tort creditors.

(C) The trust estate may be reached by O's creditors.

(D) The trust estate is reachable by O's creditors.

200. Refer to Question 199, and also assume that O had just died and that the judgment was obtained by O's creditor against O's personal representative. Which answer best describes the legal advice you would give to T?

(A) The trust estate is not reachable by O's creditors.

(B) The trust estate is not reachable by O's creditors unless they are tort creditors.

(C) The trust estate may be reached by O's creditors.

(D) The trust estate is reachable by O's creditors.

201. Refer to Question 198, but assume that the trust agreement was pursuant to an oral understanding between O and T. Which answer best describes the legal advice you would give to T under the circumstances?

(A) The trust estate is not reachable by O's creditors.

(B) The trust estate is not reachable by O's creditors unless they are tort creditors.

(C) The trust estate may be reached by O's creditors.

(D) The trust estate is reachable by O's creditors.

202. Refer to Question 198, but assume that the creditor was a creditor of T, not O, and has obtained a judgment against T arising out of a situation totally unrelated to the trust property. Which answer best describes the legal advice that you would give to T in view of these circumstances?

(A) The trust estate is not reachable by your creditors.

(B) The trust estate is not reachable by your creditors unless they are tort creditors.

(C) The trust estate may be reachable depending upon the facts and circumstances.

(D) The trust estate is reachable to satisfy your creditors.

203. Refer to Question 202, but assume that the trust agreement was pursuant to an oral agreement between O and T, and T wishes to protect the interests of C and G. What legal advice would you give to T?

ANSWER:

204. Refer to Question 198, but assume that the creditor is a creditor of C, not O. The creditor is a former business associate of C and has obtained a judgment against C related to a business transaction. Which answer best describes the legal advice you would give to T under the circumstances?

    (A) The trust estate can be attached to satisfy the debt.

    (B) Trust income can be attached to satisfy the debt.

    (C) Trust income can be attached if the creditor is a tort creditor.

    (D) The trust estate cannot be attached to satisfy the debt.

205. Refer to Question 204, but assume that the trust agreement only authorizes T to distribute to C as much income as T, in T's discretion, determines is appropriate. Which answer best describes the legal advice you would give to T under the circumstances?

    (A) The trust estate can be attached to satisfy the debt.

    (B) Trust income can be attached to satisfy the debt.

    (C) Trust income can be attached if the creditor is a tort creditor.

    (D) The trust estate cannot be attached to satisfy the debt.

206. Refer to Question 204, but assume that T, according to the terms of the trust agreement, can only distribute to C such amounts of income as are necessary for C's health, education, maintenance, or support. Which answer best describes the legal advice you would give to T under the circumstances?

    (A) The trust estate can be attached to satisfy the debt.

    (B) Trust income can be attached to satisfy the debt.

    (C) Trust income can be attached if the creditor is a tort creditor.

    (D) The trust estate cannot be attached to satisfy the debt.

207. Refer to Question 206, but assume the creditor is a hospital that provided medical services to C. Which answer best describes the legal advice you would give to T under the circumstances?

    (A) The trust estate can be attached to satisfy the debt.

    (B) Trust income estate can be attached to satisfy the debt.

    (C) Trust income can be attached only if the creditor has exhausted C's individual assets.

    (D) The trust estate cannot be attached to satisfy the debt.

208. Refer to Question 198, but assume that the creditor is a creditor of G, not O, and has a judgment against G. Which answer best describes the legal advice that should be given to T under the circumstances?

(A) The trust estate can be attached to satisfy G's debt.

(B) G's interest in the trust estate can be attached to satisfy G's debt.

(C) The trust estate must be sold in order to pay the debt.

(D) The trust estate cannot be attached.

209. Refer to Questions 204 and 208. How would your answers differ if the trust agreement included a provision stating that the beneficiaries' interests in the trust could not be attached in order to satisfy any debt of a beneficiary?

ANSWER:

210. Refer to Question 208, but assume that the only provision in the trust agreement relating to creditors of beneficiaries is one that provides that, if a creditor of C ever attempts to attach C's interest, the interest terminates and passes to G; if a creditor of G ever attempts to attach the interest of G, the interest terminates and passes to a charity. Which answer best describes the legal advice you give T under those circumstances?

(A) The provision is valid; terminate the trust by delivering the property to the charity.

(B) The provision is valid; terminate the trust by delivering the property to C.

(C) The provision is valid; G's interest has passed to the charity.

(D) The provision is not valid; the creditor can attach G's interest in the trust.

211. O, an unmarried resident of the state of X, was the settlor of a valid, enforceable irrevocable express trust. The trustee is T; the beneficiaries are two adults, C and G. According to the terms of the trust agreement, C is entitled to all of the trust income for the rest of C's lifetime; at C's death, the trustee is to distribute the trust estate to G. T has recently learned that C has assigned C's interest in the trust to Q. Q is demanding that the trustee distribute the trust income to Q. Which answer best describes the legal advice that should be given to T?

(A) The assignment is valid; you should distribute the income to Q as long as C is alive.

(B) The assignment is void; you should continue to pay C for the remainder of C's lifetime.

(C) Because the assignment is not enforceable against the trust, you should continue to pay the income to C for the rest of C's lifetime.

(D) C's interest in the trust has terminated; the remaining trust assets should be delivered to G.

212. Refer to Question 211, but assume that the trust agreement only authorizes T to deliver to C as much income as C needs for C's health, support, education, or maintenance. Which answer best describes the legal advice that should be given to T?

   (A) The assignment is valid; you should pay all the income to Q for the rest of C's lifetime.

   (B) The assignment is valid, you should distribute to Q whatever income you would have distributed to C for C's health, support, education, or maintenance.

   (C) The assignment may be valid if Q paid C good and valuable consideration in exchange for the assignment.

   (D) The assignment may be valid if Q provided services for C's health, support, education, or maintenance.

213. Refer to Question 211, but assume that the trust agreement authorized T to distribute to C only as much as income as T, in T's discretion, deems appropriate. What legal advice should you give T under the circumstances?

ANSWER:

214. Refer to Question 211, but assume that it was G, not C, that assigned G's interest in the trust estate to Q. Which answer best describes the legal advice you should give T under the circumstances?

   (A) The assignment is void; you should continue to pay the income to C and deliver the trust estate to G when C dies.

   (B) The assignment is valid; T should deliver the trust estate to Q now.

   (C) The assignment is valid; T should deliver the trust estate to Q when C dies.

   (D) The assignment is enforceable only against G; you should continue to pay the income to C and deliver the trust estate to G when C dies.

215. Refer to Question 211, but assume that both C and G assigned their interests in the trust estate to T, not Q. Which answer best explains the most likely disposition of the trust estate under those circumstances?

   (A) The assignment can be set aside by O.

   (B) The assignment is valid; T is now the beneficiary of the trust.

   (C) The assignment is valid; T acquires fee simple title to the trust estate.

   (D) The assignment may be voidable by C and G.

216. Refer to Question 214, but assume the trust agreement includes a provision that prohibits both voluntary and involuntary assignments of beneficial interests by beneficiaries. Which answer best describes the legal effect of the assignment?

(A) The assignment is unenforceable against T who can deliver the trust estate to G when C dies.

(B) The assignment is valid; T should deliver the trust estate to X when C dies.

(C) The assignment is valid only if X paid good and valuable consideration for the assignment.

(D) The assignment is voidable at the election of G.

217. O created a valid, enforceable irrevocable express trust. T is the trustee; C and G are the beneficiaries. The trust agreement provides that T is to pay to C only as much income as T, in T's discretion, determines is appropriate, as long as C is alive; at C's death, T is to deliver the remaining trust estate to G. T has been making distributions of income to C. C believes the amount is not enough; G believes the amount is too much. Which parties have standing to challenge the distributions made by T?

ANSWER:

218. Refer to Question 217. Which answer best describes who has the burden of proof on the issue of whether or not the amount of the distributions has been proper?

(A) T must prove that T distributed an appropriate amount.

(B) C or G must prove the amount distributed was not an appropriate amount.

(C) T must prove that T did not abuse T's discretion.

(D) C or G must prove that T abused T's discretion.

219. Refer to Question 218, but assume that the trust agreement authorized T to distribute to C only as much income as was necessary for C's health, support, education, or maintenance. Which answer best describes the burden of proof in litigation involving the appropriate amount?

(A) T must prove that T did not abuse T's discretion.

(B) T must prove the amount distributed was needed for C's health, support, education, or maintenance.

(C) C or G must prove the amount was not the amount needed for C's health, support, education, or maintenance.

(D) (B) or (C) must prove that T abused T's discretion.

Note: In answering Questions 220 - 257 assume UPC § 2-707 is not applicable. UPC § 2-707 is a controversial provision that significantly changes the law of future interests. See Jesse Dukeminier, The Uniform Probate Code Upends the Law of Remainders, 94 Mich. Law Review 148 (1995). A number of states that have enacted the Uniform Probate Code have not included UPC § 2-707 as part of the legislation.

220.   O created a valid, enforceable inter vivos irrevocable express trust. The terms of the trust direct T to pay all the income to M, O's mother; at the time of M's death, T is directed to deliver the remaining trust estate to A, B, and C, the children of O's sister. Following the creation of the trust and prior to M's death, (i) O's sister had an additional child, D, and (ii) A died. A was survived by A's spouse, S. A's valid will has been admitted to probate and devises all of A's property to S. M has recently died. The significant asset of the trust is Blackacre. Who will succeed to Blackacre by reason of M's death?

ANSWER:

221.   Refer to Question 220, but assume that A was also survived by a child, G. Which answer best describes who will succeed to the trust estate by reason of M's death?

(A) B and C.

(B) B, C, and D.

(C) S, B, and C.

(D) G, B, and C.

222.   Refer to Question 220, but assume that the terms of the trust directed T, at M's death, to deliver the remaining trust estate to "the children of O's sister." Who succeeds to the trust estate by reason of M's death?

ANSWER:

223.   Refer to Question 222. How would your answer differ if O's sister was pregnant at the time of M's death?

(A) My answer would not change.

(B) The "child in embryo" succeeds to an equal interest with S, B, C, and D.

    (C) If born alive, the "child in embryo" succeeds to an equal interest with S, B, C, and D.

    (D) O will decide whether "the child in embryo" receives an interest in the trust estate.

224. Refer to Question 220, but assume that the trust agreement directed T at M's death to distribute the trust estate equally to each of A, B, and C, who survived M, or all to the survivor or survivors of them who survived M. Which answer best describes who succeeds to the trust estate by reason of M's death?

    (A) B, C, and D.

    (B) B and C.

    (C) S, B, and C.

    (D) O, B, and C.

225. Refer to Question 223, but assume that the trust document directs T, at M's death, to deliver the trust estate to the children of O's sister who survived M. Which answer best describes who succeeds to the trust estate by reason of M's death?

    (A) B, C, and D.

    (B) S, B, C, and D.

    (C) B, C, D, and the "child in embryo."

    (D) B, C, D, and, if born alive, the "child in embryo."

226. Refer to Question 225. How would your answer differ if O's sister advised T that the sister intended to have at least one other child in addition to the "child in embryo?"

    (A) My answer would not change.

    (B) My answer would not change unless O's sister did, in fact, have an additional child, in which event, that child would partially divest all of the sister's other children who had already received the trust estate.

    (C) My answer would not change unless O's sister did, in fact, have an additional child, in which event, that child would partially divest only the "child in embryo."

    (D) My answer would not change unless O's sister did, in fact, have an additional child, in which event, that child would partially divest all of the sister's other children who had already received the trust estate, assuming that child was born before the statute of limitations had run.

227. Refer to Question 222, but assume that O's sister had not had any children before M died. One year following M's death, A was born to O's sister. A later died. A was survived by O's sister, who was A's only heir. O's sister intends to have more children. What is the proper disposition of the estate following M's death?

ANSWER:

228. Refer to Question 222, but assume that the trust agreement prohibited voluntary and involuntary assignments of beneficial interests in the trust. Which answer best describes the most likely disposition of the trust estate?

    (A) My answer would not change.

    (B) B, C, and D.

    (C) O, B, C, and D.

    (D) C and D.

229. Refer to Question 220, but assume that the trust agreement prohibited voluntary and involuntary assignments of beneficial interests in the trust. Which answer best describes the most likely disposition of the trust estate?

    (A) My answer would not change.

    (B) B, C, and D.

    (C) B and C.

    (D) O, B, and C.

230. O, an unmarried resident of the state of X, died several years ago. O was survived by a child, A, and a grandchild, B, the only child of A. O's valid will was admitted to probate and devised Blackacre to A for life, remainder to B; the rest, residue, and remainder of O's estate was devised to a charity. B died recently survived by A, B's spouse, S, and B's children, B1 and B2. B's will devised all of B's property to S. Which answer best describes who succeeds to the future interest in Blackacre that B owned prior to B's death?

    (A) The charity.

    (B) A.

    (C) S.

    (D) B1 and B2.

231. Refer to Question 230. How would your answer differ if Blackacre had been devised by O to A for life, remainder to B, if B survives A?

    (A) My answer would not change.

    (B) A.

    (C) The charity.

    (D) B1 and B2.

232. Refer to Question 230. How would your answer differ if B had predeceased O?
ANSWER:

233. Refer to Question 230. How would your answer differ if Blackacre had been devised to T in trust with directions for T to pay the income to A for life, and, at A's death, deliver Blackacre to B?

    (A) My answer would not change.

    (B) A.

    (C) The charity.

    (D) B1 and B2.

234. O, an unmarried resident of X, died. O was survived by a child, A, and a grandchild, B. O's valid will was admitted to probate and devised Blackacre to A for life, remainder to B if B attains age 21. The rest, residue, and remainder of O's estate passed to a charity. At the time of O's death, B was only 14. B died recently at the age of 20, survived by A, B's spouse, S, and B's child, C. B's valid will has been admitted to probate and devises B's estate to S. Which answer best describes who succeeds to the future interest in Blackacre that B owned?

    (A) The charity.

    (B) A.

    (C) S.

    (D) C.

235. Refer to Question 234, but assume that B was 22 when B died. Which answer best describes who succeeds to the future interest in Blackacre that B owned?

    (A) The charity.

    (B) A.

(C) S.

(D) C.

236. Refer to Question 234, but assume that O's will had devised Blackacre to A for life, remainder to be delivered to B when B reaches age 21. Which answer best describes the most likely disposition of Blackacre by reason of B's death?

(A) C will be entitled to possession as soon as A dies.

(B) S will be entitled to possession as soon as A dies.

(C) The charity will be entitled to possession when A dies.

(D) A has acquired fee simple title.

237. O, an unmarried resident of the state of X, died. O was survived by a child, A, and a grandchild, B. O's valid will was admitted to probate and devised Blackacre to A for life, remainder to B, if B attains age 21. The rest, residue, and remainder of O's estate passed to a charity. At the time of O's death, B was only 14. A just died, and B is only 19. Which answer best describes the disposition of Blackacre by reason of A's death?

(A) A's heirs and devisees succeed to fee simple title.

(B) A's heirs and devisees are entitled to possession until B attains age 21, if B attains age 21.

(C) The charity succeeds to fee simple title.

(D) The charity is entitled to possession until B reaches age 21, if B attains age 21.

238. O, an unmarried resident of the state of X, died. O's valid will was admitted to probate and devised Blackacre to A for life, the remainder to B, but if B is not survived by children, to Charity No. 1. The rest, residue, and remainder of O's estate was devised to Charity No. 2. Both A and B survived O; however, B died recently, survived by A, B's spouse, S, and B's child, C. B's valid will has been admitted to probate and devises B's estate to S. Which answer best describes the effect B's death has on Blackacre?

(A) Charity No. 1 acquired the remainder interest in Blackacre.

(B) Charity No. 2 acquired the remainder interest in Blackacre.

(C) B's interest passed to S.

(D) B's interest passed to C.

239. Refer to Question 238. How would your answer differ if B and C died in an automobile accident, and there is no evidence as to who survived whom?

(A) My answer would not change.

    (B) Charity No. 1 acquired the remainder interest in Blackacre.

    (C) Charity No. 2 acquired the remainder interest in Blackacre.

    (D) B's interest passed to C.

240. O, an unmarried resident of the state of X, died. O's valid will was admitted to probate and devised Blackacre to A for life, then to A's children, but, if, at A's death, A is not survived by children, to Charity No. 1. The rest, residue, and remainder of the estate is devised to Charity No. 2. At the time of O's death, O was survived by O's child, A, and A's children, C1 and C2. Prior to A's death, C3 was born to A, and C2 died. C2 was survived by C2's spouse, S, and C2's child, G. C2's will devised all of C2's property to S. Which answer best describes the effect C2's death had on Blackacre?

    (A) C1 and C3 own the remainder interest.

    (B) C1 owns the remainder interest.

    (C) C2's interest passed to S.

    (D) C2's interest passed to S, subject to divestment if no child of A survives A.

241. Refer to Question 240. How would your answer differ if O's will devised Blackacre to A for life, then to such of A's children who survive A, but if none survive A, to a charity?

    (A) My answer would not change.

    (B) C1 and C3 own the remainder interest.

    (C) C1 owns the remainder interest.

    (D) C2's interest passed to G.

242. O, an unmarried resident of the state of X, died. O's valid will has been admitted to probate and devises Blackacre to O's grandchildren, and the rest, residue, and remainder of O's estate to a charity. At the time of O's death, O was survived by O's child, A, and A's two children, G1 and G2. A was not pregnant at the time of O's death. Who acquired ownership of Blackacre by reason of O's death?

ANSWER:

243. Refer to 242, but assume A did not have any children at the time of O's death but was pregnant at the time of O's death. Which answer best explains the ownership of Blackacre by reason of O's death?

    (A) The child in embryo owns fee simple title.

    (B) The charity acquires fee simple title subject to divestment upon the birth of the first child of A, who will acquire fee simple title.

    (C) The charity acquires fee simple title subject to divestment upon the birth of the first child of A, who will acquire fee simple title subject to partial divestment if A has any more children.

    (D) The charity owns fee simple title.

244. Refer to Question 242, but assume that A did not have any children and was not pregnant at the time of O's death. Who acquired ownership of Blackacre by reason of O's death?

ANSWER:

245. Refer to 244, but assume O's will had devised "10 acres of land to each of O's grandchildren" rather than "Blackacre to O's grandchildren." Which answer best explains the ownership of the land that had been specifically devised in the will by reason of O's death?

    (A) The charity owns fee simple title.

    (B) The charity acquires fee simple title subject to divestment upon the birth of the first child of A, who will acquire fee simple title.

    (C) The charity acquires fee simple title subject to divestment upon the birth of the first child of A, who will acquire fee simple title subject to partial divestment if A has more children.

    (D) A acquired fee simple title.

246. O, an unmarried resident of the state of X, died. O's valid will has been admitted to probate and devises Blackacre to O's grandchildren who are alive 21 years following O's death, and the rest, residue, and remainder of O's estate passes to a charity. At the time of O's death, O was survived by O's child, A, and A's two children, G1 and G2. Which answer best explains the ownership of Blackacre by reason of O's death?

    (A) The charity owns fee simple title.

    (B) The charity owns fee simple title subject to the future interests of G1 and G2.

    (C) The charity owns fee simple title subject to the future interests of G1, G2 and any other children A may have following O's death.

    (D) The charity owns fee simple title subject to the future interests of any children of A who are alive on the twenty-first anniversary of O's death.

247. Refer to Question 246, but assume that A did not have any children at the time of O's death. Which answer best describes the ownership of Blackacre by reason of O's death?

    (A) The charity owns fee simple title.

    (B) The charity owns fee simple title subject to the future interests of the first born child of A.

    (C) The charity owns fee simple title subject to the future interests of any other child A may have.

    (D) The charity owns fee simple title subject to the future interests of any children of A who are alive on the 21st anniversary of O's death.

248. Refer to Question 247, but assume that (i) Blackacre was devised to O's grandchildren who are alive 100 years following O's death and (ii) A had predeceased O. Which answer best describes the ownership of Blackacre by reason of O's death?

    (A) The charity owns fee simple title.

    (B) The charity owns fee simple title subject to divestment if G1 and G2 are both alive on the 100th anniversary of O's death.

    (C) The charity owns fee simple title subject to divestment if G1 or G2 is alive on the 100th anniversary of O's death.

    (D) The charity owns fee simple title subject to divestment if any descendant of A is alive on the 100th anniversary of O's death.

249. O, an unmarried resident of the state of X, died. O's valid will has been admitted to probate and devises Blackacre to the first grandchild of O who reaches age 25 and the rest, residue, and remainder of O's estate to a charity. At O's death, O was survived by O's child, A, and A's two children, G1 and G2, ages 18 and 19, respectively. Who acquires the ownership of Blackacre by reason of O's death?

ANSWER:

250. Refer to Question 249, but assume G1 and G2 were ages 24 and 26, respectively, at the time of O's death. Which answer best explains the ownership of Blackacre by reason of O's death?

    (A) The charity owns fee simple title.

    (B) G2 owns fee simple title.

    (C) G2 owns fee simple title subject to partial divestment if G1 reaches age 25.

    (D) G2 owns fee simple title subject to partial divestment if any other children reach age 25.

251. Refer to Question 249, but assume that O's will devised Blackacre to O's "grandchildren who reach age 21." Which answer best explains the ownership of Blackacre by reason of O's death?

    (A) The charity owns fee simple title.

    (B) The charity owns fee simple title subject to divestment if G1 or G2 reaches age 21.

    (C) The charity owns fee simple title subject to divestment if any child of A reaches age 21.

    (D) A owns fee simple title.

252. Refer to Question 249, but assume that O's will devised Blackacre to O's "grandchildren who reach age 25" and that A had predeceased O by one day. A's spouse, S, was pregnant at the time of the deaths of both O and A. Which answer best describes the ownership of Blackacre by reason of the death of O?

    (A) The charity owns fee simple title.

    (B) The charity owns fee simple title subject to divestment if G1 or G2 reaches age 25.

    (C) The charity owns fee simple title subject to divestment if G1, G2, or the child in embryo reaches age 25.

    (D) The charity owns fee simple title subject to divestment only if all of A's children, including the child in embryo, reach age 25.

253. O, an unmarried resident of X, died recently. O was survived by one child, A, and two grandchildren, G1 and G2, ages 8 and 9, respectively. O, shortly prior to O's death, conveyed Blackacre to the first grandchild of O who reaches age 21. The deed was duly recorded. O's valid will has been admitted to probate and devises all of O's property to a charity. Who acquired the ownership of Blackacre by reason of the conveyance and O's death?

ANSWER:

254. O, an unmarried resident of the state of X, died recently. O's valid will has been admitted to probate and devises Blackacre to O's children for their lifetimes with a remainder to O's grandchildren. The rest, residue, and remainder of O's estate passes to a charity. At the time of O's death, O was survived by one child, A, age 85, and one grandchild, G, age 65. Which answer best describes the ownership of Blackacre by reason of O's death?

    (A) A has a life estate, and G owns the remainder interest.

    (B) A has a life estate, and G and any other children A might have in the future own the remainder interest.

(C) The charity owns fee simple title.

(D) A has a life estate, and the charity owns the remainder interest.

255. Refer to Question 254 but assume that, several years before O's death, O had conveyed Whiteacre to O's children for their lifetimes with a remainder to O's grandchildren. O's will devised O's entire estate to a charity. Who acquired the ownership of Whiteacre by reason of the conveyance and O's death?

ANSWER:

256. O, an unmarried resident of the state of X, died recently. O's will devised Blackacre to T in trust with directions for T to pay O's child, A, the income for the rest of A's lifetime; and then to pay to A's children the income for the rest of their lifetimes; upon the death of the last surviving child of A, T is to deliver the trust estate to A's grandchildren. At the time of O's death, O was survived by O's child, A, age 60, and A's children, A1, A2, and A3, ages 25, 27, and 30, respectively; each child is the parent of a child. Does all or any part of the disposition of Blackacre violate the rule against perpetuities?

ANSWER:

257. O, an unmarried resident of the state of X, died recently. O's will has been admitted to probate and devises Blackacre to A for life, then to A's widow for her remaining lifetime, and the remainder to A's children who survive A's widow. At the time of O's death, O was survived by A, A's spouse, S, and A's three children, G1, G2, and G3. Does all or any part of the disposition of Blackacre violate the rule against perpetuities?

ANSWER:

258. O, a resident of the state of X, created a valid, enforceable irrevocable express trust. The terms of the written trust agreement direct the trustee, T, to pay the income to A for the rest of A's lifetime; at the time of A's death, T is directed to deliver the trust estate to such of A's children as A appoints by will. In default of appointment, T is to deliver the trust estate to a charity. At the time the trust was created, A had two children, C1 and C2. Following the creation of the trust, A validly executed a will in which A expressly appointed the trust estate to C1 and C2. Later, A had another child, C3. All parties reside in the state of X. Which answer best describes the current beneficiaries of the trust?

(A) A.

(B) A, C1, and C2.

(C) A and the charity.

(D) A, C1, C2, and the charity.

259. Refer to Question 258, but assume A has recently died, survived by a spouse, S, as well as A's children, C1, C2, and C3. Which answer best describes who is likely to succeed to the trust estate by reason of A's death?

(A) The charity.

(B) C1 and C2.

(C) C1, C2, and C3.

(D) S, C1, C2, and C3.

260. Refer to Question 259 but assume A's will cannot be admitted to probate because A failed to comply with a technical requirement of the laws of X. What is the most likely disposition of the trust estate?

ANSWER:

261. Refer to Question 259 and assume A's will has been admitted to probate, but also assume that the will does not make any reference to A's power of appointment or the trust estate; it simply devises all of A's property to A's children. Which answer best describes the most likely disposition of the trust estate?

(A) T should distribute it to the charity.

(B) T should distribute it to C1 and C2.

(C) C1, C2, and C3 will have the court impose a constructive trust on the charity to avoid unjust enrichment.

(D) C1 and C2 will have the court impose a constructive trust on the charity to avoid unjust enrichment.

262. Refer to Question 259, but assume A never executed the will and died intestate. Which answer best describes the most likely disposition of the trust estate?

(A) T should distribute it to the charity.

(B) T should distribute it to C1 and C2.

(C) C1, C2, and C3 will have the court impose a constructive trust on the charity to avoid unjust enrichment.

(D) C1 and C2 will have the court impose a constructive trust on the charity to avoid unjust enrichment.

263. O, an unmarried resident of the state of X, died years ago. O's valid will was admitted to probate and devised Blackacre to A for life, remainder to such person or persons as A appoints by will, including A's estate, and, in default of appointment, to a charity. A, also a resident of the state of X, died recently survived by A's spouse, S, and A's child, C. A's valid, probated will did not refer to A's power of appointment, but specifically devised Blackacre to C and the rest, residue, and remainder of A's estate to S. Blackacre had a fair market value of $100,000 at the time of A's death; the value of A's property exceeded one million dollars. Which answer best describes the most likely disposition of Blackacre?

(A) It passes to the charity.

(B) It passes to C.

(C) It passes to C, subject to S's marital share.

(D) It passes to the charity, subject to S's marital share.

264. Refer to Question 263, but assume A's will simply devises all of A's property to C. There is no reference in A's will to Blackacre or A's power of appointment. Which answer best describes the most likely disposition of Blackacre by reason of A's death?

(A) It passes to C.

(B) It passes to C, subject to S's marital share.

(C) It passes to the charity.

(D) It passes to the charity, subject to S's marital share.

265. Refer to Question 263, but assume A's will devised "all of my property, including any property over which I have a power of appointment, to C." What is the most likely disposition of Blackacre?

ANSWER:

266. Refer to Question 265, but assume C predeceased A, survived by C's spouse, CS, and C's child, CC. Which answer best explains the most likely disposition of Blackacre by reason of A's death?

    (A) It passes to CC.

    (B) It passes to CS.

    (C) It passes to S.

    (D) It passes to the charity.

267. Refer to Question 266, but assume A's will expressly exercised the power of appointment in favor of C and then devised all of A's property to S. Which answer best describes the most likely disposition of Blackacre by reason of A's death?

    (A) It passes to CC.

    (B) It passes to CS.

    (C) It passes to S.

    (D) It passes to the charity.

268. Refer to Question 267, but assume that, at the time of A's death, A's liabilities exceeded A's assets. Explain the rights of A's creditors, if any, in and to Blackacre.

ANSWER:

269. Refer to Question 265, but assume that, at A's death, A's liabilities exceeded the value of A's assets. Which answer best describes the rights of A's creditors in and to Blackacre?

    (A) A's creditors have no rights in and to Blackacre.

    (B) A's creditors can attack the transfer as one in fraud of creditors.

    (C) A's creditors can demand that A's personal representatives return Blackacre to the estate to satisfy the creditors, if the probate assets are insufficient.

    (D) Blackacre will be subject to A's debts.

270. A, an unmarried resident of the state of X, created 10 years ago an irrevocable, valid, enforceable inter vivos express trust agreement with A as trustee. At the time the trust was created, A was solvent and remained solvent after the trust was funded. The terms of the written trust agreement authorize A to distribute to A as much income and/or principal as A needs for A's health, support, education, or maintenance. In addition, A may appoint any part of the trust estate to any one or more of A's children by deed during A's lifetime or at A's death by A's will. At the time of A's death, the successor trustee is to distribute any remaining trust assets to a charity. No trust assets have ever been distributed to A. A is now in financial difficulties due to bad investments made last year. A's creditors are seeking assets to attach. A creditor of A is seeking your legal advice. Which answer best describes the legal advice you should give the creditor?

(A) You cannot reach any part of the trust estate.

(B) You may be able to reach whatever assets A may distribute to A's children.

(C) You may be able to attach only what A distributes to himself.

(D) You can attach all or any part of the trust estate.

271. Refer to Question 270. How would your answer differ if the trust described would have been a "spendthrift" trust? Would your answer differ if A's parent had created and funded the trust?

ANSWER:

272. O, an unmarried resident of the state of X, died. O's valid will was admitted to probate and devised Blackacre to A for life, remainder to such of A's children as A appoints by will, and in default of appointment, to another child of O, B. The rest, residue, and remainder of O's estate was devised to B. Additionally, during O's lifetime, O had created a valid irrevocable inter vivos express trust that directed the trustee, T, to pay the income to A during A's lifetime; at A's death, T is directed to distribute the principal to anyone, including A's estate, as A may appoint by will, and, in default of appointment, to B. A died recently, intestate, and a resident of the state of X. Which answer best explains whether Blackacre and the trust estate of the trust will be included in A's gross estate for federal transfer tax purposes?

    (A) Both Blackacre and the trust estate will be included in A's gross estate.

    (B) Neither Blackacre nor the trust estate will be included in A's gross estate.

    (C) Blackacre, but not the trust estate, will be included in A's gross estate.

    (D) The trust estate, but not Blackacre, will be included in A's gross estate.

273. Refer to Question 272, but assume A had a valid will that has been admitted to probate, but the will fails to exercise either power of appointment. Which answer best explains whether Blackacre and the trust estate of the trust will be included in A's gross estate for federal transfer tax purposes?

    (A) Both Blackacre and the trust estate will be included in A's gross estate.

    (B) Neither Blackacre nor the trust estate will be included in A's gross estate.

    (C) Blackacre, but not the trust estate, will be included in A's gross estate.

    (D) The trust estate, but not Blackacre, will be included in A's gross estate.

274. Refer to Question 272, but assume A had a valid will that has been admitted to probate and that exercises both of the powers of appointment in favor of A's child, C. Will Blackacre or the trust estate be included in A's gross estate for federal transfer tax purposes?

ANSWER:

275. O, an unmarried resident of the state of X, created a valid, enforceable irrevocable inter vivos express trust. A is the trustee of the trust, and, as trustee of the trust, A is authorized to distribute to A such amounts of the income and principal as A needs for A's health, support, education, or maintenance. At A's death, the successor trustee is directed to deliver the remaining

trust estate to anyone in the world, other than A's estate or creditors, and in default of appointment, to A's sibling, B. O created a second trust with A as trustee. According to the terms of the second trust agreement, A, as trustee, can distribute to A such amounts of income and principal as A needs for A's comfort or welfare. At A's death, the successor trustee is directed to deliver any remaining trust estate of the second trust to B. A has recently died, intestate, survived by A's children, C1 and C2. Which answer best explains whether the trust estates of the two trusts will be included in A's gross estate for federal transfer tax purposes?

(A) Both trust estates will be included in A's gross estate.

(B) Neither trust estate will be included in A's gross estate.

(C) The trust estate of trust one, but not of trust two, will be included in A's gross estate.

(D) The trust estate of trust two, but not of trust one, will be included in A's gross estate.

276. O, an unmarried resident of the state of X, created a valid irrevocable inter vivos express trust with a friend of O, T, serving as trustee. The terms of the written trust agreement direct T to pay to A all of the income and such amounts of principal as T determines is appropriate for A's comfort or welfare; at A's death, T is directed to deliver the trust estate to the children of A. Additionally, when O died, O's valid will was admitted to probate and devised certain property to T with directions for T to pay to A such amounts of income or principal as T, in T's discretion, determines is appropriate; at A's death, T is directed to deliver any remaining trust estate to A's children. A died recently and was survived by A's spouse, S, and two children, C1 and C2. Which answer best describes whether the trust estates of the inter vivos trust and the testamentary trust will be included in A's gross estate for federal transfer tax purposes?

(A) The trust estates of both trusts will be included in A's gross estate.

(B) The trust estates of both trusts will not be included in A's gross estate.

(C) The trust estate of the inter vivos trust, but not the testamentary trust, will be included in A's gross estate.

(D) The trust estate of the testamentary trust, but not the inter vivos trust, will be included in A's gross estate.

277. O, a resident of the state of X, died recently. O was survived by O's spouse, S, and two children, A and B. O's valid will has been admitted to probate and devises O's entire estate to S. At the time of O's death, O owned the fee simple title to: (i) several tracts of real estate located in X, (ii) certain common stocks, (iii) numerous items of tangible personal property, and (iv) a checking account. Which of the above described assets would be included in O's gross estate for federal transfer tax purposes?

ANSWER:

278. O, an unmarried resident of the state of X, died recently. Prior to O's death, O had conveyed to A, a child of O, a remainder interest in Blackacre, expressly retaining a life estate. In addition, O had conveyed to B, another child of O, an executory interest in Whiteacre that becomes possessory at O's death. Both deeds were duly recorded prior to O's death. Which answer best explains whether Blackacre and Whiteacre will be included in O's gross estate for federal transfer tax purposes?

   (A) Both Blackacre and Whiteacre will be included in O's gross estate.

   (B) Neither Blackacre nor Whiteacre will be included in O's gross estate.

   (C) Whiteacre, but not Blackacre, will be included in O's gross estate.

   (D) Blackacre, but not Whiteacre, will be included in O's gross estate.

279. Refer to Question 278 and assume also that O had deposited $10,000 into a savings account in O's name "payable on O's death to A" and another $10,000 into a checking account in the names of O and B "with rights of survivorship." Which answer best explains whether these accounts would be included in O's gross estate for federal transfer tax purposes?

   (A) The checking account and the savings account would be included in O's gross estate.

   (B) Neither the checking account nor the savings account would be included in O's gross estate.

   (C) The checking account, but not the savings account, would be included in O's gross estate.

   (D) The checking account and one-half of the savings account would be included in O's gross estate.

280. Refer to Question 278, but assume that, at O's death, O had owned two life insurance policies; one is a term policy made payable at O's death to O's estate, and the other is a whole life policy made payable to A. Which answer best explains whether the policies would be included in O's gross estate for federal transfer tax purposes?

   (A) Both policies would be included in O's gross estate.

   (B) Neither policy would be included in O's gross estate.

   (C) The whole life policy, but not the term policy, would be included in O's gross estate.

   (D) The term policy, but not the whole life policy, would be included in O's gross estate.

281. Refer to Question 280, but assume that (i) four years prior to O's death, O had assigned the term policy to B (who then changed the beneficiary to B) and (ii) two years prior to O's death, O had assigned the whole life policy to A. Will the policies be included in O's gross estate for federal transfer tax purposes?

ANSWER:

282. Refer to Question 281, but also assume that, in addition to assigning the life insurance policies to A and B, O had also given shares of stock worth $50,000 to each of A and B when O had assigned the policies. Which answer best explains whether the shares of stock would be included in O's gross estate for federal transfer tax purposes?

    (A) The stock given to both A and B would be included in O's gross estate.

    (B) None of the stock would be included in O's gross estate.

    (C) The stock given to A, but not B, would be included in O's gross estate.

    (D) The stock given to B, but not A, would be included in O's gross estate.

283. Refer to Question 277, but assume that, prior to O's death, O had assigned all of the described assets to O as trustee of a valid, enforceable revocable express trust agreement in writing, which provided that, during O's lifetime, O could use the income and/or principal for O's health, support, education, or maintenance; at O's death, the remaining trust assets were to be delivered by the successor trustee to A and B. Will the described assets be included in O's gross estate for federal transfer tax purposes?

ANSWER:

284. O, an unmarried resident of the state of X, died recently. Immediately prior to O's death, O had been participating in a 401(K) plan created and funded by O's employer; at the time of O's death, the value of the 401(K) plan was $1,000,000. In addition, O had been voluntarily contributing to another 401(K) plan, which had a value at the time of O's death of $500,000. Prior to O's death, O had designated a child, C, as the beneficiary of both 401(K) plans. Which answer best explains whether the 401(K) plans would be included in O's gross estate for federal transfer tax purposes?

    (A) Both plans would be included in O's gross estate.

    (B) Neither plan would be included in O's gross estate.

    (C) The employer's plan, but not the voluntary plan, would be included in O's gross estate.

    (D) The voluntary plan, but not the employer's plan, would be included in O's gross estate.

285. O, an unmarried resident of the state of X, died recently. O was survived by two children, A and B, and three grandchildren, G1, G2, and G3. O's gross estate for federal transfer tax purposes has been valued at four million dollars. At the time of O's death, O owed to third parties debts secured by real estate included in O's gross estate of $400,000 and unsecured debts of $100,000. Which answer describes the proper amount that can be deducted from O's gross estate to determine the amount of O's taxable estate for federal transfer tax purposes?

    (A) $500,000.

(B) $400,000.

(C) $100,000.

(D) $0.

286. Refer to Question 285, but assume that the expenses of O's last illness amounted to $40,000, O's funeral expenses amounted to $20,000, and the expenses incurred in the administration of O's estate are $10,000. Which answer describes the proper amount that can be deducted from O's gross estate to determine the amount of O's taxable estate for federal transfer tax purposes?

(A) $70,000.

(B) $60,000.

(C) $50,000.

(D) $40,000.

287. Refer to Question 285, but assume that O married S shortly before he died, and O's will has been admitted to probate and devises property valued at $2,000,000 to S, property valued at $1,000,000 equally to A and B, and property valued at $430,000 to a charity. Which answer best describes the amount that can be deducted from O's gross estate to determine the amount of O's taxable estate for federal transfer tax purposes?

(A) $430,000.

(B) $1,430,000.

(C) $2,430,000.

(D) $3,430,000.

288. Refer to Question 287, but assume the $2,000,000 was not devised outright to S, but $1,000,000 was devised to a trustee in trust for S with directions for the trustee to distribute to S such amounts of income and principal as S would need for S's health, support, education, and maintenance. At S's death, the trustee is to deliver the remaining trust estate to A and B. The other $1,000,000 was devised in trust to a trustee with directions to pay to S all of the trust income for the remainder of S's lifetime, and at S's death, the principal is to be delivered to A and B. Which answer describes the amount that can be properly deducted from O's gross estate to determine the amount of O's taxable estate for federal transfer tax purposes?

(A) $430,000.

(B) $1,430,000.

(C) $2,430,000.

(D) $0.

289. Refer to Questions 288 and explain whether or not the trust estates of the described trusts would be included in S's gross estate at the time of her death, and if included, further explain who would be responsible for the payment of any resulting transfer taxes at S's death.

ANSWER:

290. When O died, O devised $500,000 into a valid, enforceable testamentary trust. O's spouse, S, was the trustee, and the terms of the trust directed S to pay to herself all of the income. She was also granted the authority to distribute principal to herself as needed for her health, support, or maintenance. At S's death, the trust estate is to be distributed to O's child from a prior marriage, C. At S's death, the trust estate had a fair market value of $10,000,000. S's will devised all of her property to D, her daughter from a prior marriage. What amount, if any, will be added to S's gross estate by reason of S's interests in the described trust?

(A) $0.

(B) $500,000.

(C) The value of S's life estate in the trust estate.

(D) $10,000,000.

PRACTICE FINAL EXAM

Instructions: This exam consists of 19 questions, some of which are multiple choice and some of which are short answer. Try to answer all of these questions in no more than two hours.

291. O, an unmarried resident of the state of X, died while traveling in the state of Y. In addition to the tangible personal property in O's physical possession at the time of O's death, O owned real and personal property located the state of X, but O's more valuable assets were real and personal property located in the state of Z. A creditor of O (a national bank, located in the state of Q, which issued O the credit card that O used while O was in the state of Y) has not been paid. Additionally, formal administration of O's estate is pending in each state where formal administration is proper. Which answer best describes where the creditor could properly pursue its claim against O's estate?

    (A) The state courts of X, Y, Z, and Q.

    (B) The state courts of X, Y, and Z.

    (C) The state courts of X or Q.

    (D) A federal court.

292. H and W were married and have always resided in the state of X. H died recently. During the marriage, H acquired real and personal property located in X; all assets were titled in H's name. Immediately prior to H's death, a fully-competent H acting on H's own free will (i) validly assigned to H's paramour, P, the ownership of all of the described assets and (ii) validly revoked H's will that left all of H's property equally to W and C, H's adult child by prior marriage.

    Assuming all debts and taxes have been satisfied, which answer best describes the most likely disposition of the described assets?

    (A) P retains all of the assets transferred.

    (B) P is liable to both C and W for their respective intestate shares.

    (C) P is liable to C, but not W, for C's intestate share.

    (D) P is liable to W for W's elective share.

89

293. O, an unmarried resident of the state of X, died recently. O was survived by a child from O's first marriage, C1, and another child born to O during O's second marriage, C2. In addition to C1 and C2, O was the father of a child born out of wedlock prior to even meeting O's first wife; this child is C3. C3 died intestate before O and was survived by C3's spouse and child, SP and G, respectively. G is a minor. O executed a will that leaves all of O's property to F, a friend. F has filed the will for probate. Which answer best describes the members of C3's family that have standing to contest O's will?

   (A) SP and G would have standing if C3's paternity was established prior to or after O's death.

   (B) G would have standing if C3's paternity was established prior to or after O's death.

   (C) G would have standing only if C3's paternity was established before C4's death.

   (D) Regardless of when paternity may have been established, neither SP nor G has standing.

294. O, an unmarried resident of the state of X, died. O was survived by O's only child, C, C's only child, G, and G's child GG. O's valid will has been admitted to probate and devises Blackacre to G and the rest, residue and remainder of O's estate to a charity. G filed a valid disclaimer in the probate proceedings of O's estate. Which answer best describes the effect the disclaimer has on the disposition of Blackacre following the formal administration of O's estate?

   (A) G has assigned G's interest in Blackacre to GG.

   (B) G has assigned G's interest in Blackacre to the charity.

   (C) Blackacre passes from O to GG.

   (D) Blackacre passes from O to the charity.

295. When O died years ago, O devised a life estate in Blackacre to A and the remainder interest to B. A has recently died, and A's valid, probated will devises Blackacre to C and the balance of A's estate to C and B. Which answer best describes the most likely disposition of Blackacre and A's estate?

   (A) B takes Blackacre, and B and C share the balance of A's estate.

   (B) C inherits Blackacre, and B and C share the balance of A's estate.

   (C) B and C share equally in Blackacre, as well as the balance of A's estate.

   (D) B may elect either to retain Blackacre and not share in the estate or convey Blackacre to C and share in the balance of A's estate.

296. O, an unmarried resident of the state of X, died recently, survived by an adult child, A. O's apparently valid will (i.e., a document in writing signed by O in the presence of three witnesses) leaves all of O's estate to O's live-in caretaker, F. However, the witnesses signed the will while each witness was present and while the testator was present, but before O signed the will. Which answer best explains whether the document will be admitted to probate?

    (A) Because O did not sign the will before the witnesses, the will cannot be admitted to probate.

    (B) Even though O did not sign the will before the witnesses, the will can be admitted to probate.

    (C) Even though O did not sign the will before the witnesses, the will may be admitted to probate.

    (D) I need to research the question.

297. O, an unmarried resident of the state of X, died recently, survived by one adult child, C, and several cousins. However, because O was estranged from C, O validly executed in 1990 a typewritten, witnessed will leaving all of O's estate to a friend, A. In 2000, O validly executed a new typewritten, witnessed will expressly revoking all prior wills and leaving all of O's property to another friend, B. Shortly before O's death, while O was angry with B, and while several friends were present, a competent O asked O's nurse to destroy the will. The nurse found the 2000 will in the downstairs study and tossed the will into a fire in the study. She then reported to O and the friends that the will had been destroyed. What is the most likely disposition of O's estate?

    (A) Since the 2000 will was not revoked, the 2000 will can be admitted to probate, and the estate passes to B.

    (B) Although the 2000 will was not revoked, O's intent will be carried out by imposing a constructive trust on B in favor of C.

    (C) Although the 2000 will was not revoked, O's intent will be carried out by imposing a constructive trust on B in favor of A.

    (D) The 2000 will was revoked.

298. O, an unmarried resident of the state of X, died recently, survived by O's spouse, S, and their two children, C1 and C2. O's will, which O executed after O married S but before the births of C1 and C2, leaves all of O's property to S. The will was also executed before the birth of C3, a child born of an extramarital affair of O and P. C3 died intestate several years ago. C3 was survived by C3's spouse, S3, and their child, G3; both S3 and G3 survived O. Which answer best describes the most likely disposition of O's estate?

    (A) The will can be admitted to probate; the entire estate passes to S.

    (B) The will cannot be admitted to probate; the entire estate passes to C1, C2, and C3.

(C) The will can be admitted to probate, but C1, C2, and C3 will be entitled to an intestate share of the estate, and the balance of the entire estate passes to S.

(D) The will can be admitted to probate, but C3 will be entitled to an intestate share of the estate, and the balance of the estate passes to S.

299. O, an unmarried resident of the state of X, died recently, survived by two children, S and D. O's valid will has been admitted to probate; it simply states: "I devise my home to S and the rest, residue, and remainder of my estate to D." At the time of O's death, the significant assets of the estate consisted of the home (fair market value of $100,000) and shares of a New York Stock Exchange company (fair market value of $100,000). The only debts or expenses of O's estate are (i) unsecured debts of O in the amount of $50,000 and (ii) a note signed by O and secured by the home; the outstanding balance of the note was $50,000. The will does not direct how the decedent's debts are to be paid. Which answer best explains the most likely disposition of O's estate?

(A) S receives the home, subject to the outstanding indebtedness, and D receives half of the shares of stock after the payment of the unsecured debts.

(B) S receives the home, free of any indebtedness, and D will not receive anything because the shares of stock will be sold to pay all the debts.

(C) One-half of all the debts should be paid by S, or out of the sales proceeds of the house, and the other one-half of all the debts should be paid by D, or out of the sales proceeds of part of the stock.

(D) The answer depends on the decisions the creditors make after O's death.

300. O, an unmarried resident of the state of X, died recently. O's valid will has been admitted to probate and devises O's estate to C, O's only child. C was married to S, and they had one child, G. C survived O by one week. C's valid, probated will leaves C's entire estate to S. However, a valid disclaimer of C's interest in O's estate was properly filed. S is upset that C's interest in O's estate is passing to G and not to S became of the disclaimer. Which answer best describes S's legal position in view of the disclaimer?

(A) S is entitled to have the disclaimed property included as part of C's augmented estate.

(B) S may have a valid cause of action against both C's estate and the person serving as the executor of C's estate.

(C) S may have a valid cause of action against the person serving as the executor of C's estate.

(D) S is without any remedy.

301. O, an unmarried resident of the state of X, died recently. O was survived by O's child, C, and C's child, G (age 20). O's valid will has been admitted to probate. O's will devises Blackacre to F, a friend of O, and the rest, residue, and remainder of O's estate to a charity. However,

other friends of both F and O will testify that O and F had orally agreed, prior to O's execution of the will, that F would deliver Blackacre to G when G attains age 21. It has also been discovered that O's will failed because O did not comply with a technical formality required of a will in the state of X. Which answer best describes the disposition of Blackacre under those circumstances?

(A) C acquires fee simple title.

(B) G will have the court impose a constructive trust on C to avoid unjust enrichment by C.

(C) G will have the court impose a constructive trust on F to avoid unjust enrichment by F.

(D) F acquires fee simple title.

302. O created a valid, enforceable irrevocable spendthrift express trust several years ago by a written agreement. The trustee is T; C and G are named as beneficiaries. The assets of the trust consist of real and personal property; title is in T's name. C is entitled to all of the income for the rest of C's lifetime; at C's death, T is to deliver the trust estate to G. The trust agreement also authorizes T to distribute principal, at the trustee's discretion, to or for O's benefit. A creditor of O has recently obtained a judgment against O and is trying to attach the assets of the trust. The trustee has never distributed any part of the principal to O. O was solvent prior to and right after the creation of the trust. Which answer best describes the legal advice that should be given to the trustee under those circumstances?

(A) The principal is not reachable by O's creditors.

(B) The principal is not reachable by O's creditors unless they are tort creditors.

(C) The principal may be reached by O's creditors.

(D) The principal is reachable by O's creditors.

303. O, an unmarried resident of the state of X, was the settlor of a valid, enforceable irrevocable spendthrift trust. The trustee is T; the beneficiaries are two adults, C and G. According to the terms of the trust agreement, C is entitled to all of the trust income for the rest of C's lifetime; at C's death, the trustee is to distribute the trust estate to G. C and G have recently convinced T to assign to them all of the trust estate, but T is seeking your legal advice prior to assigning the trust estate to C and G. Which answer best describes the legal advice that should be given to the trustee under those circumstances?

(A) The trustee must deliver the trust estate to C and G.

(B) The trustee, in its discretion, may deliver the trust estate to C and G.

(C) The trustee should not deliver the trust estate to C and G unless O consents.

(D) Even if O consents, the trustee may be at risk of personal liability, if the trustee delivers the trust estate to C and G.

304. O, an unmarried resident of the state of X, died recently. O's valid will has been admitted to probate and devises Blackacre to O's grandchildren who are alive 25 years following O's death, and the rest, residue, and remainder of O's estate passes to a charity. At the time of O's death, O was survived by O's child, A, and A's two children, G1 and G2. Explain the ownership of Blackacre by reason of O's death.

ANSWER:

305. O, an unmarried resident of the state of X, died recently. O's valid will, executed in 1950, has been admitted to probate and devises Blackacre to T, as trustee, with instructions for T to pay the income to A's children for their lifetimes, and, at the death of the surviving child of A, to deliver the trust estate to A's grandchildren. The rest, residue, and remainder of O's estate is devised to a charity. At the time of O's death, O was survived by O's child, A, age 85, and A's child, G, age 65. Does all or any part of the disposition of Blackacre violate the rule against perpetuities?

ANSWER:

306. O, an unmarried resident of the state of X, has entered into an irrevocable, valid, enforceable inter vivos express trust agreement with A, as trustee. The terms of the written trust agreement direct A to distribute to A as much income and/or principal as A needs for A's health, support, education, or maintenance. In addition, A may appoint any part of the trust estate to any one or more of A's children by deed during A's lifetime or at A's death by A's will; at the time of A's death, the successor trustee is to distribute any remaining trust assets to a charity. A is in financial difficulties due to bad investments. A's business creditors are seeking assets to attach. One creditor of A is seeking your legal advice. What legal advice should you give the creditor?

ANSWER:

307. O, an unmarried resident of the state of X, died. O's valid will was admitted to probate and devised Blackacre to A for life, remainder to such of A's children as A appoints by will, and in default of appointment, to another child of O, B. The rest, residue, and remainder of O's estate was devised to B. Additionally, during O's lifetime, O had created a valid irrevocable inter vivos express trust that directed the trustee, T, to pay the income to A during A's lifetime; at A's death, T is directed to distribute the principal to anyone, including A's estate, as A may appoint by will, and, in default of appointment, to B. A died recently. A's valid will

has been admitted to probate and expressly exercises the power of appointment over Blackacre in favor of C and expressly exercises the power of appointment over the trust estate to A's spouse, S. Which answer best describes whether Blackacre or the trust estate will be includable in A's gross estate for federal transfer tax purposes?

(A) Both Blackacre and the trust estate will be includable in A's gross estate.

(B) Neither Blackacre nor the trust estate will be includable in A's gross estate.

(C) Blackacre, but not the trust estate, will be includable in A's gross estate.

(D) The trust estate, but not Blackacre, will be includable in A's gross estate.

308. O, an unmarried resident of the state of X, died recently. O was survived by O's adult child, C, and C's adult child G. G's valid will has been admitted to probate; E has been appointed the executor of O's estate. The will devises O's entire estate to G. The estate is still in administration. You have been retained by E to be the "lawyer for the estate." Your fees have been paid by E out of the estate. Whom do you represent? In other words, is E your client? Are C and G clients? Can C or G sue you for a breach of duty?

ANSWER:

309. Refer to Question 308, but assume that the will was not admitted to probate because it did not meet the technical requirements of the applicable wills act due to the negligence of the lawyer who drafted the will. Notwithstanding the testimony of O's friends concerning O's intent to devise O's estate to G, the probate court found that G failed to meet the burden of proof required of UPC 2-503 the "harmless error" rule. C refused to file a disclaimer or otherwise share the estate with G. Did the lawyer who negligently drafted the will owe a duty of care to the intended beneficiary of the will?

ANSWER:

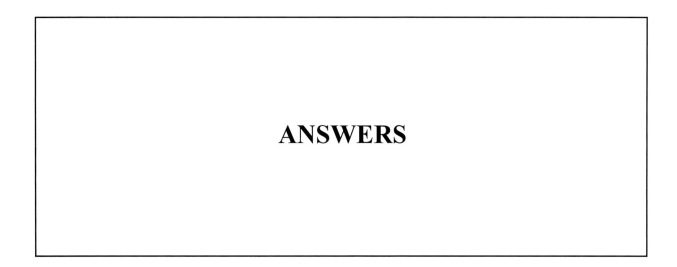

ANSWERS

1. **Answer (D) is correct.** According to general principles of conflict of laws, the substantive law of a decedent's domicile normally governs rights of succession to the decedent's personal property. Restatement (Second) of Conflict of Laws §§ 222, 260, 263 (1971) (Restatement (Second) Conflict of Laws § ___). UPC § 1-301 follows these principles. Because all of the described assets are personal property, the law of the state of X will determine whether these assets will pass (i) by intestate succession to O's heirs determined under the law of X or (ii) to devisees described in a will of O that is admitted to probate in accordance with the law of the state of X. UPC §§ 1-301, 1-302. *See* William M. McGovern, Jr. and Sheldon F. Kurtz, *Wills, Trusts, and Estates* § 1.2 (2d ed. 2001) (McGovern § ___).

    Answer (A) is incorrect. Even though the heirs may reside in different states and certain assets of O are located in different states, these facts do not trigger the application of any federal statutes to determine who owns what. The 14th Amendment does require that governing state law not violate the "due process" and "equal protection" clauses of the Constitution of the United States.

    Answer (B) is incorrect. While federal banking laws govern many of the practices of the bank, the succession of the checking account is a matter of state law. While (i) the state of Y may have jurisdiction over the shares of stock due to the corporation being a Y corporation and (ii) the state of Z has jurisdiction over the tangible personal property located in Z, the succession of those assets is a matter of the law of the state where O was domiciled, the state of X.

    Answer (C) is incorrect. While (i) the state of Y may have jurisdiction over the shares of stock due to the corporation being a Y corporation and (ii) the state of Z has jurisdiction over the tangible personal property located in Z, the succession of those assets is still a matter of the law of X. Although the Uniform Probate Code does not change the ordinary choice of law rules, a testator can generally select the law of a particular state to be used for the purpose of interpreting the will. UPC § 2-703.

2. **Answer (B) is correct.** UPC § 1-201 (38) defines the term "property" to include both real and personal property, and UPC §§ 1-301 and 1-302 appear to give the state of X the authority to determine the rights of succession to the real property in the states of Y and Z. However, conflict of laws principles provide that the substantive law of the decedent's domicile normally governs the rights of succession to the decedent's personal property, but the law of the situs of real property usually governs the rights of succession to the real property. See Restatement (Second) Conflict of Laws §§ 222, 236, 239, 260. Statutes in Y and Z may require that a final order determining testacy by a court in X "be accepted as determinative of ownership" of real property in those states." See UPC § 3-408.

Answer (A) is incorrect. Conflict of laws principles generally provide that the law of the decedent's domicile governs the succession to the decedent's personal property, but the law of the situs of real property governs the succession of the real property. A state statute may permit the probate of a will under certain circumstances even if the will was not executed in accordance with the formalities of the state's applicable wills act. See UPC § 2-506.

Answers (C) and (D) are incorrect. Assuming that the "due process" and "equal protection" clauses of the 14th Amendment of the Constitution of the United States have not been violated, the laws of X, Y, and Z control the succession of real property located in those states.

3. **Answer (C) is correct.** A proceeding to settle a decedent's estate is an in rem action. Accordingly, any state has territorial jurisdiction over the property of a decedent physically located in the state even though the decedent was domiciled in another jurisdiction. Restatement (Second) of Judgments § 6 (1980) (Restatement (Second) Judgments § ____). In addition, the state where the decedent was domiciled at the time of death also has jurisdiction over the personal property of the decedent located in another jurisdiction. Exclusive jurisdiction of real property is usually retained by the state where the real property is located. *See* 3 *American Law of Property* § 14.45 (James A. Casner ed. 1952) (Casner § ___); Restatement (Second) Conflict of Laws §§ 236, 260.

    Answers (A), (B), and (D) are incorrect. Conflict of laws principles dictate that the situs state has jurisdiction over property, both real and personal, located in that state. The domiciliary state also has jurisdiction over the decedent's personal property wherever located.

4. **Answer (C) is correct.** Conflict of laws principles dictate that the situs state has territorial jurisdiction over property, both real and personal, located in that state. Restatement (Second) Judgments § 6. The domiciliary state also has jurisdiction over the decedent's personal property wherever located. Conflict of laws principles presume that the law of the decedent's domicile governs the rights of succession to the decedent's personal property, but the law of the situs of real property governs the rights of succession to the real property. *See* Casner § 14.45; Restatement (Second) Conflict of Laws §§ 222, 236, 239, 260, 263. Statutes in Y and Z may require that a final order determining testacy by a court in X "be accepted as determinative of ownership" of real property in those states. *See* UPC § 3-408; Restatement (Second) Conflict of Laws § 239.

    Answers (A), (B), and (D) are incorrect. Conflict of laws principles generally provide that the law of the decedent's domicile governs the succession of the decedent's personal property, but the law of the situs of real property governs the succession of the real property.

5. Because a proceeding to settle a decedent's estate is an in rem action, the "situs" state has territorial jurisdiction over property, both real and personal, located in that state. Restatement (Second) Judgments § 6. The domiciliary state also has jurisdiction over the decedent's personal property wherever located. See Casner § 14.45; Restatement (Second) Conflict of Laws §§ 260, 263. Accordingly, formal administration could be opened in each of the states, X, Y, and Z. *See* UPC § 3-815. A personal representative of the decedent's estate in Y or Z would then have the responsibility to (i) marshal the decedent's assets located in that state, (ii) satisfy any obligations pursued by a creditor in that state and any taxes imposed by that state, and (iii) deliver any remaining personal property to the personal representative in the state of X, or to whomever succeeds to the personal property according to the law of X. *See* UPC § 3-816. The real property in Z passes to O's heirs determined according to the law of Z. Administration proceedings in Y and Z are referred to as "ancillary" administrations; the probate proceeding in X is referred to as the "principal," "primary," or "domiciliary" administration.

6. **Answer (B) is correct.** Because O owned only a life estate in Blackacre, O's interest in Blackacre terminated at O's death; A's remainder interest became fee simple title by the terms of the original grant; and C inherited no interest in Blackacre. Thomas E. Atkinson, *Handbook of the Law of Wills and Other Principles of Succession, Including Intestacy and Administration of Decedents' Estates* § 28 (2d ed. 1953) (Atkinson § ___). Because O's remainder interest in Whiteacre was not expressly made subject to the condition that O survive B, C inherited O's remainder interest, but still subject to B's life estate. Atkinson § 27. Consequently, only O's remainder interest in Whiteacre is part of O's probate estate, which C inherits.

    Answers (A), (C), and (D) are incorrect. Because O's interest in Blackacre terminated at O's death, C only inherited the remainder interest in Whiteacre. An interest in property does not need to be a possessory interest in order to become part of a decedent's probate estate and subject to formal administration and the claims of the decedent's creditors.

7. **Answer (C) is correct.** O's life estate in Blackacre terminated at O's death; A's remainder interest passed as part of A's probate estate to A's heirs; C inherited no interest in Blackacre. When B died, O's remainder interest in Whiteacre became a fee simple. At O's death, Whiteacre became part of O's probate estate. See Atkinson §§ 27, 28.

    Answers (A), (B), and (D) are incorrect. O's life estate in Blackacre did not become part of O's probate estate. C acquired no interest in Blackacre by reason of O's death. O's remainder interest in Whiteacre became a fee simple interest at B's death and passed (subject to possible formal administration and the claims of O's creditors) to C.

8. Absent a statute, a disposition of property intended to take effect at the transferor's death, which is not executed with testamentary formalities, must be sustained under the theory of contract, gift, or trust. See Atkinson, Chapter 4. However, legislation exists in most states that validates many types of nonprobate dispositions of property that become effective at the transferor's death. See UPC, Article VI. Consequently, while O owned both the savings account and the policy, neither asset is part of O's probate estate at O's death, and C acquired no interest in either asset. The savings account became the property of D at O's death because O had entered into a contract with the bank that controls the disposition of the account. The proceeds of the policy passed to E because of the contract between O and the insurance company. See Atkinson § 39. The savings account and life insurance policy are examples of "nonprobate" or "nontestamentary" dispositions.

9.   **Answer (A) is correct.** The fact that O had entered into contracts with the bank and insurance company that control the dispositions of the assets at O's death did not give D and E ownership interests in the assets during O's lifetime. O retained fee simple title during O's lifetime. The intended beneficiary must survive the transferor in order to be entitled to the account or insurance proceeds. *See* UPC §§ 6-211(c), 6-212(b)(2). The account and proceeds became part of O's probate estate and are subject to formal administration, but the policy's proceeds may be exempt from the claims of O's creditors.

      Answers (B), (C), and (D) are incorrect. D and E were "third party beneficiaries" of contracts prior to their deaths. Their deaths terminated their contractual rights under the contracts. Because D and E had mere "expectancies" and not future interests, the heirs of D and E did not inherit any interest in the account or policy.

10.   **Answer (B) is correct.** O's probate estate includes only Whiteacre. Blackacre, the account, and the policy proceeds are not part of the probate estate. Because O's will has been admitted to probate, C has been divested, and F succeeds to the ownership of the assets included in O's probate estate. Atkinson § 1.

      Answers (A), (C), and (D) are incorrect. Because O died testate, F succeeded to the ownership of the probate assets in the same way C inherited the assets in the probate estate when O died intestate. Of the four described assets, only O's interest in Whiteacre is included in the probate estate and subject to formal administration and the claims of O's creditors.

11.   **Answer (C) is correct.** Because O died testate, F succeeded to the ownership of the probate assets in the same way C inherited the assets in the probate estate when O died intestate. Atkinson § 1. Of the four described assets, only Blackacre is not included in O's probate estate. When O died, O's interest in Blackacre terminated. A owns Blackacre. F inherited Whiteacre, the account, and the policy proceeds; these assets became part of O's probate estate and are subject to formal administration, but the policy's proceeds may be exempt from the claims of O's creditors.

      Answers (A), (B), and (D) are incorrect. O's probate estate includes Whiteacre, the account, and the policy proceeds because B, D, and E died before O. Blackacre passed to A at O's death because O only had a life estate, which is not included as a part of O's probate estate.

12.   The answer depends on the marital property law of the state of X, and marital property laws vary considerably from state to state. If X is a community property state, or a state which has enacted the Uniform Marital Property Act (1983) (thereby enacting the "partnership theory" of marriage), W may have owned an ownership interest in half of the property prior to H's death; H may have owned half of the assets held in W's name; and only H's half interest in the community property passes to C. W's interest in some community property may have been subject to formal administration in H's probate estate. McGovern § 3.8. In most other states, the property belonged exclusively to H prior to H's death. While most of these

states have abolished the common law concepts of dower and curtesy, W may be entitled to an elective share amount or percentage payable out of the probate estate and other nonprobate transfers. In Georgia, W is not entitled to claim any portion of H's probate estate. *See* McGovern § 3.7. In community and non-community property states, W may also have other rights in and to H's estate, such as homestead, exempt property, or family allowance, depending on state law. *See* UPC §§ 2-401 – 2-405; McGovern § 3.4.

13. **Answer (C) is correct.** Because H failed to designate a third party beneficiary of the life insurance, the proceeds are payable to H's personal representative and become part of the probate estate. Most pensions are subject to ERISA, a federal law that may require the death benefit to be paid to the employee's spouse in the form of an annuity. Employee Retirement Income Security Act of 1973 § 205(a), 29 U.S.C. § 1055(a) (2002) (ERISA § ___). Both death benefits are taken into consideration in determining the augmented estate in order to compute W's elective share amount. UPC §§ 2-203, 2-206. *In a community property state, W may be entitled to half of the proceeds of the life insurance, if H's interest in the policy were community property.*

    Answer (A) is incorrect. ERISA preempts the law of X as it would otherwise apply to the pension plan.

    Answer (B) is incorrect. ERISA does not require the proceeds of a group life policy be made payable to the employee's spouse.

    Answer (D) is incorrect for the reasons given.

14. **Answer (D) is correct.** Because H and W were married for 10 years, W's elective share percentage is 30% of the "augmented estate" of O and W. *See* UPC § 2-202. However, if the value of the property W owned prior to H's death, when added to the value of Greenacre (plus most other assets passing to W by reason of H's death), exceeds the 30% amount, W will not receive anything else. If not, the difference is paid out of O's probate estate and other nonprobate transfers. *See* UPC § 2-209. *In a non-UPC state, the results may vary, and the surviving spouse may have to elect between the amount devised in the will and the elective share amount. See McGovern § 3.7. In a community property state, the residuary estate is typically limited to the decedent's half of any community property. In those states, W retains W's half of any community property and also inherits what H devised to W.*

    Answers (A), (B), and (C) are incorrect for the reasons given.

15. **Answer (A) is correct.** C, an adult child of O from O's prior marriage, is not entitled to any share of O's probate estate. Because O's will was presumably executed after C's birth and O's subsequent marriage, C is not "omitted" or "pretermitted" as that term is defined in UPC § 2-302. *Statutes in some non-UPC states may afford C the status of a "pretermitted heir." See* McGovern § 3.5.

Answer (B) is incorrect. C would be entitled to an intestate share of H's probate estate only if O died intestate. H died testate and can devise H's estate to W, thereby disinheriting C. *Parents can intentionally disinherit their children in all but one state. Louisiana still retains the civil law concept of "legitime" or "forced heirship" under some circumstances. The "pretermitted child" statute in some non-UPC states may protect C from an unintentional disinheritance, if O's will does not expressly disinherit C. See* McGovern § 3.2.

Answers (C) and (D) are incorrect. Because C is an adult, neither O nor O's estate following O's death had a legal obligation to support C, absent a contract that would have created a debt of the estate. *If C were an adult suffering from a disability, the family law of a state may impose some legal obligation on O's estate to support C following O's death.*

16. If H had a legal obligation to support C, C would have been entitled to a reasonable allowance for C's maintenance during the period of administration. If O's estate is insolvent, the allowance cannot extend for a period of time in excess of one year. However, if O were not legally obligated to support C under the family law of the state of X, C would have been totally disinherited. *See* UPC § 2-404. Absent a contractual obligation to the contrary, a general rule of family law is that a parent's legal obligation of support ends at the parent's death. *See* John DeWitt Gregory et al., *Understanding Family Law* § 9.06 (2d ed. 2001). *States that have not enacted the Uniform Probate Code typically provide for some type of support for minor or dependent children during formal administration. See* McGovern 3.4.

17. **Answer (A) is correct.** Because H and W were married for 10 years, W is entitled to an elective share percentage of 30% of the augmented estate. However, H's will devised to W the residuary estate, and the value of the residuary, when added to the value of other property received by W by reason of H's death, as well as W's own property, is likely to exceed the 30% amount. *See* UPC §§ 2-207, 2-209.

Answer (B) is incorrect. W did not own an interest in Greenacre at O's death, and it is likely that Greenacre will not be needed to satisfy W's elective share percentage. *In a community property state, W would not likely retain W's half of Greenacre and also inherit O's residuary estate. W would be put to an election: (i) retain W's half of the community assets and disclaim W's rights under H's will or (ii) accept W's rights under H's will and allow W's half of Greenacre to pass to C. See* McGovern § 3.8.

Answer (C) is incorrect. In some non-UPC states, the surviving spouse must elect between what is devised to the spouse in the will or the elective share amount. *See* McGovern § 3.7.

Answer (D) is incorrect. C, an adult child of H from H's prior marriage, is not entitled to any share of H's probate estate. Because H's will was presumably executed after C's birth and H's subsequent marriage, C is not "omitted" or "pretermitted." UPC § 2-302.

18. **Answer (C) is correct.** Because all of the described assets comprise H's probate estate, W is entitled to an amount equal to the value of her elective share percentage of the augmented estate, less the value of W's property included in the augmented estate, and P will inherit the balance. *See* UPC §§ 2-202–2-210. *In a community property state, a spouse's testamentary power of disposition is typically limited to the spouse's half of the community probate property, because the surviving spouse retains half of the community property. See* McGovern § 3.8.

    Answer (A) is incorrect. UPC §§ 2-209 – 2-210 prevent P from succeeding to H's entire probate estate notwithstanding the terms of H's will unless the value of W's property included in the augmented estate exceeds the percentage share amount. *If X is a non-community property state that has neither adopted the augmented estate concept followed in the Uniform Probate Code nor adopted an elective share system, Answer (A) would be correct.*

    Answers (B) and (D) are incorrect. C, as H's heir, is entitled to an intestate share of O's probate estate only if O died intestate. Because there is a valid will, C does not receive anything.

19. **Answer (D) is correct.** The Uniform Probate Code revokes a pre-divorce beneficiary designation of a transfer-on-death account. As a result, the accounts pass as if W had died immediately before the divorce. UPC § 2-804. *In a state that has not enacted the Uniform Probate Code, or a statute similar to UPC § 2-804, the result may differ. Absent a statute, courts have allowed the former spouse to enforce the terms of the contract.* McGovern § 5.5.

    Answers (A), (B), and (C) are incorrect for the reasons given.

20. The designation of W as beneficiary of the policy was revoked by the divorce. UPC § 2-804. However, notwithstanding state law to the contrary, the designation of W as the beneficiary of the pension plan may still be enforceable by W. ERISA's preemption clause has been invoked to override state statutes similar to UPC § 2-804 where the death benefit was provided by the employer as part of an employee benefit plan. *Egelhoff v. Egelhoff ex rel. Breiner*, 532 U.S. 141 (2001). *See* comment to UPC § 2-804 and ERISA § 514(a). *Many non-UPC states have statutes similar to* UPC § 2-804. *Absent a statute, courts have allowed the former spouse to enforce the terms of the contact. See comment to* UPC § 2-804.

21. **Answer (C) is correct.** The answer appears to depend initially on whether the property law of the state of X presumes that co-owners are joint tenants with rights of survivorship or tenants in common. See McGovern § 4.8. However, because neither O nor C2 survived the other by 120 hours, half of Whiteacre passes to C2's devisee, S2, and the other half passes to O's heirs or their devisees, G2, G3, and S4. UPC § 2-702(a). Each half will become part of the respective owner's probate estate and subject to the claims of creditors. *Many states that have not enacted the Uniform Probate Code have statutes similar to UPC § 2-702.*

Answer (A) is incorrect. C2 did not survive O by the requisite 120 hours. *Absent a statute that changed the common law rule, S2 would inherit all of Whiteacre, if O and C2 held title as joint tenants with rights of survivorship and S2 could prove that C2 survived O by an "instant" of time."*

Answer (B) is incorrect. O did not survive C2 by 120 hours. *Absent a statute that changes the common law rule, O's heirs would inherit all of Whiteacre, if O and C2 held title as joint tenants with rights of survivorship and the heirs can prove O survived C2 by an "instant of time.*

Answer (D) is incorrect for the reasons given.

22.   **Answer (A) is correct.** At O's death, O's life estate terminated, and C2's remainder interest became a possessory fee interest that was devised by C2 to S2. The "120 hour" rule does not apply because the will of O's father did not condition C2's vested remainder interest on C2 surviving O, and conditions of survivorship are not implied. *See* UPC § 2-702(b) and comment to UPC § 2-707. *The result would likely be the same in non-UPC states. See* Atkinson §§ 27, 28.

Answer (B) is incorrect. C2's interest passed to S2 pursuant to C2's will subject to formal administration as part of C2's estate and the claims of C2's creditors.

Answer (C) is incorrect. O only had a life estate that terminated at O's death.

Answer (D) is incorrect. O's father did not condition C2's remainder interest on C2 surviving O, or on C2 surviving O by a certain amount of time.

23.   **Answer (C) is correct.** O was survived by children. The charity's shifting executory interest did not become possessory and terminated because O was survived by children. Accordingly, Brownacre passed to O's heirs or their devisees. *See* McGovern § 10.1.

Answer (A) is incorrect. Even if C4 had not survived O by 120 hours, the "120 hour rule" of UPC § 2-702 should not apply, and Brownacre passed to O's heirs subject to formal administration and the claims of O's creditors.

Answer (B) is incorrect. Because C2 and C3 are deemed to have predeceased O, their children take by representation the interests C2 and C3 would have inherited from O had they survived O by 120 hours. UPC §§ 2-104, 2-106.

Answer (D) is incorrect. C4 survived O by 120 hours. Therefore, C4's interest passes to C4's devisee, S4, subject to formal administration and the claims of C4's creditors.

24.   According to the common law, O had acquired a fee simple subject to an executory inter-
       est, and the event occurred that triggered the condition subsequent attached to O's interest
       in Brownacre, thereby divesting O; Brownacre is not part of O's probate estate, and the char-
       ity's executory interest became a possessory fee simple interest. *See* Restatement of Property
       § 267 (1936) (Restatement, Property § ___). *However, statutes in some states have modified
       the common law by construing the limitation to refer to the person having died before the
       original transfer took effect (i.e., death of O's father). See* McGovern § 10.1.

25.   **Answer (D) is correct.** The only parties with standing to contest the probate of a will are, generally, the decedent's heirs at law. *See* McGovern § 12.1. Notwithstanding their divorce, H and W were O's parents and O's only heirs at law. *See* UPC §§ 2-103, 2-114. *The result is likely to be the same in a non-UPC state.*

       Answer (A) is incorrect. Other than a decedent's surviving spouse, a person related to the decedent only by marriage is not an heir at law.

       Answers (B) and (C) are incorrect. Because H and W both survived O, neither the ancestors of H and W nor the descendants of those ancestors are O's heirs at law.

26.   **Answer (C) is correct.** The only parties with standing to contest the probate of a will are, generally, the decedents's heirs at law. *See* McGovern § 12.1. Notwithstanding their divorce, H and W were O's parents and O's only heirs at law. *See* UPC §§ 2-103, 2-114. *The result is likely to be the same in a non-UPC state.*

       Answers (A) and (B) are incorrect. O's siblings are not O's heirs because both of O's parents survived O. *See* UPC § 2-103. It does not matter if the siblings were born of the same, or a prior, or a subsequent, marriage of O's parents.

       Answer (D) is incorrect. The identity of the parent awarded custody during the divorce proceedings is irrelevant in determining O's heirs at law.

27.   **Answer (D) is correct.** While O would likely have had a right to inherit from H, if H had died intestate before O, H would not have a right to inherit from O, if O died intestate. H2 is an heir. *See* UPC § 2-114 (b) and comment. Accordingly, H would not have standing to contest the probate of the will. *The same result is likely to occur in a non-UPC state. See* McGovern § 2.10.

       Answers (A) and (C) are incorrect. H2's adoption of O, typically, eliminates H's status as an heir of O.

       Answer (B) is incorrect. H2 is treated as a parent of O. Consequently, W is not O's sole heir at law.

28.   **Answer (A) is correct.** Notwithstanding (i) the divorce of H and W and (ii) O's adoption by W's husband, H2, O is still considered to be one of H's heirs at law. *See* UPC § 2-114 (b). *The same result is likely to occur in a non-UPC state. See* McGovern § 2.10.

Answers (B), (C), and (D) are incorrect. All of H's children are his heirs at law regardless of the identity of their mothers. UPC § 2-114 (b).

29.   Because W is also the mother of S1 and S2, she is not H2's sole heir unless the value of the probate estate is less than $100,000 (plus the value of exemptions and allowances set aside to W). *See* UPC § 2-102 (2-102A). Assuming the value of H2's probate exceeds $100,000 (plus the value of any exemptions or allowances set aside for W), all of H2's children (whether born to or adopted by him) are entitled to a share of H2's probate estate. Stepchildren are excluded as heirs unless adopted. The Uniform Probate Code has adopted these generally accepted principles. UPC §§ 1-201(5), 2-114(b). *See* McGovern § 2.10. Accordingly, O, S4, S5, and S6 are heirs of H2. S1 and S2 are stepchildren of H2 and excluded as heirs of H2. *In some community property states, the decedent's half of the community property passes to the surviving spouse only if all the decedent's descendants are also descendants of the surviving spouse.*

30.   **Answer (D) is correct.** S5's mother is S5's sole heir at law, if she survived S5. UPC § 2-103 (2). *The results may differ in a non-UPC state; the surviving siblings may share the estate with S5's mother.*

       Answers (A), (B), and (C) are incorrect. UPC § 2-103 (2) describes S5's mother as the sole heir. If S5's mother did not survive S5, S6 would still not be S5's sole heir even though S5 and S6 were born to the same parents. Kindred of the half blood inherit the same share as kindred of the whole blood. S6, S4, and O would be S5's heirs and share equally in the probate estate. *See* UPC § 2-107. *If S5's mother did not survive S5, S6 would be S5's sole heir in a jurisdiction that had not enacted the Uniform Probate Code and whose statutes exclude as heirs siblings of the half blood unless there are no siblings of the whole blood. The law in some jurisdictions provides that children of the half blood receive only half as much as children of the whole blood.* Atkinson § 19.

31.   **Answer (B) is correct.** O's siblings, who are either born to or adopted by either H or W, are O's heirs at law, have standing to contest the probate of the will, and will share equally in the estate, if they are successful. UPC §§ 2-103, 2-107.

       Answer (A) is incorrect. S4 is related to O by marriage and excluded as an heir unless W adopted S4.

       Answer (C) is incorrect. S3 is a child of W and is an heir.

       Answer (D) is incorrect. S2 and S3, children of H and W, respectively, are also heirs of O per UPC § 2-107. *However, in some non-UPC jurisdictions, Answer (D) is correct because siblings of the half blood are not heirs unless there are no siblings of the whole blood.* Atkinson § 19.

32. **Answer (D) is correct.** O's heirs at law have standing to contest the probate of the will. Because O was survived by children, O's heirs are C1 and C2, who would share O's probate estate equally, if O died intestate. C3 is a stepchild and excluded, unless O had adopted C3. UPC §§ 1-201(5), 2-103. Because C1 and C2 are minors, surrogates acting on their behalf (presumably their surviving parents) would need to initiate the will contest. *The result is likely to be the same in a non-UPC state.* Atkinson § 18.

     Answers (A), (B), and (C) are incorrect. Neither S nor C3 is an heir at law. S is excluded because O was survived by children.

33. C4 is likely to be an heir. State statutes that exclude non-marital children from inheriting from their biological fathers have been held to violate the equal protection clause of the 14th Amendment of the U. S. Constitution. See *Trimble v. Gordon*, 430 U.S. 762, 776 (1977). UPC § 2-114 directs that the parent-child relationship may be established under relevant state law, such as the Uniform Parentage Act (2002). *States typically have procedures allowing a child to establish that a man was the child's biological father either before or after the man's death even if the father never acknowledged the child as his own.* See McGovern § 2.9.

34. **Answer (D) is correct.** C4 is O's only heir. The identity of a child's other parent or the parent who was awarded custody is irrelevant. However, in order to be an heir, one must not only survive the intestate, but survive by 120 hours. If one survives the intestate but dies within 120 hours, that person is deemed to have died before the intestate. UPC §§ 2-103, 2-104. *Most states which have not enacted the Uniform Probate Code have statutes that require an heir to survive by 120 hours.* See McGovern § 2.2.

     Answer (A) is incorrect. C1 did not survive O. *Even if applicable state law did not require an heir to survive by 120 hours, the common law required an heir to survive the intestate by an "instant" of time.*

     Answers (B) and (C) are incorrect. Typically, state statutes require heirs to survive the decedent by 120 hours. Prior to the enactment of statutes that require survivorship by 120 hours, many states had statutes that would have created the presumption that C2 died before O. Absent proof to the contrary, in those states, C3 and C4 would be O's heirs.

35. **Answer (C) is correct.** Because of the "120 hour rule" of UPC § 2-104, C4 would appear to be O's only heir. However, the "representation rule" of UPC §§ 2-103, 2-106 would substitute G2 and G3 as heirs in place of C2 and C3. Accordingly, O's probate estate would be delivered equally to G2, G3, and C4's devisee, S4. If G2 and G3 are minors their respective shares would be delivered to a guardian or other surrogate pursuant to local law. *The result would be the same in most states that have not enacted the Uniform Probate Code.* McGovern § 2.2.

     Answers (A) and (B) are incorrect. The "120 hour rule" excludes C2 and C3 as heirs. Consequently, their devisees are not entitled to any part of O's estate.

Answer (D) is incorrect. C4 survived O by 120 hours and was one of the heirs. At C4's death, C4's interest passed to S4 subject to formal administration in C4's estate.

36. **Answer (C) is correct.** An individual in gestation at the time of the intestate's death is treated as living at the time of the intestate's death, if the individual lives for at least 120 hours after birth. UPC § 2-108. G6, having been adopted by C3, is an heir of O as well. UPC § 2-114. Consequently, G5 and G2, as well as G6 and G3, succeed to the one-third interests that their parents would have been entitled had the parents survived O by 120 hours. UPC §§ 2-104, 2-106, 2-114. *The result would be the same in most states that have not enacted the Uniform Probate Code.* McGovern §§ 2.2, 2.10.

    Answers (A), (B), and (D) are incorrect for the reasons given.

37. G2, G5, G3, G6, and G4 will share the estate equally. None of the children of O survived O. Consequently, their heirs and devisees did not inherit an interest in O's probate estate from the children. UPC § 2-106 (b) adopts the system of representation called "per capita at each generation" (i.e. equal shares to those equally related). Consequently, the grandchildren share equally in O's probate estate because none of the children survived O. *The result is likely to differ in a non-UPC state that has not enacted a statute similar to UPC § 2-106(b). Some state statutes provide for a "per stirpes" system of representation; other states have enacted different systems (such as the pre-1999 Uniform Probate Code approach — "per capita with representation"). If the applicable statute is a strict "per stirpes" statute, one-third would pass to G2 and G5, one-third would pass to G3 and G6, and one-third would pass to G4. See* McGovern § 2.2.

38. **Answer (D) is correct.** According to UPC § 2-106 (b), O's probate estate is divided into five equal shares for each grandchild who survived O (G2, G3, G5, G6) and one share for the deceased grandchild who left a descendant who survived O (G4). *The result may differ in a non-UPC state. See* McGovern § 2.2.

    Answers (A) and (B) are incorrect. GG succeeded to the interest in O's estate that G4 would have inherited had G4 survived O.

    Answer (C) is incorrect. This answer would be correct in a state with a strict "per stirpes" system of representation.

39. **Answer (D) is correct.** O's probate property passes ("escheats") to the state of X because there are no heirs as defined in UPC §§ 2-103, 2-105. *See* McGovern § 2.2. *Some states that have not enacted the Uniform Probate Code have adopted a similar "parentelic" system; however, not all parentelic systems are the same. Other states have adopted a "next of kin" system to apply in this situation. See* McGovern § 2.2.

    Answers (A), (B), and (C) are incorrect. Neither A nor B is an heir. *However, in some states both A and B would be the heirs of O. In other states, only A would be an heir.*

40.   **Answer (C) is correct.** According to UPC § 2-103(4), a descendant of deceased grand-parents takes by representation. Accordingly, C would inherit O's probate estate. *The result may differ in a non-UPC state. See* McGovern § 2.2.

      Answers (A) and (B) are incorrect. The state takes only if there is no taker under UPC § 2-103.

      Answer (D) is incorrect. B would be an heir under other "parentelic" systems.

41.   Early common law prohibited aliens from acquiring land by descent, a rule followed in some modern cases and adopted by statute in some states. The modern view is that non-citizens can acquire property unless a state's statute provides otherwise. Atkinson § 24. UPC § 2-111 does not disqualify an heir because he or she is an alien. *The result may differ in a non-UPC state. However, even if a state statute purports to limit an alien's inheritance, federal law may override it, if the United States has a treaty with the alien's country. See* Atkinson, § 24.

42. In the absence of a statute, the gift may have been presumed to be an advancement of C2's inheritance and would be taken into account in determining C2's share of O's probate estate. If the value of Blackacre exceeded the value of C2's share of the "hotchpot estate," C2's share of the probate estate would be reduced using the "hotchpot" method. C2 would not be required to reimburse C1 or to restore Blackacre to the probate estate. *See* Atkinson § 129. Uniform Probate Code § 2-109 and similar statutes enacted in most non-UPC states require written evidence of the intent that a gift is to be treated as advancement when the donor dies. *See* McGovern § 2.6.

43. **Answer (D) is correct.** C4 is O's only heir. In order to be a heir, one must not only survive the intestate, but survive by 120 hours. If one survives the intestate but dies within 120 hours, that person is deemed to have died before the intestate. UPC §§ 2-103, 2-104. *Many states that have not enacted the Uniform Probate Code have statutes that require an heir to survive by 120 hours. See* McGovern § 2.2.

    Answers (A), (B), and (C) are incorrect for the reasons given.

44. **Answer (C) is correct.** Because of the "120 hour rule" of UPC § 2-104, C4 would appear to be O's only heir. However, the "representation rule" of UPC §§ 2-103, 2-106 would substitute G2 and G3 as heirs in place of C2 and C3. Accordingly, O's probate estate would be delivered equally to G2, G3, and C4's devisee, S4. If G2 and G3 are minors, their respective shares would be delivered to a guardian or other surrogate pursuant to local law. *The result would be the same in most states that have not enacted the Uniform Probate Code. See* McGovern § 2.2.

    Answers (A), (B), and (D) are incorrect for the reasons given.

45. **Answer (A) is correct.** Absent written evidence that O intended the conveyance to be an advancement (or that C4 acknowledged the gift was an advancement), S4 not only inherited Blackacre when C4 died but also succeeded to C4's interest in O's probate estate. UPC § 2-109. *The result may differ in states that have not enacted the Uniform Probate Code. See* McGovern § 2.6.

    Answers (B) and (C) are incorrect. In order for the gift to be treated as an advancement and either reduce or eliminate S4's interest in O's probate estate, written evidence of O's intent to treat the gift as an advancement must be produced. UPC § 2-109. *In a non-UPC state the gift may be presumed to be an advancement.*

Answer (D) is incorrect. Even if the gift is treated as an advancement, Blackacre was owned by C4 and passed to S4 at C4's death subject to formal administration in C4's estate. Neither C4 nor S4 is under a legal obligation to reimburse O's other heirs or restore Blackacre to O's probate estate.

46.   **Answer (C) is correct.** Because the gift was to G4, it has no effect on C4's inheritance from O that passed to S4 when O died. The gift is not an advancement. UPC § 2-109; Atkinson § 129.

      Answers (A), (B), and (D) are incorrect. The facts do not create an advancement situation under the Uniform Probate Code, similar statutes in non-UPC states, or the common law. Even a written agreement between O and G4 defining the transaction as an advancement may not be binding on C4. Had C4 been a party to the agreement and agreed the gift would be taken into account in determining C4's share of O's probate estate, S4 may be bound by the agreement, or estopped to deny that the advancement to G4 should not be taken into account in determining C4's share of O's probate estate.

47.   **Answer (A) is correct.** Even if there is written evidence of O's intent to treat the gift as an advancement to C4, C4 died before O, and G4 succeeded to the interest in O's probate estate that C4 would have inherited had C4 survived O. UPC §§ 2-103, 2-106. Accordingly, unless the written evidence of the advancement provides otherwise, Blackacre is not taken into account in determining G4's share of O's probate estate. UPC § 2-109(c). *The result may differ in states that have not enacted the Uniform Probate Code.* Atkinson § 129.

      Answers (B) and (C) are incorrect. Absent written evidence that O not only intended for the gift to C4 to be an advancement but that O also intended for the advancement to be taken into account in the event C4 preceded O, the gift is not treated as an advancement. UPC § 2-109(c). *In non-UPC states, G4 may be "burdened by representation."*

      Answer (D) is incorrect. Even if the gift was an advancement, neither C4, C4's heirs and devisees, nor C4's descendants taking by representation have a legal obligation to restore Blackacre to O's probate estate.

48.   Absent written evidence that O intended the gift to be an advancement to G4, the gift is not taken into account in determining G4's share of O's probate estate. UPC § 2-109. *The same result is likely to occur in a state that has not enacted the Uniform Probate Code because the presumption of advancement may not be applicable, because G4 was not an "heir apparent" at the time of the gift. At common law, the gift had to have been made to one who would have been an heir at the time of the gift in order to create the presumption of advancement.* Atkinson § 129.

49. **Answer (A) is correct.** At the time of the assignment, C3 had no property interest in O's probate estate that C3 could transfer; C3 had an expectancy, not a property interest that could have been assigned. O still owned fee simple title. *See* Atkinson § 131. Because C3 was not an heir of O due to UPC § 2-104, G4 succeeded to the interest in O's probate estate that C3 would have inherited if C3 was not deemed to have predeceased O. UPC § 2-106. *The same result would likely occur in states that have not enacted the Uniform Probate Code.*

    Answers (B) and (C) are incorrect. C3 did not own a property interest in O's property that could be given or sold to the assignee. Had C3 survived O by more than 120 hours, the assignee may have been able to enforce the assignment against C3 and C3's estate, if the assignment had been supported by fair consideration.

    Answer (D) is incorrect. The assignee may be a creditor of C3 or C3's estate, but O's estate is not legally obligated to C3's assignee.

50. **Answer (B) is correct.** As soon as O died, O's heirs succeeded to their respective interests in O's estate subject to the 120 hour rule, as well as the debts and other obligations of O and O's estate. Accordingly, C4's expectancy in O's property became a property interest at the time of O's death and could be assigned by C4 to the third party. McGovern § 2.2. Of course, the assignee cannot acquire an interest greater than the one C4 owned at the time of the assignment.

    Answer (A) is incorrect. C4 has assigned C4's interest in O's probate estate.

    Answer (C) is incorrect. An assignment does not need good and valuable consideration to be effective. It may have been a gift.

    Answer (D) is incorrect. The third party is not a creditor of O; the third party acquired whatever interest in O's probate estate that C4 inherited.

51. At the time of the assignment, C4 had an expectancy in O's property. Such an expectancy is not a future interest in O's property; it's not even a property interest. Therefore, the assignment did not transfer any property interest in O's property to the assignee. At O's death, C4's expectancy, in effect, matured into a property interest. State law may provide the third party with a remedy to enforce the assignment as a contract, if the third party paid good and valuable consideration. If no consideration was paid by the third party to C4, the transaction may be viewed as an unenforceable promise of C4. *See* Atkinson § 131. If the assignment was a conveyance of real property, the doctrine of "after acquired title" may be applicable. Roger A. Cunningham et. al., *The Law of Property* § 11.5 (2d ed. 1995).

52. **Answer (A) is correct.** Because C3 is deemed to have predeceased O, C3 is not an heir and did not acquire a property interest in O's probate estate that could be attached by a creditor of C3. UPC § 2-104. *Most states that have not enacted the Uniform Probate Code have statutes similar to the UPC § 2-104.* McGovern § 2.2.

Answers (B), (C), and (D) are incorrect. UPC § 2-104 or a similar statute in a non-UPC state prevents C3 from acquiring an interest in O's probate estate that could be attached by C3's creditor. *In a state that still follows the common law rule, a creditor could attach C3's interest subject to the rights of O's creditors and other administration issues, because the common law required that C3 survive only O by only an "instant" of time.*

53. **Answer (B) is correct.** Because C3 survived O by more than 120 hours and O's debts and other obligations have been satisfied by O's personal representative, C3's one-third interest in O's probate estate is reachable by C3's creditor. McGovern § 2.2. O's personal representative should deliver C3's share to the creditor, if the personal representative has been properly placed on notice of the attachment.

    Answer (A) is incorrect. C3's property interest can be attached.

    Answer (C) is incorrect. It does not matter what kind of debt C owed.

    Answer (D) is incorrect. The creditor is not a creditor of O and does not have to follow the procedures required of O's creditors.

54. **Answer (B) is correct.** Because C3 survived O by 120 hours, the lien can attach to C3's interest in O's probate estate that passed to S3 when C3 died. McGovern § 2.2. However, C3's interest in O's estate is still subject to administration by O's personal representative, as well as O's debts and other obligations. The creditor cannot acquire an interest greater than the one C3 inherited.

    Answer (A) is incorrect. The lien can attach to C3's interest in O's probate estate.

    Answer (B) is incorrect. The nature of the debt is irrelevant.

    Answer (D is incorrect. The creditor is not a creditor of O and does not have to follow the procedures required of O's creditors.

55. The early common law did not allow a decedent's heirs to refuse to accept their inheritances. Modern statutes in most states, such as UPC §§ 2-1105, 2-1106, authorize an heir to disclaim the heir's interest in the decedent's estate so that the property to which the heir would have been entitled passes as if the heir had predeceased the decedent. Statutes in some states, such as UPC § 2-1105, permit an heir's court appointed surrogate, guardian, conservator, or personal representative to execute the disclaimer. However, the law varies from state to state on the effect the disclaimer will have on the disclaimant's creditors. Federal law will control if the disclaimant is in bankruptcy. McGovern § 2.8.

56. **Answer (A) is correct.** Assuming the disclaimer satisfied the requirements of both applicable state law and the relevant provisions of the Internal Revenue Code, the one-third interest in O's probate estate that C4 would have inherited had it not been for the disclaimer

passes from O to G4. UPC § 2-1106(b)(3). No part of the disclaimed property is included in C4's gross estate for estate tax purposes, and C4 did not make a gift to G4 for gift tax purposes. I.R.C. § 2518 (2000) (IRC § ___). *See* McGovern § 2.8.

Answers (B), (C), and (D) are incorrect for the reasons given.

57.   In most states, if O's probate estate is otherwise solvent (i.e., the assets exceed the liabilities), whether or not the debt is valid and enforceable, the concept of "retainer" provides that C4's share of O's estate should be reduced by $8,000 so that the other two heirs' shares of the probate estate are increased by a like amount in order to create equality among the heirs similar to the application of the will construction principle of "advancement." *See* Atkinson § 141. However, UPC § 3-903 gives C4 the benefit of any defense that would be available in a direct proceeding for recovery of the debt. If O's estate is insolvent (i.e., the liabilities exceed the assets) and the debt is a valid and enforceable obligation of C4, C4's estate should pay into O's estate $12,000 in order for the personal representative to have funds to pay O's debts. If neither C4's estate nor S4 pays what is owed, O's personal representative should pursue the $12,000 debt against C4's estate. Atkinson, Chapter 13. If O's estate is insolvent and the debt is no longer enforceable (i.e., collection is barred by the statute of limitations), neither C4's estate nor S4 has any obligation to pay any amount into O's estate.

58.   **Answer (B) is correct.** UPC § 2-803(b) provides that an heir who feloniously and intentionally kills the intestate forfeits the heir's intestate share. It also provides that the intestate's probate estate passes as if the killer disclaimed the killer's interest in the intestate's estate. Accordingly, the interest C4 would have received passes from O to G4. *A number of states that have not enacted the Uniform Probate Code have similar statutes.* See McGovern § 2.7.

Answer (A) is incorrect. Because C4 is deemed to have disclaimed the interest, the interest does not pass to C4's devisee, S4.

Answer (C) is incorrect. UPC § 2-803(b) provides that C4's interest passes as if C4 had disclaimed C4's interest. *However, in some states, the applicable "slayer's rule" directs that C4's interest would be forfeited and C4's interest passes to O's other heirs. Accordingly, in those states, G2 and G3 would take C4's interest, and G4 is excluded because C4, in fact, survived O.* McGovern § 2.7.

Answer (D) is incorrect. UPC § 2-803(b) provides a legal remedy that avoids having to resort to equitable principles. *However, in states that do not have a "slayer's rule" statute, the other heirs may be able to resort to the constructive trust as a remedy to prevent unjust enrichment.*

59.   **Answer (A) is correct.** It is generally accepted that delivery and acceptance are necessary for a valid inter vivos gift. Neither the cash nor the deed was delivered to C3 during O's lifetime. Accordingly, unless the law of X relaxes the delivery and acceptance requirements of a gift under "gift causa mortis" theory, both the house and cash would pass to O's heirs. *See* Atkinson § 45.

       Answers (B) and (D) are incorrect. The concept of "gift causa mortis" has been limited in most jurisdictions to gifts of personal property only.

       Answer (C) is incorrect. If the described assets were still part of O's probate estate, the assets would pass to O's heirs. However, if O made an inter vivos gift of the assets prior to O's death, the assets would have already been owned by the donee prior to O's death. Delivery during the donor's lifetime is an essential element of a gift. Because the deed was not delivered while O was alive, the house is still part of the probate estate. However, states that recognize the concept of "gift causa mortis" may relax the delivery and acceptance requirements. Accordingly, in those states the cash may have been given to C3 and then passed to S3 at C3's death subject to formal administration in C3's estate.

60.   **Answer (D) is correct.** O died intestate. The Uniform Probate Code requires that wills be in writing. O's oral statements as to O's testamentary wishes do not control the disposition of any of O's probate estate. UPC § 2-502. The home and its contents are part of O's probate estate and pass subject to formal administration equally to O's heirs, C1 and C2. *The same result is likely in states that have not enacted the Uniform Probate Code. However, there are limited situations in some states that may give rise to a valid oral will. See* McGovern § 4.4.

       Answers (A), (B), and (C) are incorrect. Whether real or personal property, testamentary dispositions require a writing executed pursuant to the requisite testamentary formalities. The Uniform Probate Code's liberal choice-of-law rule related to will execution is limited to written wills. UPC § 2-506.

61.   **Answer (A) is correct.** O died intestate. UPC § 2-502 requires that testamentary wishes be reduced to a writing executed with the requisite testamentary formalities. It is irrelevant how many witnesses heard O's oral statements and when they heard the statements. *The same result is likely in states that have not enacted the Uniform Probate Code. There are limited situations in some states that may give rise to a valid oral will. See* McGovern § 4.4.

       Answers (B), (C), and (D) are incorrect. A testamentary disposition requires a writing executed with testamentary formalities. UPC § 2-502. The Uniform Probate Code's liberal choice-of-law rule related to will execution is limited to written wills. UPC § 2-506.

62.   Because there is no writing signed by O evidencing the contract, UPC § 2-514 would appear to prevent C1 from enforcing the terms of the oral agreement assuming the contract was agreed to after the effective date of the Uniform Probate Code. Thus, because O died

intestate, the probate estate, including the home and its contents, passed to C1 and C2. However, because C1 rendered good and valuable consideration to O during O's lifetime, C1 may seek recovery against O's estate in quantum meruit for the value of the services rendered. *See* comment to UPC § 2-514. *The result may differ in states that have not adopted UPC § 2-514 or a similar statute. See McGovern § 4.9. For example, C1's partial performance of the agreement may excuse any writing requirement.*

63. **Answer (D) is correct.** O still died intestate. However, C1 appears to have a valid, enforceable contract claim to enforce against O's estate. UPC § 2.514. *See* McGovern § 4.9. Accordingly, C can possibly seek from O's estate specific performance or the imposition of a constructive trust, or ask for money damages.

     Answers (A), (B), and (C) are incorrect. Even though O died intestate, C1 may wind up with the home and contents, as provided in the contract.

64.   **Answer (A) is correct.** O appears to have died intestate. Because the letter was typewritten by O and not signed by the friends, the document does not meet the requirements for a valid will. UPC § 2-502. However, UPC § 2-503 allows a probate court to "excuse a harmless error" and probate a defectively executed document if there is "clear and convincing evidence" that the otherwise defective document represents the decedent's testamentary intent. C1 will likely argue that the letter manifests testamentary intent and for the application of UPC § 2-503. *Most states do not have a statute similar to UPC § 2-503.*

        Answers (B), (C), and (D) are incorrect. Unless C1 meets the burden of proof required in UPC § 2-503, the letter cannot be admitted to probate. UPC § 2-502. The comment to UPC § 2-502 notes there is no requirement that the witnesses sign before the testator's death so long as the reasonable-time requirement is met. However, the limited case authority available indicates that the will is still invalid in this situation. Lawrence H. Averill, Jr., *Uniform Probate Code in a Nutshell* § 9.02 (5th ed. 2001) (Averill § ___).

65.   **Answer (A) is correct.** O appears to have died intestate. Unless the material provisions of the will are in O's handwriting, a writing that does not include the signatures of two witnesses cannot be admitted to probate. UPC § 2-502. Delivery is not a prerequisite to a will. However, UPC § 2-503 allows the probate of a defectively executed will if there is "clear and convincing evidence" that the otherwise defective document represents the decedent's testamentary intent. *See* Question 64. *Most states do not have a statute similar to UPC § 2-503.*

        Answers (B), (C), and (D) are incorrect. C1 may argue that C2 had agreed with O that C1 was to receive the house and its contents and that the court should impose a constructive trust on C2 to prevent C2 from being unjustly enriched. Restatement (Third) Trusts § 18 (2003) (Restatement (Third) Trusts § ___).

66.   **Answer (B) is correct.** UPC § 2-502(b) recognizes "holographic" wills. Accordingly, assuming the letter properly manifested O's intent to make a disposition effective at O's death, the will can be admitted to probate, and the home and its contents pass to C1. If not, the letter is not a will, and O died intestate. *Some states that have not enacted the Uniform Probate Code have similar statutes. However, a number of states do not recognize holographic wills unless properly witnessed.* McGovern § 4.4.

        Answer (A) is incorrect. UPC § 2-502(b) recognizes holographic wills. However, answer (A) would be the correct answer in a number of states.

        Answers (C) and (D) are incorrect. In a state that recognizes holographic wills, a properly executed holographic will can devise both real and personal property.

67.   **Answer (C) is correct.** Wills are revocable dispositions of property that take effect upon the testator's death. The execution of a joint will does not create a presumption of a contract not to revoke the will. UPC § 2-514. Accordingly, absent written evidence of a contract, A had the power and right to revoke the 1990 will, which she did by the execution of the 2000 will. UPC §§ 2-507(c), 2-514. *Many non-UPC states have similar statutes. Absent a statute, the common law of a state may create a presumption that the parties intended to have a contractual will when they executed the joint will.* McGovern § 4.9.

        Answer (A) is incorrect. The 1990 document was intended by A and B to be a will. In order for it to be effective, the 1990 will must be admitted to probate. However, it was apparently revoked by A when A executed the 2000 will.

        Answer (B) is incorrect. The 1990 will was revoked. Further, there is no evidence that A ever revoked the 2000 will.

        Answer (D) is incorrect. UPC § 2-514 creates a presumption that the 1990 will was not executed pursuant to a contract not to revoke it. Accordingly, unless B can establish that a contract existed pursuant to UPC § 2-514, B is without a cause of action. Even if a contract can be established, A revoked the 1990 will, and B's remedy is typically limited to a breach of contract action. Atkinson § 48.

68.   The provision in the will stating the material provision of the parties' agreement allows B to enforce the terms of the contract. UPC § 2-514. However, the prevailing view is that A did have the power to revoke the 1990 will, and the 2000 will can be admitted to probate. A's interest in Blackacre passes to F. Consequently, B is typically limited to bringing a breach of contract action against A's estate and/or F and seeking specific performance, the imposition of a constructive trust, or money damages. Atkinson § 48. *The same result would occur in most other states. However, in some jurisdictions, a contract may not have existed because A did not comply with the terms of the agreement (i.e., she revoked the will and devised the property to F). Under this approach, the agreement was actually an offer by B to be accepted by A, and A did not accept B's offer. Consequently, B has no cause of action. See* McGovern § 4.9.

69.   **Answer (A) is correct.** Assuming that the intent expressed in the 1990 document is not testamentary in nature, but is a valid agreement to create a right of survivorship, A and B converted their tenancy in common into a joint tenancy with rights of survivorship. Atkinson § 40. Consequently, at A's death, A's interest passed nonprobate to B. A's will only controls the disposition of A's probate estate (i.e., property that would otherwise pass by intestate succession). UPC § 1-201(55). *The same result would likely occur in states that have not enacted the Uniform Probate Code.*

        Answer (B) is incorrect. The 1990 document was not intended to be a will and was not executed with the requisite testamentary formalities.

Answers (C) and (D) are incorrect. While the 2000 will devises A's probate estate to F, Blackacre passed nonprobate to B.

70. **Answer (A) is correct.** UPC § 2-514 creates the presumption that the joint 1990 will was not contractual. Because the 2000 will was found not to be valid, the 1990 will was not revoked, and Blackacre passed to B when it was probated. Absent another written document establishing a contract, B has the power and the right to devise Blackacre to anyone, and C would not have a valid cause of action against B or B's estate. *Many non-UPC states have similar statutes that would create the same result. The result may be different in some states that have not enacted the Uniform Probate Code or a similar statute. In these states, the execution of a joint will may raise a presumption that a contract does exist.* McGovern § 4.9. *Answers* **(B), (C), and (D) are incorrect** for the reasons given.

71. **Answer (C) is correct.** UPC § 2-514 will now allow C to enforce the terms of the contract as the third party beneficiary of the contract of A and B. However, in most jurisdictions, C cannot stop B from executing a new will. Atkinson § 48. At B's death, B's new will can be admitted to probate, and if B does not devise Blackacre to C, C's remedy is typically limited to a breach of contract action against B's estate, and B may seek specific performance, a constructive trust, or money damages. A few cases have allowed a suit by the third party beneficiary of the contract during the promissor's lifetime. McGovern § 4.9.

    Answer (A) is incorrect. The provisions of UPC § 2-514 have been met.

    Answer (B) is incorrect. A will by its nature is a revocable disposition to take effect at death. Accordingly, a will can be revoked. C's cause of action will not accrue until B's death.

    Answer (D) is incorrect. The terms of the 1990 will did not devise to C a remainder interest.

72. **Answer (A) is correct.** B's contract with A required B to devise Blackacre to C when B dies. Because a will does not become effective until the testator dies, C's rights under the contract were arguably dependent on C surviving B. Atkinson § 48.

    Answers (B) and (C) are incorrect. C would have had to survive B in order for B to have been obligated to devise Blackacre to C.

    Answer (D) is incorrect. The terms of the 1990 will did not devise to C a remainder interest. However, the terms of the 1990 will could have been worded so that C would have inherited a remainder interest at A's death.

73. **Answer (D) is correct.** Because the contract can be established pursuant to UPC § 2-514, had C not died, C would likely have been in a position to bring a breach of contract cause of action against B's estate, if B did not devise the property to C. Atkinson § 48. If B does not revoke the 1990 will, at B's death, C's child, J, would be able to probate the 1990 will

as B's will, and Blackacre would pass to J pursuant to the "antilapse" provisions of UPC § 2-603. Accordingly, if B devises the property to G, J may have a breach of contract action against B's estate. G will argue that J was not the intended third party beneficiary of the contract. *Most states that have not enacted the Uniform Probate Code have statutes similar to UPC § 2-603.* McGovern § 8.3.

Answer (A) is incorrect. UPC § 2-603 may give J a breach of contract action.

Answer (B) is incorrect. The terms of the 1990 will did not devise to C a remainder interest.

Answer (C) is incorrect. Any cause of action J may have will generally not accrue until B's death. A few cases have allowed a suit during the promissor's lifetime. McGovern § 4.9.

74.   **Answer (C) is correct.** Because B intends to devise to C something other than Blackacre, the proposed will would put C to an "equitable election." At B's death, C would likely be required to either (i) accept the devise in B's will and not pursue the breach of contract action or (ii) disclaim what was devised to C in the will and pursue the breach of contract action. Atkinson § 138.

Answers (A), (B), and (D) are incorrect for the reasons given.

75.   Although a contract not to revoke a will can be established if the provisions of UPC § 2-514 are met, if B devises Blackacre to G when B dies, the personal representative of B's estate will be in a position to argue "failure of consideration" as a defense to any breach of contract action brought by C. Because A and B owned Blackacre as joint tenants with rights of survivorship, B acquired A's half of Blackacre by reason of the form of ownership, not pursuant to A's will. Atkinson § 40. Arguably, B's promise to devise Blackacre to C was not supported by consideration. C will likely argue there was, in fact, consideration, if the law of the state of X permits joint tenants to unilaterally sever the joint tenancy. *See* McGovern § 4.9.

76.   **Answer (C) is correct.** Although Blackacre passed nonprobate to B due to the survivorship rights associated with the joint tenancy, B is put to an "equitable election," and B cannot accept any benefits under A's will without agreeing, in effect, to convey Blackacre to F. If B accepts any benefits under the will, F will be entitled to Blackacre. C's rights as a third party beneficiary under the original contract would then be effectively revoked by the original parties' subsequent modification of the original agreement. *See* Atkinson §§ 40,138.

Answers (A), (B), and (D) are incorrect for the reasons given.

77. **Answer (B) is correct.** Due to the joint tenancy, A acquired fee simple title to Blackacre by reason of B's death. Atkinson § 40. At A's death, Blackacre passes to F, and the residuary estate is divided between F and B1, who takes as a substituted taker for B pursuant to UPC § 2-603(b)(1). If A's promise to B to devise Blackacre to C was not supported by any consideration, C is without a legitimate cause of action. If consideration is found, C may have a breach of contract cause of action against A's estate. McGovern § 4.9. *Most states that have not enacted the Uniform Probate Code have statutes similar to UPC § 2-603.* McGovern § 8.3.

Answers (A) and (C) are incorrect for the reasons given.

Answer (D) is incorrect. It is arguable that A's promise to B not to revoke the 1999 will was not supported by any consideration. However, C will likely argue that A's promise was supported by consideration, if the law of the state of X permits a joint tenant to unilaterally sever a joint tenancy.

78. **Answer (B) is correct.** A testator must be at least 18 years of age and be of sound mind in order to validly execute a will. UPC § 2-501. In a contested probate proceeding, F will have the burden to prove the facts of (i) O's death, (ii) the court's venue, and (iii) the due execution of the will. However, A will have the burden to prove O did not have testamentary capacity. UPC § 3-407. *In many jurisdictions, F would have the burden to prove O had testamentary capacity at the time O executed the will.* Atkinson § 100.

    Answer (A) is incorrect. A diagnosis of Alzheimer's alone is not likely to be considered prima facie evidence of the lack of O's testamentary capacity.

    Answer (C) is incorrect. According to the Uniform Probate Code, the burden of proof on the issue of testamentary capacity is on the contestant.

    Answer (D) is incorrect. The test for the capacity necessary to execute a will differs from the test for incapacity in a guardianship or conservatorship proceeding. In order to determine whether a testator had testamentary capacity, courts typically look at various factors, such as the testator's ability to understand the nature of a testamentary act, to remember the "natural" objects of the testator's bounty, and to understand the nature and extent of the testator's property. McGovern § 7.1.

79. **Answer (B) is correct.** A has the burden to prove O lacked testamentary capacity when the will was executed. UPC § 3-407. The fact that O was found to be incapacitated in a guardianship proceeding after the will was executed may be evidence of incapacity but is not conclusive. Different tests for capacity are used in guardianship proceedings and probate proceedings. *F would have the burden to prove O had testamentary capacity in many non-UPC jurisdictions.* Atkinson § 100.

    Answers (A), (C), and (D) are incorrect for the reasons given.

80. **Answer (C) is correct.** A has the burden to prove O lacked testamentary capacity when the will was executed. UPC § 3-402. However, introduction of evidence that O had previously been found to be incapacitated in a guardianship proceeding may be evidence that O lacked testamentary capacity. McGovern § 7.2. *In many non-UPC jurisdictions the burden of proof is on F to prove O had testamentary capacity.* Atkinson § 100.

    Answers (A), (B), and (D) are incorrect for the reasons given.

81. **Answer (C) is correct.** The will of a testator with the requisite testamentary capacity can still be denied probate if the devisee improperly influenced the testator during the execution of the will. Accordingly, A has the burden to prove F's undue influence. UPC § 3-407. *States that have not enacted the Uniform Probate Code typically place the burden on the contestant for the issue of undue influence. However the contestant may be able to rely on a presumption of undue influence if a person who prepared the will was in a confidential relationship with the testator.* McGovern § 7.3.

    Answers (A) and (B) are incorrect. Undue influence is an issue separate and distinct from testamentary capacity, although evidence of one is relevant to the other.

    Answer (D) is incorrect. The burden of proof is typically on the contestant even in a state where the burden of proof on capacity is on the proponent.

82. A will must be in writing and signed by the testator. UPC § 2-502. However, a testator does not need to sign the testator's legal name or even the name typically used by the testator. If whatever was actually written on the will by the testator was intended by the testator to be a signature, the will has been signed by the testator. Accordingly, if O wrote O's first name and intended it to be O's signature, the will was signed; if the evidence shows O intended to write both the first and last names, but was unable to complete the task, some courts have held the will was not signed. McGovern § 4.2. *The same result is typically reached in states that have not enacted the Uniform Probate Code.*

83. **Answer (C) is correct.** Whatever a testator intends to be a signature can be a signature. It is not unusual for a testator to make a "mark" on the will rather than sign the testator's name. If the "mark" was intended to be a signature, the will has been signed. McGovern § 4.2. The burden of proof is on F to prove due execution. UPC § 3-407. *States that have not enacted the Uniform Probate Code typically place the burden of proof on the proponent of the will.*

    Answers (A), (B), and (D) are incorrect. If F can prove O intended the mark to be O's signature, the will can be admitted to probate.

84. **Answer (C) is correct.** UPC § 2-502 (a)(2) authorizes what is commonly called a "proxy signature." If the testator's name is signed by another in the testator's "conscious" presence and at the testator's direction, the will can be admitted to probate. Accordingly, F has the burden to prove the requisites of a "proxy signature." *While most states that have not enacted the Uniform Probate Code permit "proxy signatures," they may differ on what is required for a "proxy signature" to be effective.* Comment to UPC § 2-502.

    Answer (A) is incorrect. A will can have a proxy signature.

    Answer (B) is incorrect. F will have to prove by a preponderance of the evidence that the witness signed O's name at O's direction and in O's "conscious" presence.

Answer (D) is incorrect. UPC § 2-502 (a)(2) requires that the witness sign O's name in O's "conscious" presence. *In some non-UPC states the "proxy signature" may need to have been done in O's "visual presence" or "line of sight." If so, because O could not see the witness sign the will, the will may not be valid.*

85.   UPC § 2-502 does not require that the testator "publish" the document as a will. Accordingly, it is not necessary to prove that the witnesses were aware the document they were signing was O's will. If F can prove that the witnesses signed after they observed O sign the document, or that the witnesses signed after O acknowledged O's signature, the will can be admitted to probate, even if they were not aware what they signed was actually a will. *In states that have not enacted the Uniform Probate Code, the technical requirements for will execution vary. For example, the testator may be required to "publish" the will; in others, the testator must at a minimum acknowledge to the witnesses that the document is the testator's document. Some states require that the testator request the witnesses sign the document.* McGovern § 4.3.

86.   **Answer (C) is correct.** UPC § 2-502 (a)(3) does not require the witnesses observe a testator sign the will. If it can be established that the witnesses signed the will within the reasonable time after they observed the testator acknowledge the testator's signature or the will itself, the will can be admitted to probate. *In a state that has not enacted the Uniform Probate Code, the state's attestation requirements may be significantly different.* McGovern § 4.3.

        Answers (A) and (B) are incorrect for the reasons given.

        Answer (D) is incorrect. Not a good answer to give the client! The Uniform Probate Code only requires that each witness observe one of the following: (i) the testator sign the will, (ii) the testator acknowledge the testator's signature, or (iii) the testator acknowledge the document as the testator's will. *In a state that has not enacted the Uniform Probate Code, the state's attestation requirements may be significantly different, and the will may not be valid.*

87.   **Answer (C) is correct.** The Uniform Probate Code does not require that each witness sign in the presence of the other witnesses so long as they otherwise comply with UPC § 2-502 (a)(3). *Some states which have not enacted the Uniform Probate Code may require the witnesses to sign in each other's presence.* McGovern §4.3.

        Answers (A) and (B) are incorrect for the reasons given.

        Answer (D) is incorrect. Not a good answer to give the client! The Uniform Probate Code only requires that each witness observe one of the following: (i) the testator sign the will, (ii) the testator acknowledge the testator's signature, or (iii) the testator acknowledge the document as the testator's will. *In a state that has not enacted the Uniform Probate Code, the state's attestation requirements may be significantly different, and the will may not be valid.*

88.   **Answer (B) is correct.** UPC § 2-502 (a)(3) does not require the witnesses sign the will in the presence of the testator. Assuming the other requirements of UPC § 2-502 can be proven by F, the will can be admitted to probate. *Many states which have not enacted the Uniform Probate Code require that the witnesses sign the will in the presence of the testator.* McGovern § 4.3.

    Answers (A) and (C) are incorrect for the reasons given

    Answer (D) is incorrect. Not a good answer to give the client! The Uniform Probate Code does not require that the testator observe the witnesses sign the will. *In those jurisdictions that require the witnesses sign in the presence of the testator, research may be necessary to determine if the law of the state requires "conscious" presence or "visual" or "line of sight" presence. If so, the will may not be valid.*

89.   The Uniform Probate Code does not require that the witnesses sign the will in the testator's presence, and the comment to UPC § 2-502 suggests that they can even sign the will after the testator's death. Accordingly, if F can prove that the witnesses did sign within "a reasonable time" after they observed O sign the will, or O acknowledge O's signature, or O acknowledge the document as O's will, the will may be admitted to probate. *The statutes in most states which have not enacted the Uniform Probate Code require the witnesses sign in the testator's presence, and many courts have rejected wills signed by witnesses after the testator's death.* McGovern § 4.3.

90.   **Answer (B) is correct.** The Uniform Probate Code only requires two witnesses. UPC § 2-502 (a)(3). *Most American jurisdictions require two witnesses, but Vermont still requires three witnesses and Louisiana, five, in some circumstances.* McGovern § 4.3.

    Answers (A) and (C) are incorrect. If the will is otherwise valid, the will can be admitted to probate with only two witnesses.

    Answer (D) is incorrect. The Uniform Probate Code does not require three witnesses. *In those jurisdictions that do require more than two witnesses, research may be necessary to see if the state has a "harmless error" statute, or if the courts have otherwise relaxed the doctrine of "strict compliance," or whether their statutes include an applicable choice of law exception similar to* UPC § 2-506.

91.   **Answer (C) is correct.** Unlike statutes in some states, the Uniform Probate Code does not require that the testator sign the will at the end of the document. UPC § 2-502 (a)(2). F must prove that O intended the writing of O's name in the first line to be O's signature. *The result may be different in a non-UPC state.* McGovern § 4.2.

    Answers (A) and (B) are incorrect. The fact that the testator did not sign at the end is not necessarily a bar to the will's probate. Nevertheless, the fact the testator wrote the testator's name in the body of the will may not constitute a "signature".

Answer (D) is incorrect. The Uniform Probate Code does not require the testator's signature to be at the end of the will. *In a state that has not enacted the Uniform Probate Code, research may be necessary to determine if the applicable statute requires the testator's signature to appear at the end of the will. If so, the will may not be valid.*

92.   C1 inherits the entire estate. O did not comply with the statutory requirements of revocation or execution. The 1990 will was not revoked by O prior to O's death. It is generally accepted that a will may be revoked by either a subsequent valid will or an authorized act done to the will. UPC § 2-507 confirms this principle. Accordingly, notwithstanding O's expressed intent to revoke the 1990 will and leave O's property to G, O's intent was not expressed in a writing that met the requirements of a valid will. See UPC § 2-502. The email did not meet the statutory requirements of a will. *The result is likely to be the same in a state that has not enacted the Uniform Probate Code.* McGovern §§ 5.1, 5.2. *If UPC § 2-503 is applicable in this situation and G can meet the burden of proof required by the statute, O's stated testamentary intent may be carried out.*

93.   **Answer (B) is correct.** The 1990 will was not revoked by O. It is generally accepted that a will may be revoked by either a subsequent valid will or an authorized act done to the will. UPC § 2-507 confirms this principle. Accordingly, notwithstanding O's express intent to revoke the 1990 will and leave O's property to G, O's intent has not expressed in a writing that meets the requirements of a valid will. *See* UPC § 2-502. *The result is likely to be the same in a state that has not enacted the Uniform Probate Code.* McGovern §§ 5.1, 5.2.

Answers (A) and (D) are incorrect for the reasons given.

Answer (C) is incorrect. The letter was not a valid will unless the court finds UPC § 2-503 is applicable, and G meets the burden of proof required by the statute.

94.   **Answer (C) is correct.** UPC § 2-502(b) provides that a will that is not properly witnessed can still be valid, if the material provisions of the will are in the testator's handwriting. Accordingly, if the letter manifests "testamentary" intent (i.e. the letter indicates it was intended to have dispositive effect and not just a casual expression of what a future will should contain), it's a will that revokes the old will and devisees O's probate estate to G. Proof of testator's intent can be made with extrinsic evidence. UPC § 2-502(c). In a significant departure from the generally accepted view, UPC § 3-407 places on the contestants the burden of establishing O's lack of testamentary intent. *Some states that have not enacted the Uniform Probate Code do not recognize unwitnessed holographic wills; other states may require that the evidence of the testator's intent be found in the will itself; most states place the burden of proof on the proponent.* Atkinson § 47.

Answers (A), (B), and (D) are incorrect for the reasons given.

95.   **Answer (B) is correct.** The 1990 will was not revoked. The document found in the box is not a valid will. UPC § 2-502(b) provides that a will that is not properly witnessed must be in the testator's handwriting. *The result is likely to be the same in a state that has not enacted the Uniform Probate Code.* McGovern § 5.1.

       Answers (A) and (D) are incorrect. O was survived by both children but did not die intestate.

       Answer (C) is incorrect. The document in the safe deposit box is not a valid will unless the court finds UPC § 2-503 is applicable and G meets the burden of establishing O intended the document to be O's will.

96.   UPC § 2-502(b) provides that a will that is not properly witnessed can still be valid, if the material provisions of the will are in the testator's handwriting. Accordingly, the new will impliedly revoked the old will due to the inconsistent dispositive provisions and devises O's probate estate to G. *Some states that have not enacted the Uniform Probate Code do not recognize unwitnessed holographic wills; other states require the testator's intent to be found within the four corners of the will.* McGovern § 4.4.

97.   **Answer (C) is correct.** UPC § 2-502 (b) requires that only the "material portions" of the will be in the testator's handwriting. *In some non-UPC states, the 1990 will was not revoked because the new will was not properly witnessed. In other states, a court may determine that O intended for the date to be part of the new will and that the new will is, therefore, not wholly in the testator's handwriting and invalid. Another state may find that the name of the hotel and the date were "surplus" and that the new will was wholly in the testator's handwriting and valid.* McGovern § 4.4.

       Answers (A), (B), and (D) are incorrect for the reasons given.

98.   **Answer (A) is correct.** O died intestate. The 1990 will was revoked by O. It is generally accepted that a testator can revoke a will by lining through the testator's signature. And, because the 1990 will was found in O's safe deposit box, most courts would presume that O placed the "X" on O's signature, thereby revoking the will. McGovern § 5.2. UPC § 2-507 adopts this principle. This answer assumes O had testamentary capacity at all relevant times.

       Answers (B), (C), and (D) are incorrect for the reasons given.

99.   **Answer (B) is correct.** The 1990 will was not revoked. While it is generally accepted that a will can be revoked by the testator destroying the same or another individual destroying the same at the direction of the testator, a "proxy" revocation must be done in the "presence" of the testator. UPC § 2-507 (a) (2) adopts this principle. It is doubtful that the lawyer's destruction of the 1990 will will be found to have been done in O's presence. *Like the Uniform Probate Code, the law in some non-UPC states adopts a "conscious" presence test;*

other states use a more conservative "visual presence" or "line of sight" test. McGovern § 5.2.

Answers (A) and (D) are incorrect. The will was not destroyed in O's presence. C2 may argue that the proxy revocation was done in O's presence, if the lawyer destroyed it while O was on the phone and O heard the lawyer destroy it. If C2 is successful, C1 may argue for the application of the "doctrine of dependent relative revocation" to negate the revocation because O's intent to devise O's estate to G cannot be carried out.

Answer (C) is incorrect. There is no writing documenting O's intent to devise the probate estate to G.

100. It appears that O revoked the most current will in favor of G, causing O's probate estate to pass by intestate succession to C1 and C2. The 1990 will would not be revived by the revocation of the later will. *See* UPC § 2-509. However, G will likely argue that O did not have the requisite mental capacity to revoke the will. Alternatively, the common law doctrine of "dependent relative revocation" may be applicable, if G can prove that O's mistaken belief of G's death caused her to revoke the will. McGovern § 5.3. If either argument is successful, the new will could be probated notwithstanding its destruction. A will that cannot be produced may be admitted to probate in most jurisdictions upon adequate proof of its contents and the execution. Atkinson § 97. *Some states, which have not enacted the Uniform Probate Code, have held that the revocation of a revoking document does have the effect of reviving the earlier revoked will.* McGovern § 5.3.

101. **Answer (B) is correct.** According to UPC § 2-509 (a), the 1990 will is likely to have been revived because it is evident from the circumstances and O's contemporary declarations that O intended the 1990 will to take effect at O's death. *The result may be different in a state that has not enacted the Uniform Probate Code. Some courts have held that, because a will is ambulatory, the earlier will is not actually revoked until the testator dies and the later will is admitted to probate. Other courts follow the rule that the earlier will was revoked when the later one was executed. The rule in some states distinguishes between express and implied revocations.* Atkinson § 92.

Answer (A) is incorrect. UPC § 2-509(c) is likely to revive the 1990 will, so O did not die intestate. *However, in some non-UPC states, the 1990 will is not revived and O died intestate.*

Answer (C) is incorrect. The 2000 will was revoked.

Answer (D) is incorrect. Even if O died intestate, the cousins would not be considered heirs despite the estrangement between O and C.

102. **Answer (B) is correct.** The 1990 will was "impliedly" revoked by the execution of the 2000 will due to the wills' inconsistent provisions. UPC § 2-507(c). Because the 2000 will was revoked, UPC § 2-509 (a) is likely to revive the 1990 will. *In some non-UPC states, the 1990 will was not revoked by the execution of the 2000 will, because the 2000 will was revoked before O died. In other states, the 1990 will was revoked by the execution of the 2000 will and was not revived when the 2000 will was revoked. The rule in some states distinguishes between express and implied revocations. Atkinson § 92.*

Answers (A), (B), and (C) are incorrect for the reasons given.

103. **Answer (B) is correct.** The 1990 will was revoked by the execution of the 2000 will but is likely to have been revived by O's destruction of the 2000 will. UPC § 2-509(a). It is irrelevant that the 2000 will was a holographic will. UPC § 2-507. *Non-UPC states that recognize holographic wills are likely to adopt the same rule. Atkinson § 87. If the state does not recognize holographic wills, the 1990 will was never revoked.*

Answers (A), (B), and (C) are incorrect for the reasons given.

104. **Answer (A) is correct.** It is generally accepted that, if a will was last known to have been in the testator's possession, the will is presumed to have been revoked by the testator destroying the same when it cannot be found after the testator's death. McGovern § 5.2. A will argue that O's statements to the friends revived the 1990 will. UPC § 2-509(a). However, without proof of when O destroyed the 1990 will, O likely died intestate.

Answer (B) is incorrect. The 1990 will is presumed revoked. If A can prove that O destroyed the 1990 will before the unsigned 2000 will was destroyed, UPC § 2-509(a) may revive the 1990 will, if its contents can be proven. C will argue that UPC § 2-509(c) is not applicable in this situation.

Answer (C) is incorrect. The 2000 will was never executed by O.

Answer (D) is incorrect. Even if O died intestate, the cousins would not be considered heirs.

105. A is likely to inherit the entire estate. The 1990 will is likely to have been revived by the revocation of the 2000 will. UPC § 2-509 (a). The fact that the 1990 will was destroyed by the lawyer is not determinative, if its contents can otherwise be established. The lawyer's destruction of the will was not a "proxy revocation." UPC § 2-507 (a) (2). *The result may be different in a non-UPC state which would hold that the 1990 will was revoked when the 2000 will was executed and not revived by the revocation of the 2000 will. Atkinson § 92. In those states, O died intestate, and C inherits.*

106. **Answer (B) is correct.** The 2000 will was revoked by the nurse tossing it in the fire at O's direction and in O's presence. UPC § 2-507(a)(2) adopts the generally accepted concept of "proxy revocation." The revocation of the 2000 will is likely to have revived the 1990 will.

UPC § 2-509(a). *The result may be different in some non-UPC states which would hold that the 1990 will was revoked when the 2000 will was executed and not revived by the revocation of the 2000 will.* Atkinson § 92.

Answer (A) is incorrect. UPC § 2-509(a) is likely to revive the 1990 will, so O does not die intestate. *However, in some non-UPC states, the 1990 will is not revived, and O dies intestate.*

Answer (C) is incorrect. The 2000 will was revoked by O.

Answer (D) is incorrect. Even if O died intestate, the cousins would not be considered heirs.

107.   Because the will was not executed, it cannot be admitted to probate. The comment to UPC § 2-503 seems to indicate that the situation described is not one that could be corrected by the court admitting the unexecuted will to probate. However, G may be successful in requesting the court to impose a constructive trust on C1 and C2 due to C1's wrong doing in order to prevent unjust enrichment by both C1 and C2. Even though only one of the heirs did anything wrong, a court may impose the constructive trust on both the wrong doing and the innocent parties, because the innocent party would not have inherited any part of the estate had it not been for the bad acts of the other person. McGovern § 6.1.

108.   **Answer (B) is correct.** The will is not valid, and upon proof of the circumstances surrounding its execution, it will not be admitted to probate. Although the document was executed with the requisite testamentary formalities, it did not express O's actual testamentary intent. Atkinson § 55.

Answers (A), (C), and (D) are incorrect. The will did not reflect O's actual testamentary intent so it should not be admitted to probate.

109.   **Answer (A) is correct.** Although the will was destroyed, it was not revoked because O lacked the requisite intent to revoke the will due to C1's coercion. Atkinson § 86.

Answers (B), (C), and (D) are incorrect. O lacked the intent to revoke when O destroyed the will.

110.   **Answer (C) is correct.** Because the will was not revoked, it can be admitted to probate. The comment to UPC § 2-503 seems to indicate that the situation described is not one that could be corrected by the court denying the will's probate. However, due to G1's wrongdoing, C may be successful in requesting the court to impose a constructive trust on G1 and G2 to prevent their unjust enrichment. McGovern § 5.2.

Answer (A) is incorrect. The will can be admitted to probate, unless C can convince the court that UPC § 2-503 is applicable. In any event, the court may impose a constructive trust on both G1 and G2.

Answer (B) is incorrect. The will was not revoked. It may be admitted to probate.

Answer (D) is incorrect. The court may impose a constructive trust on both G1 and G2 to prevent their unjust enrichment due to G1's wrongdoing.

111. Like the law in all states, UPC § 2-507 (a) (2) provides that a will may be revoked by the testator performing a revocatory act with the intent and for the purpose of revoking the will. In order to have the required intent, the testator must have testamentary capacity. UPC § 3-407 places the burden on a will's contestant to prove that the testator revoked a will; this rule suggests that the contestant must establish that O had the requisite mental capacity to revoke the will; however, that same section requires a will's contestant to prove that the testator lacked testamentary intent or capacity. That section fails to expressly describe who has the burden of proof where the issue is the testator's capacity to revoke a will. The overall intent of the Uniform Probate Code suggests that testators are presumed to have the capacity to both execute and revoke wills. *The common law typically placed the burden of the capacity issue on the party trying to establish a will had been executed or revoked. The law in some non-UPC states places the burden on a will's proponent to prove the will was not revoked.*

112. **Answer (D) is correct.** Because its material provisions are in the testator's handwriting, the note is a valid will even though it was not signed by any witnesses. UPC § 2-502(b). The earlier will was revoked even though it was signed by two witnesses. UPC § 2-507(a)(1). *In a non-UPC state that does not recognize holographic wills, the earlier will would not have been revoked absent the application of a "harmless error" statute. However, in most non-UPC states that allow holographic wills, a holographic will can revoke an attested one.* McGovern § 5.1.

Answer (A) is incorrect. The earlier will has been revoked.

Answer (B) is incorrect. O did not die intestate. The note not only revoked the earlier will but also devised O's probate estate to C1.

Answer (C) is incorrect. O did not die intestate, and even if O had died intestate, O was survived by C1 and C2.

113. **Answer (B) is correct.** UPC § 1-201(55) defines the term "will" to include a testamentary instrument that merely revokes another will, and UPC § 2-507 says a will can be revoked by a subsequent will. Because the new will did not contain a new disposition of O's estate, O's probate estates passes to O's heirs at law. *The same result is likely to occur in states that have not enacted the Uniform Probate Code.*

Answers (A), (C), and (D) are incorrect for the reasons given.

114. O's marriage to S after the execution of the will did not revoke the will. UPC § 2-508. However, S is generally entitled to what S would have received had H died intestate. UPC § 2-301. The amount is deducted from the augmented estate to determine S's elective share amount as defined in UPC § 2-202. In addition, S will be entitled to assert any rights she might have under local law in or to the homestead, homestead allowance, exempt property, and family allowance. *In a community property state, the surviving spouse is generally entitled to half of any community property. The rights of the "forgotten" or "pretermitted" spouses, if any, in other non-UPC states will vary from state to state. In some states, the will may have been revoked by operation of law.* Atkinson § 85.

115. **Answer (C) is correct.** O generally has the right to devise O's estate to whomever O chooses, subject to S's elective share percentage amount. UPC § 2-202. In addition, S will be entitled to assert any rights she might have under local law in or to the homestead, homestead allowance, exempt property, and family allowance. *In a community property state, a surviving spouse generally retains half of any community probate property. In non-community property states (other than Georgia) that have not adopted the Uniform Probate Code, surviving spouses have a right to some share of the estate.* McGovern § 3.7.

     Answer (A) is incorrect. S will be entitled to an elective share amount as described above. In addition, S will be entitled to assert any rights S might have under local law in or to the homestead, homestead allowance, exempt property, and family allowance.

     Answers (B) and (D) are incorrect. The will is valid; O did not die intestate.

116. According to UPC § 2-804 (b), the divorce revoked any dispositive provision of O's will in favor of S. Because the will devised all of O's probate estate to S, the probate estate passes by intestate succession to O's heirs. If S is named as the executor of O's estate, the divorce also revoked O's nomination of S as executor. *Statutes in most non-UPC states would produce the same result, and in some states, even without a statute, case law may work a revocation by operation of law due to the change of circumstances. In a few states, a divorce revokes the entire will and not just the provisions in favor of the former spouse.* McGovern § 5.4.

117. **Answer (A) is correct.** Because O's will devised all of O's estate to their surviving parent, C1 and C2 will not receive an interest in O's probate estate even though they were omitted from the will. UPC § 2-302 (a) (1). Their births did not revoke the will. UPC § 2-508. *In almost every state that has not enacted the Uniform Probate Code, statutes grant "omitted" or "pretermitted" children certain rights in their parents' estates under some circumstances; the details vary from state to state.* McGovern § 3.5.

     Answers (B), (C), and (D) are incorrect for the reasons given.

118. **Answer (A) is correct.** The "omitted children" provisions of the Uniform Probate Code provide protection from unintended disinheritance under certain circumstances only for children born or adopted after the execution of the will. See UPC § 2-302. *The "pretermitted" child statutes in states that have not enacted the Uniform Probate Code vary considerably from state to state.* McGovern § 3.5.

Answers (B), (C), and (D) are incorrect for the reasons given.

119. **Answer (D) is correct.** C3, who was omitted from the will, will receive an intestate share of O's probate estate. UPC § 2-302(a)(1). *In almost every state that has not enacted the Uniform Probate Code, statutes grant marital and non-marital "omitted" or "pretermitted" children certain rights in their parents' estates under some circumstances; the details vary from state to state.* McGovern § 3.5.

Answer (A) is incorrect. C3 is an "omitted child" and entitled to the share C3 would have received had O died intestate.

Answer (B) is incorrect. The birth of the children after the execution of the will did not revoke the will.

Answer (C) is incorrect. Because S is the surviving parent of C1 and C2, they are not entitled to an interest in O's estate.

120. **Answer (A) is correct.** O's probate estate passes to O's heirs but subject to formal administration by a court-appointed personal representative and the rights of O's creditors, as well as any expenses in incurred in the administration of O's estate. UPC § 3-101. However, C could agree to become a "universal successor" and assume personal responsibility for O's debts. UPC § 3-312. *In states that have not enacted the Uniform Probate Code, a personal representative also discharges the decedent's debts out of the probate estate.* McGovern § 12.2.

   Answers (B), (C), and (D) are incorrect for the reasons.

121. Even though C resides in state Y, the law of X applies. UPC § 2-401. Accordingly, C may have a right to an amount payable out of O's probate estate equal to $15,000 for the homestead allowance. UPC § 2-402. In addition, C may be entitled to a value not to exceed $10,000 in household furnishings, furniture, automobiles, and personal effects. UPC § 2-403. Also, if O had an obligation to support C, C will be entitled to a reasonable allowance for maintenance for a period not to exceed one year. UPC § 2-404. The balance of the estate will be used to satisfy the debts and expenses. *A minor child's right to these types of allowances will vary considerably in those states that have not enacted the Uniform Probate Code.* McGovern § 3.4.

122. **Answer (A) is correct.** Absent a provision in the state constitution of X that either (i) grants a decedent's surviving spouse a right to occupy the home owned by the deceased spouse regardless of the solvency of the estate and who actually inherits the home and/or (ii) exempts the family home from the claims of unsecured creditors and estate administration expenses, if the owner is survived by a spouse, the home will likely be sold to raise cash to pay allowances and the obligations. *See* UPC § 2-402A. *The availability of the homestead to satisfy a decedent's general obligations will vary from state to state.* McGovern § 3.4.

   Answers (B), (C), and (D) are incorrect. Unless the constitution of X creates a homestead right in S as described above, the home will be sold to pay expenses and debts.

123. **Answer (A) is correct.** UPC § 2-607 provides that a specific devise passes subject to any indebtedness secured by the property unless the will provides otherwise. *In those states that have not enacted the Uniform Probate Code, or a statute similar to UPC § 2-607, the common law rule of exoneration creates a presumption that a testator intends a devisee to inherit a specific devise, free of indebtedness. In those states, half of the stock would be sold to raise the cash to pay the note.* McGovern § 8.2.

Answers (B) and (C) are incorrect. The Uniform Probate Code creates a presumption of "non-exoneration." Jurisdictions that still follow the common law rule of "exoneration of liens" grant S the right to receive the home free of debt.

Answer (D) is incorrect. In some jurisdictions the secured creditor can elect either to have the debt paid in due course of administration or pursuant to the terms of the creditor's contract with the decedent. This decision should not affect whether S or D bears the burden of the debt.

124.   **Answer (A) is correct.** Because the will does not direct the order of "abatement," the debt should be paid out of residuary devise. UPC § 3-902. *Many non-UPC states have abatement statutes that are similar to UPC § 3-902; other states follow common law abatement, which would produce the same result under these circumstances.* McGovern § 8.2.

Answers (B) and (C) are incorrect. The debts paid by the executor should be paid out of the residuary devise.

Answer (D) is incorrect. The source of the debt payment depends on the relevant abatement rule.

125.   An executor will typically use the most liquid non-exempt asset of the estate that has not been specifically devised by the testator in the will. If the cash is used, the executor may also need to sell the stocks and bonds to raise the cash necessary to satisfy the pecuniary bequest owing to B. UPC § 3-902. In this situation, C is not likely to receive anything upon final settlement of O's estate because the executor must distribute to B either $100,000 in cash or stocks and bonds worth $100,000 on the date distributed to B. B can demand cash. UPC § 3-906. *States that have not enacted the Uniform Probate Code are likely to have statutes or common law rules that reach a similar result. However, some states' laws will require the executor to satisfy the pecuniary bequest in cash unless the devisee agrees to a distribution "in-kind."* McGovern § 12.10.

126.   **Answer (A) is correct.** Absent a provision in the will that provides otherwise, UPC § 3-902 prescribes how the probate estate abates in order to satisfy the decedent's debts. Real estate has a priority over personal property only within the four categories of probate assets: (i) property not disposed by will, (ii) residuary devises, (iii) general devises, and (iv) specific devises. *States that have not enacted the Uniform Probate Code will typically have a similar statute or a common law rule that reaches a similar result.* McGovern § 8.2.

Answer (B) is incorrect. If the executor uses the cash to pay the debts, the home and its contents may have to be sold to raise the $100,000 to satisfy the bequest to B.

Answer (C) is incorrect. C was specifically devised all of the stocks and bonds.

Answer (D) is incorrect. UPC § 3-902 prescribes how the probate estate abates in order to satisfy the decedent's debts.

127. **Answer (A) is correct.** The executor will typically use the most readily available liquid non-exempt asset available to pay the creditors. Pursuant to UPC § 3-906(a)(2)(i), the executor may need to sell other assets, like the stocks and bonds, to raise the cash necessary to satisfy B's pecuniary bequest. *McGovern §§ 8.2, 12.10.*

   Answers (B), (C), and (D) are incorrect for the reasons given.

128. **Answer (A) is correct.** UPC § 2-605 directs that A is entitled to the ExxonMobil stock. UPC § 2-606(a)(5) directs that Whiteacre passes to B. *The results may differ in states that have not enacted the described provisions of the Uniform Probate Code or similar statutes. Under the common law, the rule of "ademption by extinction" may cause the entire probate estate, including the stock and land, to pass to C.* McGovern § 8.1.

   Answer (B) is incorrect. UPC § 2-606(a)(5) directs that B is entitled to Whiteacre because O acquired it as a replacement for Blackacre. *Many non-UPC states have enacted statutes similar to UPC § 2-605, but not statutes like UPC § 2-606. In those states, Answer (B) would be correct.*

   Answers (C) and (D) are incorrect. The Uniform Probate Code has replaced the common law's strict "identity" test with a more liberal "change of form" rule.

129. UPC § 3-902 directs that the debts are to be paid from the residuary devise, and if it is not sufficient, from the general devisees. After the debts and expenses are paid, specific devises are distributed, general devises are paid to the extent assets are available, and if there is anything remaining, it is delivered to the residuary devisee. Accordingly, after the home and the stocks and bonds are sold to pay the debts, A will receive the proceeds paid by the insurance company for the damage to the car. UPC § 2-606(a)(3). B will receive the balance. C will receive nothing. *In states that have not enacted the Uniform Probate Code or similar statutes, the common law rule of ademption by extinction may limit A to only $1,000, the value of the car at the time of O's death, and the balance would pass to B.* Atkinson § 134.

130. **Answer (A) is correct.** An inter vivos gift to a person named as a devisee in the donor's will is not treated as the "satisfaction" of the testamentary devise unless the will provides for a deduction of the gift or there is a written document in which the donor or donee indicates that the gift is to be taken into account at the time of the donor's death. See UPC § 2-609. *States that have not enacted the Uniform Probate Code or similar statutes may still follow the common law rule that presumes a gift to devisee of a general or residuary devise is either a partial or total "satisfaction" of the testamentary devise.* Atkinson § 133.

   Answers (B) and (C) are incorrect. Where applicable, the doctrine of satisfaction generally applies to both general and residuary devises.

Answer (D) is incorrect. Absent written evidence to the contrary in the will or another written document, the gifts are not to be taken into account when O dies.

131. **Answer (B) is correct.** An executor in every jurisdiction has a duty to expend reasonable efforts to collect any valid debts due and owing the decedent, including one owed by a devisee, particularly if the estate is insolvent. *See* UPC § 3-709.

    Answer (A) is incorrect. O's death does not extinguish the debt.

    Answer (C) is incorrect. Because the estate is insolvent, B is obligated to repay the entire $10,000.

    Answer (D) is incorrect. Because the estate is insolvent, neither A, B, nor C receives any part of O's estate.

132. **Answer (D) is correct.** Because the estate's assets exceed the debts by more than $10,000, the executor has enough non-exempt liquid assets on hand to pay the creditors what they are owed and to pay A the pecuniary bequest of $10,000. From a practical perspective, there is no reason for the executor to collect the $10,000 from B who, in effect, owes half of that amount to himself or herself as a residuary devisee. UPC § 3-903. *The result is likely to be the same in a non-UPC state pursuant to the common law concept of "retainer."* Atkinson § 141.

    Answers (A), (B), and (C) are incorrect for the reasons given.

133. **Answer (A) is correct.** The debt cannot be collected by the executor because it appears to be barred by the statute of limitations.

    Answers (B) and (C) are incorrect for the reasons given.

    Answer (D) is incorrect. Because the estate is insolvent, B does not have a residuary share to reduce by the amount of the debt.

134. **Answer (A) is correct.** UPC § 3-903 provides that, while a debt of a devisee is to be offset against the devisee's share of the estate, the devisee has the benefit of "any defense" that would be available in a proceeding for recovery of the debt, including the statute of limitations. *In states that have not enacted the Uniform Probate Code or similar statutes, the result may be different.* Atkinson § 141.

    Answers (B) and (C) are incorrect. The debt is not collectible due to the statute of limitations.

    Answer (D) is incorrect. UPC § 3-903 grants B "any defense," including the statute of limitations. *In some non-UPC states, B's share of the residuary will be reduced by half of the debt.*

135. Because a will is a disposition of property that becomes effective at the testator's death, the common law required a devisee to survive the testator by an "instant" of time. Most states have enacted statutes that require devisees to survive testators by 120 hours unless the will provides otherwise. The Uniform Probate Code has adopted this rule. See UPC § 2-702. UPC § 2-604(a) adopts the common law rule that a lapsed specific devise becomes part of the residuary devise. *See* Atkinson § 140. Accordingly, only C survived O by 120 hours, and the entire estate, including the two tracts of land, passed (subject to formal administration in C's estate) to C's spouse.

136. **Answer (D) is correct.** UPC § 2-702 requires that a devisee survive the testator by 120 hours unless the will provides otherwise. Because A and B did not survive O by 120 hours, their devises "lapsed." However, UPC § 2-604 is not applicable, and the two tracts do not become part of the residuary devise. UPC § 2-603 directs that the two tracts pass to the children of A and B. *Most states that have not enacted the Uniform Probate Code have similar "antilapse" statutes.* McGovern § 8.3.

    Answers (A), (B), and (C) are incorrect. They fail to take into consideration both UPC §§ 2-702 and 2-603.

137. **Answer (D) is correct.** Because all three children died before O, their devises lapsed, and O's probate estate passes by intestate succession. O's closest relatives that survived O were the cousins. Atkinson § 140.

    Answers (A), (B), and (C) are incorrect. The devisees named in O's will died before O; their gifts lapsed. UPC § 2-603, or a similar statute in a non-UPC state, is not applicable because the children did not have descendants.

138. The devisees to A, B, and C lapsed because they died before O. The antilapse provisions of UPC § 2-603 do not apply to any devisee but only to certain categories of devisees. No part of O's estate passes to the spouses or children of A, B, and C. O's probate estate passes by intestate succession to D. *In a state that has not enacted the Uniform Probate Code, the result may differ depending on the terms of the applicable "antilapse" statute. However, most states have statutes that would create the same result as* UPC § 2-603 *under these circumstances.* McGovern § 8.3.

139. **Answer (C) is correct.** A died before O; B is deemed to have died before O because of the 120 hours rule. UPC § 2-702. Their gifts lapsed, but the "antilapse" provisions of UPC § 2-603 direct that the two-thirds they would have received pass to their children. *Most states that have not enacted the Uniform Probate Code have similar statutes.* McGovern § 8.3.

    Answers (A), (B), and (C) are incorrect. The testamentary gifts to A and B "lapsed" but their children succeed to what they would have been entitled had they survived O by 120 hours.

140. **Answer (A) is correct.** Because A and B did not survive O by 120 hours, their gifts lapsed. UPC § 2-702. According to UPC § 2-604 (b), the interests in O's probate estate they would have received pass to C. *In states that have not enacted the Uniform Probate Code or similar statutes, the result may be different. The common law typically applied the "lapsed fractional gift" rule to this type of situation, and the two-thirds of the estate devised to A and B would pass by intestate succession to O's heirs.* Atkinson § 140.

   Answers (B) and (C) are incorrect. The gifts to A and B lapsed.

   Answer (D) is incorrect. The gifts to A and B lapsed, and the two-thirds of O's probate estate they would have received pass to C. The common law rule typically resulted in the two-thirds passing to O's heirs, C and D.

141. **Answer (A) is correct.** O's will devised O's probate estate to three individuals, not including E. Only "omitted children," not omitted grandchildren, have rights under UPC § 2-302. *"Pretermission" statutes in some non-UPC states may afford rights to descendants of omitted children.* McGovern § 3.5.

   Answers (B), (C), and (D) are incorrect. E is not entitled to any portion of O's probate estate.

142. **Answer (A) is correct.** A testator may devise property to a "class" of beneficiaries, rather than to several named individuals. According to UPC § 2-603(b)(2), the "antilapse" provisions apply to certain class gifts. So, A1 and B1 succeed to the interests A and B would have had they survived O by 120 hours. *In states that have not enacted the Uniform Probate Code or similar statutes, the result may differ.* McGovern § 8.3.

   Answers (B), (C), and (D) are incorrect for the reasons given.

143. The "antilapse" provisions UPC § 2-603(b) prescribe a rule of construction to apply in the absence of a contrary intention in O's will. However, UPC § 2-603(b)(3) also provides that words of survivorship like "my surviving children" are not, in the absence of additional evidence, a sufficient indication of "contrary intention." Accordingly, A1 and B1 take the two-thirds their parents would have received had they survived O by 120 hours, and C takes the balance. *The view in many states that have not enacted the Uniform Probate Code, or a statute similar to UPC § 2-603 (b)(3), is that words of survivorship attached to a devise, like "who survive me," are sufficient to negate the applicable "antilapse" statute. In those states C would inherit the entire estate.* McGovern § 8.3.

144. **Answer (D) is correct.** The "class" of devisees opened at O's death and included E and C, as well as the substituted takers, A1 and B1. *See* UPC § 2-603. *The same result would occur in states that have not enacted the Uniform Probate Code but have a similar "antilapse" statute that applies to "class" gifts.* McGovern § 8.3.

Answers (A), (B), and (C) are incorrect. These answers do not take into account both the nature of "class gifts" and the applicable "antilapse" statute. *In a state that does not extend its "antilapse" provisions to class gifts, C and E would share the estate equally.* McGovern § 8.3.

145. **Answer (A) is correct.** At the time of O's death the "class" of devisees "opened" and "closed"; C was the only member of the class that survived O. Restatement (Second) of Property (Donative Transfers) § 27.2 (1983) (Restatement (Second) Donative Transfers § ___).

     Answers (B) and (C) are incorrect for the reasons given

     Answer (D) is incorrect. A and B did not survive O by 120 hours before they died.

146. **Answer (D) is correct.** A died before O; B is deemed to have died before O because of the 120 hours rule. UPC § 2-702. Their gifts lapsed, but UPC § 2-603's "antilapse" provisions do not direct to their children the two-thirds they would have received. Stepchildren of the testator's children are not included among the devisees whose gifts can be saved by the antilapse statute. UPC § 2-604(b) directs that C succeed to the entire residuary estate. *States that have not enacted the Universal Probate Code typically do not extend their "antilapse" provisions to stepchildren. However, in some non-UPC states, the two-thirds of the estate that A and B would have received pass to O's heir, D, pursuant to the common law's "lapsed fractional gift" rule.* Atkinson § 140.

     Answers (A), (C), and (D) are incorrect. The testamentary gifts to A and B "lapsed" but their children do not succeed to what they would have been entitled had they survived O by 120 hours.

147. The initial question is, who were the intended beneficiaries of O's probate estate? Absent evidence of contrary intent in the will, stepchildren of a child would normally be excluded from the class of intended beneficiaries, the grandchildren (unless they were adopted by the child). The Uniform Probate Code appears to have adopted this prevailing view. *See* UPC § 2-705. Because this rule excludes C (as well as substituted takers A1 and B1 under UPC § 2-603), and because D did not have any children, O did not have any grandchildren who survived him. O's sole heir, D, appears to have inherited the entire estate. C will argue that extrinsic evidence should be admitted to prove that S's stepchildren were the "grandchildren" O intended to benefit in the will. The comment to UPC § 2-601 appears to encourage courts to look at extrinsic evidence for the purpose of rebutting a rule of construction. If C is not successful, state law will determine if D inherits fee simple title, or fee simple title subject to possible divestment, if D has any children in the future.

148. **Answer (B) is correct.** When a devisee disclaims, the property disclaimed passes as if the disclaimant had predeceased the testator. UPC § 2-1106(b)(3). The "antilapse" provisions of UPC § 2-603 create a "substitute gift" in favor of the disclaimant's descendants, if any. *The same result is likely to occur in a state that has not enacted the Uniform Probate Code.* McGovern §§ 2.8, 8.3.

Answers (A), (C), and (D) are incorrect for the reasons given.

149. **Answer (A) is correct.** When a devisee disclaims, the property disclaimed passes as if the disclaimant had predeceased the testator. UPC § 2-1106(b)(3). The "antilapse" provisions of UPC § 2-603 provide a "substitute gift" in favor of the disclaimant's descendants. However, stepchildren of the testator's children do not qualify as devisees whose deaths before the testator qualify for "antilapse" treatment. The entire estate passes to O's only heir, D. *The same result may occur in a state that has not enacted the Uniform Probate Code. Antilapse statutes vary considerably from state to state.* McGovern §§ 2.8, 8.3.

Answers (B), (C), and (D) are incorrect for the reasons given.

150. Modern statutes, such as UPC § 2-1105, authorize heirs and devisees to disclaim their interests in decedents' estates. However, the law varies from state to state on the effect a disclaimer has on the rights of the disclaimant's creditors. Federal law will control, if the disclaimant is in bankruptcy. McGovern § 2.8. In any event, Blackacre passes (subject to any rights G's creditors may retain) as if G had predeceased O to the charity under the residuary clause pursuant to UPC §§ 2-604(b), 2-1105(f).

151. **Answer (B) is correct.** A's will may dispose of property by reference to facts that have significance independent from their effect on the disposition made by the will. Accordingly, the stocks pass to A, and the jewelry passes to B. UPC § 2-512 codifies this generally accepted concept. McGovern § 6.2. The described personal property will pass to C even though the memo was not executed with testamentary formalities because the will refers to it. UPC § 2-513. *Results may differ in states that have not enacted the Uniform Probate Code or similar statutes. Absent a statute similar to UPC § 2-513, the prevailing view is, the personal property passes to the residuary devisee, D.* McGovern § 6.2.

Answers (A), (C), and (D) are incorrect for the reasons given.

152. Because the will makes no reference to the intended trust, a testamentary trust was not created. *See* Restatement (Third) Trusts § 17. If F does not volunteer to perform as agreed, the court will admit evidence of the oral agreement in order to impose a constructive trust on F in favor of C and G to prevent F from being unjustly enriched. F will ordinarily be ordered to transfer the property to another person who will carry out the intended purposes of the oral agreement. Restatement (Third) Trusts § 18.

153. **Answer (D) is correct.** An express inter vivos trust was not created when the agreement was signed or during O's lifetime because property had not been transferred to F. Restatement (Third) Trusts §§ 2, 3, 10. Because the will makes no reference to the intended trust, a testamentary trust was not created. Restatement (Third) Trusts § 17. However, the court would likely impose a constructive trust on F in favor of C and G. Restatement (Third) Trusts § 18. *See* Question 152.

    Answer (A) is incorrect. An express inter vivos trust was not created when the agreement was signed because property had not been transferred to F during O's lifetime. Because the will makes no reference to the intended trust, a testamentary trust was not created. The comment to UTC § 401 notes that a trust instrument signed during the settlor's lifetime is not invalid because the trust was not funded until after the settlor's death. Accordingly, it is arguable that an express trust was created when O devised Blackacre to F. However, the Restatement takes the position that an express trust is not created if the settlor fails during life to complete the contemplated transfer. Restatement (Third) Trusts § 16.

    Answer (B) is incorrect. Equity will not allow F to be unjustly enriched.

    Answer (C) is incorrect. The situation does not fit the limited circumstances that justify the imposition of a resulting trust.

154. **Answer (D) is correct.** Although O's will manifests an intent to create an express trust, other elements essential to the creation of a testamentary trust are not in the will. Accordingly, a testamentary trust was not created. Restatement (Third) Trusts § 17. The Restatement takes the position that the court should impose a constructive trust on F in favor of C and G, if F does not volunteer to perform as agreed. Restatement (Third) Trusts § 18. However, some courts may impose a resulting trust on F in favor of the charity notwithstanding the modern trend adopted by the Restatement. *See* comment to Restatement (Third) Trusts § 18.

    Answer (A) is incorrect. Because the will failed to identify the beneficiaries, an express trust was not created.

    Answer (B) is not correct. The modern view is to impose a constructive trust in favor of C and G.

    Answer (C) is incorrect. The situation does not fit the circumstances that justify the imposition of a resulting trust in favor of O's heirs.

155. Although O's will manifests the intent to create an express trust, other elements essential to the creation of a testamentary trust, such as the purposes of the trust, are not in the will. Further, the purposes of the trust cannot be inferred from the will. Restatement (Third) Trusts § 17. Accordingly, an express testamentary trust was not created. However, evidence of the oral agreement is admissible to impose a constructive trust on F in favor of C and G in order to carry out O's intent if F does not volunteer to perform as agreed. Restatement

(Third) Trusts § 18. If evidence of the oral agreement is not admissible or not proven, even if admissible, the trust is "passive," and the intended beneficiaries are entitled to the property as tenants in common. The statute of uses, or a similar statute, may merge legal and equitable title in C and G. Restatement (Third) Trusts § 6.

156. **Answer (B) is correct.** Obviously, O did not intend for F to inherit fee simple title, but the will did not create an express trust because the terms of the intended trust were not included in the will. A constructive trust is not available because there is no evidence of the intended beneficiaries or the purpose of the trust. When a settlor's attempt to create an express trust fails, the courts will typically impose a resulting trust on the intended trustee in favor of the settlor or the settlor's successor in interest. In this case, the charity will likely succeed to Blackacre. *See* Restatement (Third) Trusts § 8.

Answer (A) is incorrect. An express trust was not created because the will did not name the beneficiaries or describe the terms of the intended trust. Further, there is no evidence of any pre-existing agreement between O and F.

Answer (C) is incorrect. The charity, not O's heir, is O's successor in interest and has standing to seek the imposition of the resulting trust.

Answer (D) is incorrect. Obviously, O did not intend for F to acquire fee simple title.

157. **Answer (D) is correct.** The trust is "passive," and the legal and equitable titles merge in C and G. UTC § 402 has codified this common law concept. Restatement (Third) Trusts § 6. *In a state that does not have a statute of uses, or a similar statute, the intended beneficiary is entitled to possession upon demand to the person in possession.*

Answer (A) is incorrect. An express trust was not created because the will did not impose on F any affirmative duties.

Answer (C) is incorrect. O did not die intestate.

Answer (B) is incorrect. The charity, as the residuary beneficiary, inherits only those probate assets that have not been specifically or generally devised.

158. **Answer (D) is correct.** Only G has standing to seek the imposition of a constructive trust, if F does not volunteer to convey Blackacre to G pursuant to the oral agreement. *See* Restatement (Third) Trusts § 18.

Answer (A) is incorrect. Because the will makes no reference to the intended trust, a testamentary trust was not created. *See* Restatement (Third) Trusts § 17.

Answer (B) is incorrect. Equity will not allow F to retain the property upon proof of the oral agreement between O and F.

Answer (C) is incorrect. In view of the oral agreement between O and F, a constructive trust in favor of G is the appropriate remedy.

159. Although a testamentary trust was not created, C will have standing to seek the imposition of a constructive trust on F, if F does not volunteer to distribute the income to C, as agreed. Restatement (Third) Trusts §§ 17, 18. Because G was not alive when O died, O's equitable reversion passed to the charity, as O's successor in interest. If F fails to convey Blackacre to the charity following C's death, the charity will seek to have the court impose a resulting trust on F in favor of the charity. *See* Restatement (Third) Trusts §§ 7, 8.

160. **Answer (D) is correct.** F died before O devised Blackacre to F; neither F's spouse nor F's child acquired an interest in Blackacre. The gift to F lapsed, and Blackacre passed to the charity. UPC § 2-604. C and G will argue that the court should impose a constructive trust in their favor on the charity to avoid the charity from being unjustly enriched. A constructive trust typically arises out of an intended express trust that is unenforceable because of the failure to satisfy the applicable wills act. Restatement (Third) Trusts § 18. The imposition of a resulting trust is not appropriate because O's successor, the charity, already has acquired title.

Answers (A) and (B) are incorrect. Because F died before O, neither F's spouse nor F's child acquired an interest in Blackacre.

Answer (C) is incorrect. C is not O's successor in interest and does not have standing to seek a resulting trust.

161. **Answer (C) is correct.** Because (i) O's attempt to create an express trust failed, and (ii) the trust intention does not appear in the will, O's successor in interest, the charity, will have the court impose a constructive trust on F to prevent F from being unjustly enriched. Restatement (Third) Trusts § 18.

Answers (A) and (B) are incorrect. Because G did not survive O, neither GS or GG has standing to impose a constructive trust.

Answer (D) is incorrect. Although it appears from the will that F has inherited Blackacre, equity will not allow F to retain it once satisfactory evidence of the oral agreement is produced.

162. **Answer (C) is correct.** F should be able to accept the specific devise of Blackacre and convey the property to C and G, if they are both competent adults. After accepting the deed, C and G, as the intended beneficiaries, can decide the ultimate disposition of the property. Because an express trust was not created, UPC § 2-707 should not be applicable. If UPC § 2-707 is applicable, G's remainder interest is contingent on G surviving C, and the charity may have inherited O's reversionary interest. If C and G do not agree to the proposed conveyance, or if either is not a competent adult, F should consider asking for court author-

ity to convey the property to another party who would agree in writing to carry out the purposes of the original oral agreement. Alternatively, F may want to consider disclaiming the property.

Answer (A) is incorrect. F can refuse to accept Blackacre by filing a qualified disclaimer. If F disclaims, Blackacre would vest in the charity, and C and G will have to deal with the charity concerning the oral agreement. They may have to incur expenses in convincing a court to impose constructive trust on the charity to avoid its unjust enrichment. Restatement (Third) Trusts § 18.

Answer (B) is incorrect. If F disclaims, Blackacre passes to the charity. UPC §§ 2-604(b)(3), 2-1106(b)(3).

Answer (D) is incorrect. An express trust was not created. Restatement (Third) Trusts § 17.

163. Because the will makes no reference to the intended trust, a testamentary trust was not created. Restatement (Third) Trusts § 17. If F accepts the stock under the will, equity will not allow F to retain it for F's own use. Parole evidence is admissible to explain the oral agreement. C and G will likely seek to impose a constructive trust on F, if F accepts the stock and does not volunteer to perform as agreed, or on the charity, if F disclaims the stock. Restatement (Third) Trusts § 18.

164. **Answer (B) is correct.** If the only proof of the oral trust is G's testimony of what O told G about the conveyance, it is likely that F will retain the fee simple title. G's testimony is hearsay. Accordingly, there is no admissible evidence of the oral agreement.

Answers (A), (C), and (D) are incorrect. Even if G can produce other evidence of the oral agreement between F and O, G must also be able to prove that F procured the transfer by fraud, duress, or undue influence or that O and F were in a confidential relationship at the time of the transfer. If G can meet the burden of proof, a constructive trust is the appropriate remedy. Restatement (Third) Trusts § 24.

165. **Answer (B) is correct.** The statute of frauds requires a writing for the inter vivos creation of enforceable express trusts of interests in real property. Restatement (Third) Trusts § 22. Because there is no writing evidencing the trust, F may retain Blackacre, notwithstanding F's acknowledgment of the oral agreement unless G can prove that F procured the transfer by fraud, duress, or undue influence or that O and F were in a confidential relationship at the time of the transfer. Comments h-j to Restatement (Third) Trusts § 24.

Answers (B), (C), and (D) are incorrect. Assuming there is no other evidence of F's intent at the time of conveyance or of a special relationship existing between O and F at the time of the conveyance, a constructive trust is not appropriate. The prevailing view is a constructive trust can be imposed on a grantee of a deed only if the grantee did not intend to perform as agreed when the promise was made. McGovern § 6.4. There are, however, cases suggesting the use of a constructive trust to prevent the unjust enrichment of a grantee who orally agrees but later refuses to hold in trust. Comments h-j to Restatement (Third) Trusts § 24.

166. **Answer (D) is correct.** Because of the pre-existing fiduciary relationship that existed between O and F, F will have to prove that the transaction was fair to O. If F does not meet that burden, a court is likely to impose a constructive trust on F in favor of O's heir, C, to avoid unjust enrichment by F. Restatement (Third) Trusts § 24.

Answers (A) and (C) are incorrect. The only proof of the oral trust is hearsay and inadmissible. If there is other admissible evidence of the oral agreement, G would be the one who could seek the imposition of the constructive trust on F.

Answer (B) is incorrect. Because of the pre-existing fiduciary relationship between O and F, equity will not likely permit F to retain Blackacre.

167.   Because the statute of frauds requires a writing for the creation of an inter vivos trust of real property, the oral express trust is not enforceable if F is not willing to perform as agreed, notwithstanding the willingness of the friends to testify as to the oral agreement. See comment to Restatement (Third) Trusts § 24. According to the prevailing view, F would be allowed to retain Blackacre unless G was able to prove that F acquired Blackacre by fraud, undue influence, or duress, or that F, at the time of the transfer, was in a confidential relationship with O. *There appears, however, to be a modern trend developing toward the use of the constructive trust to prevent F's unjust enrichment under these circumstances. Some cases favor the intended beneficiaries; others favor the settlor, or his or her successor in interest. Comments h-j to* Restatement (Third) Trusts § 24.

168.   **Answer (B) is correct.** The testimony of the other friends is likely to be the evidence needed to prove the creation of the oral express trust and its terms. Like most states, X does not require a writing to create an inter vivos express trust of personal property. Restatement (Third) Trusts § 20. However, UTC § 407 does require "clear and convincing evidence" of the creation of the oral trust and its terms. *Some states that have not enacted the Uniform Trust Code may require only a "preponderance of the evidence."*

Answer (A) is incorrect. Assuming G has "clear and convincing" evidence of the oral agreement, G can simply bring an action to enforce the express trust.

Answer (C) is incorrect. O's attempt to create the express trust did not fail for lack of a beneficiary or for failure of the trust's purpose.

Answer (D) is incorrect. Sufficient evidence is available to prevent F from retaining the stock for F's own use.

169.   **Answer (C) is correct.** Because the oral trust agreement does not satisfy the statute of frauds, G cannot enforce the express trust. Restatement (Third) Trusts § 24. The parole evidence rule will allow the friends to testify to confirm that O did not intend F to take Blackacre for F's own use, thereby leading to the imposition of a resulting trust in favor of C, as O's successor in interest. Restatement (Third) Trusts §§ 7, 8, 21, 24.

Answer (A) is incorrect. In order to satisfy the requirements of the statute of frauds, the writing must not only manifest trust intention, but also identify the trust property, the beneficiaries, and the purposes of the trust.

Answer (B) is incorrect. In most states, C, as O's successor in interest, has standing to require F to return the property unless it is proven that F acquired Blackacre by fraud, duress, or undue influence or that O and F were in a pre-existing confidential relationship. Restatement (Third) Trusts § 24. *Some states may allow G to impose the constructive trust to avoid C's unjust enrichment. Comment g to* Restatement (Third) Trusts § 24.

Answer (D) is incorrect. Equity will not allow F to retain the property.

170. **Answer (B) is correct.** F can carry out the terms of the oral trust, if the creation and the terms of an oral trust can be proven by clear and convincing evidence. Only F can assert the statute of frauds as a defense and take advantage of the oral trust being unenforceable. Restatement (Third) Trusts § 24. If F elects to take advantage of the statute of frauds or cannot prove the existence of the oral agreement, the trust is "passive," and G can demand the transfer of the property to G. If the statute of uses, or a similar statute is applicable, F's legal title merges with G's equitable title, and G already owns fee simple title. Restatement (Third) Trusts § 6. *While* UTC § 407 *requires clear and convincing evidence to prove an oral trust, many non-UTC states require proof by only a preponderance of the evidence.*

    Answers (A), (C), and (D) are incorrect for the reasons given.

171. If a valid, enforceable trust has been created, Blackacre is not subject to the personal obligations of F. Restatement, Third, Trusts § 42. UTC § 507 has codified this generally accepted principle. However, because there is not a written evidence of the trust, UTC § 407 requires that the creation of the trust and its terms be proven by "clear and convincing evidence." Will the court accept F's acknowledgment of the trust as sufficient proof of the existence of the trust and its terms? If F and G fail to meet the burden of proof, the creditors can attach the property. *In states that have not enacted the Uniform Trust Code, the creation of the trust and its terms may have to be proven by only a preponderance of the evidence.*

172. If a valid, enforceable trust can be established, Blackacre is not subject to F's personal obligations. Restatement (Third) Trusts § 42. UTC § 507 has codified this generally accepted principle. Even if the terms of the trust agreement can be established by G, F can plead the statute of frauds in most states, thereby making the trust unenforceable and allowing the creditor to attach Blackacre unless G can meet the burden of proof to have a constructive trust imposed on F. Restatement (Third) Trusts § 24. Alternatively, F can acknowledge the oral trust, not plead the statute of frauds, and prevent Blackacre from being attached, if there is clear and convincing evidence of the oral trust. UTC § 407. *In states that have not enacted the Uniform Trust Code, the creation of the trust and its terms may have to be proven by only a preponderance of the evidence.*

173. **Answer (A) is correct.** Because an enforceable express trust exists, Blackacre is not the subject to the personal obligations of F. Restatement (Third) Trusts § 42. UTC § 507 codifies the generally accepted principle.

    Answer (B) is incorrect. Because a valid, enforceable express trust has been established, the trust property is not subject to the personal obligations of F.

    Answers (C) and (D) are incorrect. Because an express trust exists, Blackacre is not the subject to the personal obligations of F. If you allow the creditor to attach Blackacre, you will breach your fiduciary duties to G.

174.   **Answer (C) is correct.** At common law, conditions of survivorship were not implied with respect to future interests. *See* comment to UPC § 2-707. However, UPC § 2-707(b) provides that a future interest under the terms of an express trust is contingent on the beneficiary surviving the distribution date. Because G predeceased O, GG is the substituted taker of G's interest pursuant to UPC § 2-707(b)(1). *In a state that has not enacted the Uniform Probate Code, or a similar statute, the result is likely to differ.* Restatement (Third) Trusts § 55.

   Answers (A) and (D) are incorrect. An express trust was created; the death of the beneficiary does not generally extinguish the trust. C may ask for the imposition of a resulting trust if C can convince the court that the trust was fully performed or failed upon the deaths of O and G. Restatement (Third) Trusts § 7. If G had not been survived by any lineal descendants in a UPC state, the property would have passed to O's heir, C. UPC § 2-707(d).

   Answer (B) is incorrect. UPC § 2-707 provides that GG acquires G's interest. *However, in some non-UPC states, S would have succeeded to G's vested remainder interest in the trust estate.*

175.   **Answer (C) is correct.** At common law, conditions of survivorship were not implied with respect to future interests. *See* comment to UPC § 2-707. However, UPC § 2-707(b) provides that a future interest under the terms of an express trust is contingent on the beneficiary surviving the distribution date. Because G predeceased O, GG is the substituted taker of G's interest pursuant to UPC § 2-707(b)(1). *In a state that has not enacted the Uniform Probate Code, or a similar statute, the result is likely to differ.* Restatement (Third) Trusts § 55.

   Answers (A) and (D) are incorrect. An express trust was created; the death of the beneficiary does not generally extinguish the trust. C may ask for the imposition of a resulting trust if C can convince the court that the trust was fully performed or failed upon the deaths of O and G. Restatement (Third) Trusts § 7. If G had not been survived by any lineal descendants in a UPC state, the property would have passed to O's heir, C. UPC § 2-707(d).

   Answer (B) is incorrect. UPC § 2-707 provides that GG is the substituted taker of G's interest. *However, in most non-UPC states, S would have succeeded to G's vested remainder interest in the trust estate.*

176.   Because the "terms of the trust" are not in writing, the generally accepted view is that the express trust is not void, but merely unenforceable by the intended beneficiary. *See* comment a to Restatement (Third) Trusts § 24. In other words, the common law treated G as acquiring a vested equitable remainder interest, which was devised to S when G died. Restatement (Third) Trusts § 55. If F does not acknowledge the trust, S has standing to seek the imposition of a constructive trust to prevent F from being unjustly enriched. Contrary to this generally accepted view, UPC § 2-707b indicates that GG, not S, acquired the interest G would have retained had G survived O, and it is GG who has standing to seek the constructive trust. In order to have a constructive trust imposed, most American jurisdictions require G's suc-

cessor, GG or S, to prove that F committed a fraud or exerted undue influence or duress on O, or that F was in a pre-existing confidential relationship with O. *Some more recent cases suggest that F's breach of promise alone may be all that is needed to justify the constructive trust to prevent F's unjust enrichment. See comments h-j to Restatement (Third) Trusts § 24.*

177. **Answer (A) is correct.** O retained a reversionary interest in Blackacre when the trust was created because the remainder interest was not assigned to G because G was already dead. C inherited O's reversionary interest when O died and has standing to seek the imposition of a resulting trust because the trust now lacks a beneficiary. *See* Restatement (Third) Trusts §§ 7, 8.

Answer (B) is incorrect. The traditional remedy when a settlor attempts but fails to create an express trust is the resulting trust.

Answers (C) and (D) are incorrect. Because G was not alive when the trust was created, G did not own an interest that GG acquired pursuant to UPC § 2-707, or that S inherited in a non-UPC state.

178. **Answer (A) is correct.** O retained a reversionary interest in Blackacre when the trust was created because the remainder interest was not assigned to G because G was already dead when the oral express trust was created. C inherited O's reversionary interest when O died and has standing to seek the imposition of a resulting trust because the trust now lacks a beneficiary. The lack of a writing does not prevent the imposition of a resulting trust. *See* Restatement (Third) Trusts §§ 7, 8.

Answer (B) is incorrect. The traditional remedy when a settlor attempts but fails to create an express trust is the resulting trust.

Answers (C) and (D) are incorrect. Because G was not alive when the trust was created, G did not own an interest that GG acquired pursuant to UPC § 2-707, or that S inherited in a non-UPC state.

179. **Answer (B) is correct.** Because the "terms of the trust" were not reduced to writing, the generally accepted view is that the trust is not void, but unenforceable by the intended beneficiaries. Restatement (Third) Trusts § 24. However, because G was already dead, O retained the equitable title, which passed to C at O's death. If F does not acknowledge the trust, C has standing to seek the imposition of a constructive trust to prevent F's unjust enrichment. Comment d to Restatement (Third) Trusts § 24.

Answer (A) is incorrect. The trust did not fail for the lack of a beneficiary; it is unenforceable. The constructive trust is the traditional remedy.

Answers (C) and (D) are incorrect. Because G was not alive when the trust was created, G did not own an interest that GG acquired pursuant to UPC § 2-707, or that S inherited in a non-UPC state.

180. **Answer (A) is correct.** A valid, enforceable express trust has been created. UTC § 401 and 402 codify the generally accepted principles for the creation of an express trust. Restatement (Third) Trusts § 22.

Answers (B), (C), and (D) are incorrect. Assuming O had the mental capacity, O transferred the property to F and indicated an intent for F to hold and manage the trust property for O and G.

181. **Answer (A) is correct.** An enforceable express trust was created; the death of G did not terminate the trust. At common law, conditions of survivorship were not implied with respect to future interests. *See* comment to UPC § 2-707. However, UPC § 2-707(b) provides that a future interest under the terms of a trust is contingent on the beneficiary surviving the distribution date. Because G was not survived by any lineal descendants, the property passed to O's heir, C, at D's death. UPC § 2-707(d).

Answers (B) and (C) are incorrect. At common law, conditions of survivorship were not implied with respect to future interests. *See* comment to UPC § 2-707. However, UPC § 2-707(b) provides that a future interest under the terms of a trust is contingent on the beneficiary surviving the distribution date. Because G predeceased O, neither C nor M inherited G's interest in the trust. *In a state that has not enacted UPC § 2-707, or a similar statute, the result is likely to differ. G's interest would likely be inherited by G's heirs, C and M.* Restatement (Third) Trusts § 55.

Answer (D) is incorrect. In any event, F does not retain the property for F's personal use.

182. **Answer (B) is correct.** Absent additional evidence of O's intentions, UPC § 2-707(b)(3) directs that the trustee deliver the property to C. *In states that have not enacted the Uniform Probate Code, G's contingent remainder failed, and O's reversionary interest passed to C, as O's heir.* Restatement (Third) Trusts §§ 8, 55. *However, if G would have been survived by a child, the child would have acquired G's interest notwithstanding the "survivorship" language. According to* UPC § 2-707(b)(3), *words of survivorship are not, in absence of additional evidence, a sufficient indication of contrary intent to negate the "substitute gift" rule of* UPC § 2-707(b). *See comment to* UPC § 2-707(b). *In a state that has not enacted the Uniform Probate Code, the result will likely differ. Comment a to* Restatement (Third) Trusts § 55.

Answer (A) is incorrect. The death of the surviving trust beneficiary does not generally pass fee simple ownership to the trustee.

Answers (C) and (D) are incorrect. G's contingent remainder interest failed.

183. Because the trust document did not address the issue of whether O could revoke the trust, the answer depends on several factors. Most importantly is the law of the state that governs the administration of the trust. In some states, trusts are presumed revocable unless the terms of the trust expressly provide that the trust is irrevocable. The Uniform Trust Code adopts this position. *See* UTC § 602(a). Most states have retained the common law rule that a trust is presumed irrevocable unless the terms of the trust expressly provide that the trust is revocable. Restatement (Third) Trusts § 63. The second factor is the effective date of the statute, if any, which reversed the common law rule. The third factor is the date the trust was created, because the law in effect at that time will control whether O retained the right to revoke the trust, thereby requiring the trustee to deliver the property as the settlor directs. If O retained the right to revoke, neither F nor O's estate is liable to G. If not, F breached fiduciary duties owing to G. O's estate may also be liable because O conspired with F to breach the terms of the trust agreement.

184. **Answer (D) is correct.** An express trust is created in a will only if the testator manifests the intent to impose on the devisee legally enforceable duties to manage the property for another. However, only such manifestations of intent that are admissible as proof in a judicial proceeding may be considered. Restatement (Third) Trusts § 13. The Uniform Trust Code has codified these generally acceptable common law principles. *See* UTC § 402 and commentary. Accordingly, without additional proof of O's intent, the language in O's will is likely to be found to be "precatory" rather than "mandatory."

    Answer (A) is incorrect. The use of the words "with the request" by O generally is considered to be "precatory" rather than "mandatory."

    Answer (B) is incorrect. Either C has fee simple title or an express trust was created for the benefit of G.

    Answer (C) is incorrect. An express trust was created for the benefit of G or C owns the stock beneficially.

185. **Answer (A) is correct.** It is evident that O did not intend C to acquire the stock for C's personal use and benefit. All of the elements of an express trust are present. Restatement (Third) Trusts §§ 13, 17. The Uniform Trust Code has codified these generally accepted common law principles. *See* UTC §§ 401, 402.

    Answer (B) is incorrect. An express trust has been created. G will seek to enforce the terms of the express trust.

    Answer (C) is incorrect. All of the elements of an express trust are present.

    Answer (D) is incorrect. C inherited the legal title only: G inherited an equitable interest in the stock.

186. **Answer (B) is correct.** Because G died before O, an express trust was not created. Restatement (Third) Trusts § 17. The devise to C fails, and O's executor should deliver the stock to O's residuary beneficiary, the charity. Restatement, Third, Trusts § 8. The Uniform Probate Code has codified this generally accepted common law principle. *See* UPC § 2-604.

Answer (A) is incorrect. O's attempt to create an express trust for the benefit of G failed because G died before the trust was created. G's heirs did not acquire any interest in the stock.

Answer (C) is incorrect. The executor should not deliver the stock to C. If C already has the stock, the charity may need to seek the imposition of a resulting trust to acquire the stock as O's successor in interest.

Answer (D) is incorrect. It is evident that O did not intend C to acquire the stock for C's personal use and benefit.

187. The court should appoint a successor trustee to manage Blackacre until G attains age 21. An express trust can be created by the settlor's declaration that the settlor holds identifiable property for another. Restatement (Third) Trusts § 10. The Uniform Trust Code has codified this generally accepted common law principle. *See* UTC § 401. The fact that O's declaration of trust was oral is problematic. However, the Uniform Trust Code has adopted the view that, absent a statute to the contrary, an express trust does not need to be evidenced by a trust instrument, if the creation of the oral trust and its terms can be established by clear and convincing evidence. UTC § 407. Assuming that the friends' testimony will be accepted by the court as "clear and convincing" evidence of the creation of the express trust, an express trust was created. *The result will differ in a state where the statute of frauds requires a signed writing in order for trusts of real property to be enforceable. The statute of frauds in many jurisdictions requires oral declarations of trust to be in writing. In those states, C, as O's heir, would likely retain Blackacre. Restatement (Third) Trusts § 22. However, a possible exception exists that may permit G to seek a constructive trust on C to prevent C's unjust enrichment. See comment j to Restatement (Third) Trusts § 24.*

188. **Answer (A) is correct.** An express trust can be created by the settlor's declaration that the settlor hold identifiable property for another. Restatement (Third) Trusts § 10. The Uniform Trust Code has codified this generally accepted common law principle. *See* UTC § 401. The fact that O's declaration was oral is problematic. However, the Uniform Trust Code has adopted the view that, absent a statute to the contrary, an express trust does not need to be evidenced by a trust instrument, if its creation and terms can be established by clear and convincing evidence. UTC § 407. *The result will differ in a state where the statute of frauds requires a signed writing for declarations of trusts of personal property.* Restatement (Third) Trusts § 22.

Answer (B) is incorrect. Assuming that the friends' testimony will be accepted by the court as "clear and convincing" evidence of the creation of the trust, an express trust was created. *The statute of frauds in many jurisdictions requires oral declarations of trust to be in writing. In those states, C, as O's heir, would likely retain the stock.*

Answer (C) is incorrect. The traditional view is that a constructive trust is an appropriate remedy when a transferee committed a fraud, exerted undue influence, or breached a confidential relationship. Neither O nor E committed any of those acts. However, a possible exception exists that may permit G to seek a constructive trust on C to prevent C's unjust enrichment. *See* comment j to Restatement (Third) Trusts § 24.

Answer (D) is incorrect. It is not the role of a personal representative to manage the settlor's inter vivos trust.

189. **Answer (A) is correct.** An express trust can be created by the settlor's declaration that the settlor was holding identifiable property for the benefit of another. Restatement (Third) Trusts § 10. The Uniform Trust Code has codified this generally accepted common law principle. *See* UTC § 401. *The same result is likely to happen in a non-UTC state because the writing requirement of an applicable statute of frauds is satisfied.* Restatement (Third) Trusts § 23.

Answer (B) is incorrect. All of the elements of a valid, enforceable express trust are present.

Answer (C) is incorrect. If C has possession and refuses to cooperate when G seeks to enforce the express trust, the court may need to impose a constructive trust.

Answer (D) is incorrect. It is not the role of a personal representative to manage the settlor's inter vivos trust.

190. **Answer (A) is correct.** Assuming the Uniform Trust Code was in effect at the time the express trust was created, the settlor may revoke the trust unless the terms of the trust provide the trust is irrevocable. UTC § 602(a). The Uniform Trust Code has reversed the generally accepted common law rule that trusts are presumed to be irrevocable. See Restatement (Third) Trusts § 63. Presumably, a court would likely find that O's conveyance to F was clear and convincing evidence of O's intent to revoke the trust. *The result is likely to be different in a state that does not presume inter vivos trusts are revocable. See* Restatement (Third) Trusts § 63.

Answers (B) and (C) are incorrect. O retained the power to revoke the trust. See UTC § 602. In a state that has not adopted the Uniform Trust Code approach, or if the trust was created before the state adopted that approach, G can file suit for breach of fiduciary duty by O. If successful, the court may impose a constructive trust on F since F was not a good faith purchaser.

Answer (D) is incorrect. While a court may impose a constructive trust on a third party who participates in a trustee's breach of trust, the third party is generally not personally liable to the beneficiary, if the third party is not aware of the trust. UTC § 1012.

191. **Answer (D) is correct.** It appears as if a valid enforceable express trust was created during O's lifetime, even though title remained in O's name until O died. UTC §§ 401, 402. At O's death, Blackacre is a nonprobate asset, and F's equitable remainder interest became possessory. *The result is likely to be the same in states that have not enacted the Uniform Trust Code.* Restatement (Third) Trusts § 10.

    Answers (A) and (B) are incorrect. An express inter vivos trust does not need to be executed with testamentary formalities. *See* UTC § 402. Blackacre passes pursuant to the terms of the trust, not by the will or by intestate succession.

    Answer (C) is incorrect. Because O did not change the title to Blackacre when the trust was created, Blackacre still appears to be a probate asset, and F will need to take steps to establish the existence of the trust and F's ownership under the trust.

192. **Answer (D) is correct.** The facts that there was no transfer of title before O's death and that O retained the power to revoke the trust do not affect the trust's validity. UTC §§ 401, 402. *See* Restatement (Third) Trusts § 10. Because O did not revoke the apparently valid, enforceable express trust prior to O's death, the terms of the trust control the disposition of Blackacre. Because the trust was created by O's declaration of trust, at O's death, Blackacre is a nonprobate asset, and F's equitable remainder interest became possessory. *The result is likely to be the same in states that have not enacted the Uniform Trust Code. See comment to UTC § 401.*

    Answers (A) and (B) are incorrect. An express trust does not need to be executed with testamentary formalities. *See* UTC § 402.

    Answer (C) is incorrect. Because O did not change the title to Blackacre when the trust was created, Blackacre still appears to be a probate asset, and F will need to take steps to establish the existence of the trust and F's ownership under the trust.

193. **Answer (A) is correct.** At common law, conditions of survivorship were not implied with respect to future interests. *See* comment to UPC § 2-707. The Uniform Probate Code has reversed this presumption and requires a future interest owner in a trust to survive until the interest becomes possessory. *See* UPC § 2-707. Because F died before O without a descendant surviving O, F's contingent remainder failed, and O's reversionary interest in Blackacre passed under O's will to G. *The result may differ in a state that has not adopted the UPC approach.* See Restatement (Third) Trusts § 55.

    Answer (B) is incorrect. O's reversionary interest passes to G under O's will.

Answers (C) and (D) are incorrect. UPC § 2-707 required F to survive O. *In states that have not adopted the UPC approach, F's vested remainder is likely to have passed to M and D. George T. Bogert, Trusts § 38 (6th ed. 1987) (Bogert § __). However, a successor trustee may need to be appointed in order to have the property conveyed to M and D as F's successors in interest.*

194. Because the express trust was irrevocable, the divorce did not affect W's income interest. *See* UPC § 2-804. However, G1's death terminated G1's interest, and a substituted gift was created in GG. GG will have to survive W to take; if not, GG's contingent remainder interest may fail, and O's reversionary interest in Blackacre may pass to O's successor in interest, presumably the devisee under O's will, G2. *See* UPC § 2-707. *The result is likely to differ in a state that has not adopted the UPC approach as it relates to the substituted gift in favor of GG. G1's interest is likely to have been a vested remainder that passed to S when G1 died.* Restatement (Third) Trusts § 55; Bogert § 38.

195. **Answer (D) is correct.** The divorce had the effect of revoking W's income interest because the trust was revocable. UPC § 2-804 (b). Because G1 died before O, G1's contingent remainder failed, and GG is the substituted taker pursuant to UPC § 2-707 (b). *However, in a state that has not adopted the UPC approach, W may still retain her income interest, and G1's vested remainder may have passed to S.* Restatement (Third) Trusts §§ 25, 55.

Answer (A) is incorrect. The rules of construction are different for revocable trusts. See UPC § 2-804.

Answers (B) and (C) are incorrect. The substituted taker, GG, survived until the distribution date, O's death. *In a non-UPC state, S may have succeeded to G1's vested remainder.* Bogert § 38.

196. Because the stocks and Blackacre are probate assets, the executor of O's estate will have to use them to satisfy O's debts. According to UPC § 3-902, shares of distributees abate without any preference between real or personal property. The stocks and real property should be abated proportionately. *States that have not adopted the Uniform Probate Code approach typically provide that personal property should be abated prior to real property within the same classification of devises. Atkinson § 136. Accordingly, in a non-UPC state, the stock may need to be sold to pay the debts and the real property will pass to G1 assuming the state allows testamentary additions to inter vivos trusts. Most states have statutes similar to UPC § 2-511 which do allow probate assets to "pour over" into the trust. If testamentary additions to inter vivos trusts are not allowed, C1 and C2 would succeed to the estate remaining after debts are paid.* McGovern § 6.2.

197. **Answer (B) is correct.** S is entitled to an elective share amount equal to the sum of the decedent's net probate estate augmented by the $100,000 in the revocable trust. UPC §§ 2-203, 2-205. *The answer may differ in a state that has not adopted the UPC approach.* Restatement

(Third) Trusts § 25. *For example, in a community property state, the surviving spouse will likely be entitled to half of the community probate assets and to be compensated for half of what the decedent contributed to the trust. See* McGovern §§ 3.7, 3.8.

Answer (A) is incorrect. The trust is valid.

Answers (C) and (D) are incorrect. The augmented estate consists of the net probate estate and certain nonprobate dispositions.

198. **Answer (C) is correct.** If the creation and funding of the trust were in fraud of O's creditors, the creditors can pursue their claims against the trust estate pursuant to X's law on fraudulent transfers. The transfer may also constitute a voidable preference in bankruptcy. *See* comment to UTC § 505. If O was not insolvent by reason of the creation of the trust, the trust estate is not reachable to satisfy O's debts. UTC § 505 adopts this generally accepted principle. *Bogert § 48.*

Answers (A) and (B) are incorrect. If the creation and funding were in fraud of the creditors, they can still reach the trust estate.

Answer (D) is incorrect. The trust assets are not reachable by the creditors unless the creation and funding of the trust were in fraud of the creditors.

199. **Answer (D) is correct.** During the lifetime of the settlor, the trust estate of a revocable trust is subject to claims of the settlor's creditors. See UTC § 505 (a) (1). *The result is likely to be the same in a state that has not adopted the Uniform Trust Code. See* Restatement (Third) Trusts § 25.

Answers (A), (B), and (C) are incorrect for the reasons given.

200. **Answer (D) is correct.** Following the settlor's death, the trust estate of a revocable trust continues to be subject to claims of the settlor's creditors. UTC § 505(a)(3) adopts this widely accepted principle. *See* Restatement, Third, Trusts § 25. *The result may differ in a non-UTC state. See* Bogert, Trusts § 148.

Answers (A), (B), and (C) are incorrect for the reasons given.

201. **Answer (C) is correct.** Assuming the terms of the trust, including its irrevocability, can be established by clear and convincing evidence, the fact that the express trust was created pursuant to an oral agreement should not be determinative of the issue. UTC § 407. If the transfer to T were in fraud of O's creditors, the creditors can pursue their claims against the property transferred. If not, the property is not reachable to satisfy O's debts. UTC § 505. *The same result is likely to occur in a non-UTC state.* Bogert § 48.

Answers (A), (B), and (D) are incorrect for the reasons given.

202. **Answer (A) is correct.** The trust property is not subject to the personal obligations of the trustee. UTC § 507 has codified this generally accepted principle. *See* Restatement (Third) Trusts § 42.

   Answers (B), (C), and (D) are incorrect. Trust property is not subject to the trustee's personal debts.

203. As long as the creation of the oral trust and its terms can be established, the trust property cannot be reached by the trustee's personal creditors. Restatement (Third) Trusts § 42. Because the trust is oral, the UTC requires "clear and convincing evidence" of the terms of the trust. *See* UTC § 407. The lack of a writing does not affect the validity of the trust as to the real property, and the trustee can properly perform notwithstanding the statute of frauds. Restatement (Third) Trusts § 24. *In a state that has not adopted the UTC approach, the existence of the trust may need to be proven by only a "preponderance of the evidence."* Restatement (Third) Trusts § 20.

204. **Answer (B) is correct.** Absent a "spendthrift" or "forfeiture" provision in the trust agreement, the court may authorize a creditor to reach a beneficiary's interest in the trust by attachment of either present or future distributions. UTC § 501 has codified this generally accepted common law principle. *See* Restatement (Third) Trusts § 56.

   Answer (A) is incorrect. C's interest is limited to the income the trust generates during C's lifetime.

   Answer (C) is incorrect. It doesn't matter whether the debt is tortious or contractual in nature.

   Answer (D) is incorrect. To the extent a beneficiary's interest is not subject to a "spendthrift" or "forfeiture" provision, it is generally available to satisfy the beneficiary's creditors.

205. **Answer (D) is correct.** Whether or not the trust agreement contains a "spendthrift" or "forfeiture" provision, a creditor of a beneficiary generally does not have standing to compel a trustee to make a discretionary distribution from the trust to the creditor or the beneficiary. UTC § 504. However, the creditor may be able to attach the beneficiary's interest, and although the interest is not subject to execution sale, the trustee may be held personally liable to the creditor for any amount paid by the trustee to the beneficiary if the trustee has been served with notice of the attachment. Comment c to Restatement (Third) Trusts § 60.

   Answer (A) is incorrect. C's interest is effectively limited to whatever income, if any, is distributed to C in T's discretion. *The Restatement takes the position that the creditor is entitled to "judicial protection from abuse of discretion by the trustee." However, it also acknowledges that the trustee's refusal to make a distribution under these circumstances may not be an abuse of discretion. Comment e to* Restatement (Third) Trusts § 60.

Answer (B) is incorrect. C does not have a mandatory right to the income.

Answer (C) is incorrect. Generally, the only creditor that may be excepted from the general rule is a child, spouse, or former spouse of the beneficiary with a judgment or order against C for support. UTC § 504(c)(2).

206. **Answer (D) is correct.** Whether or not the trust agreement contains a "spendthrift" or "forfeiture" provision, a creditor of a beneficiary cannot compel a discretionary distribution from the trust, even if the trustee has failed to comply with a standard of distribution. *See* UTC § 504. However, the creditor may be able to attach the beneficiary's interest, and although the interest is not subject to execution sale, the trustee may be held personally liable to the creditor for any amount paid by the trustee to the beneficiary if the trustee has been served with notice of the attachment. *The Restatement limits the portion to which a creditor is entitled to the excess of the beneficiary's actual needs as set by the court. See comment c to* Restatement (Third) Trusts § 60. *The result may differ in a state that has not adopted the UTC or the Restatement approach because C's interest in the trust estate is limited to whatever income is necessary for C's health, education, maintenance, or support, and when C dies, G is entitled to the income not properly distributed to C. The Restatement takes the position that the creditor is entitled to "judicial protection from abuse of discretion by the trustee." However, it also acknowledges that the trustee's refusal to make a distribution under these circumstances may not be an abuse of discretion. Comment e to* Restatement (Third) Trusts § 60.

Answers (A), (B), and (C) are incorrect. The only creditor that may be excepted from the general rule is a child, spouse, or former spouse of a beneficiary with a judgment or order against C for support. UTC § 504(c)(2).

207. **Answer (D) is correct.** A creditor of a beneficiary cannot compel a discretionary distribution from a trust, even if the trustee has failed to comply with a standard of distribution. UTC § 504. *The result may differ in a state that has not adopted the Uniform Trust Code approach. Here, C's interest is limited to whatever income is distributed to C pursuant to the described standard of distribution, and the hospital rendered medical services and should be able to garnish C's interest in the trust. See Alan Newman, The Rights of Creditors of Beneficiaries Under the Uniform Trust Code: An Examination of the Compromise, 69 Tenn. L. Rev. 771 (2002).*

Answers (A), (B), and (C) are incorrect for the reasons given. *While* UTC § 504 *appears to prohibit the creditor from compelling a distribution, states that have not adopted the Uniform Trust Code approach may allow the hospital to collect from the trustee out of the trust's income if the trust agreement does not contain a "spendthrift" or "forfeiture" provision. See* Restatement (Second) of Trusts §§ 154, 155, 157 (1959) (Restatement (Second) Trusts § ___).

208.   **Answer (B) is correct.** Absent a "spendthrift" or "forfeiture" provision in the trust agreement, the court may authorize a creditor to attach a beneficiary's future interest in the trust estate. The Uniform Trust Code codifies this generally accepted common law principle. *See* UTC § 501. The court may even order a sale of the beneficiary's future interest. Restatement (Third) Trusts § 56. However, the value of G's remainder interest is diminished by it being contingent on G surviving O. UPC 2-707.

      Answer (A) is incorrect. The creditor cannot divest C's interest in the trust.

      Answer (C) is incorrect. While a creditor, in theory, may force a judicial sale of a beneficiary's interest, such a sale cannot adversely affect the interests of other beneficiaries.

      Answer (D) is incorrect. Only G's future interest can be attached.

209.   In most jurisdictions, a settlor has the power to include as part of the terms of the trust a provision that prevents a creditor from reaching a beneficiary's interest in the trust or a distribution by the trustee before its actual receipt by the beneficiary. This so-called "spendthrift" provision is generally valid in most states so long as it prohibits both voluntary and involuntary transfers of beneficial interests. *See* Restatement (Third) Trusts § 58. These generally accepted principles have been codified in UTC § 502. Accordingly, the creditor cannot attach the beneficiaries' interests in the trust, and the creditors must wait until there are actual distributions to the beneficiaries. If valid under state law, the spendthrift provision will be effective in bankruptcy. *See* comment a to Restatement (Third) Trusts § 58. *A few states do not recognize the effectiveness of "spendthrift" provisions.* McGovern § 13.1.

210.   **Answer (C) is correct.** Even in jurisdictions that do not accept the effectiveness of "spendthrift" provisions, a settlor can generally place a "condition subsequent" on a beneficiary's interest, causing the beneficiary's interest to terminate or change, if there is an attempted involuntary or voluntary alienation. Restatement (Third) Trusts § 57.

      Answer (A) is incorrect. C's interest is not affected by the termination of G's interest.

      Answer (B) is incorrect. C's interest is not enhanced by the termination of G's interest.

      Answer (D) is incorrect. Most jurisdictions accept the effectiveness of these so called "forfeiture" provisions.

211.   **Answer (A) is correct.** As a general rule, the court may authorize an assignee of a beneficiary's interest to reach the beneficiary's interest by attachment of present or future distributions. Restatement (Third) Trusts § 51. The Uniform Trust Code has codified this generally accepted common law principle. *See* UTC § 501.

      Answers (B), (C), and (D) are incorrect. As a general rule, to the extent a beneficiary's interest is not subject to a "spendthrift" provision or a "forfeiture" provision, or statute limiting the beneficiary's power of alienation, the interest is assignable. Restatement (Third) Trusts § 51.

212. **Answer (B) is correct.** Absent a "spendthrift" or "forfeiture" provision or a state statute limiting beneficiary's power of alienation, an assignee can reach the beneficiary's interest by attachment of present or future distributions. UTC § 501. In other words, the assignee is entitled to receive any distributions the trustee makes, or is required to make, after the trustee has knowledge of the transfer. However, an assignee cannot acquire an interest greater than the one owned by the beneficiary prior to the assignment. *See* Restatement (Third) Trusts § 60. UTC § 504 prohibits a creditor from compelling a discretionary distribution. Can an assignee compel a distribution? Restatement (Third) Trust § 60 says, "yes." *The law may differ in a state that has not adopted the Restatement approach.*

     Answer (A) is incorrect. An assignee cannot acquire an interest greater than the one the assignor owned prior to the assignment. *The Restatement takes the position that the assignee is entitled to "judicial protection from abuse of discretion by the trustee." However, it also acknowledges that the trustee's refusal to make a distribution under these circumstances may not be an abuse of discretion. Comment e to* Restatement (Third) Trusts § 60.

     Answers (C) and (D) are incorrect for the reasons given. *However, the law in some states may follow* Restatement (Second) Trusts § 154 *and prohibit assignments of support interests unless they were made for the purpose of acquiring goods or services for C's support, assuming that the interests were not limited by a "spendthrift" or "forfeiture" provision, or a statute limiting the beneficiaries' powers of alienation.*

213. Absent a "spendthrift" or "forfeiture" provision, or a state statute that limits the beneficiary's power of alienation, a beneficiary's assignee has a right to receive discretionary distributions to which the beneficiary would otherwise be entitled. Restatement (Third) Trusts § 60. However, the assignee cannot compel the trustee to make a distribution, if the beneficiary could not do so. In a discretionary trust, the assignee would have to prove the trustee abused its discretion after consideration of the beneficiary's circumstances and the effect the decision will have on G in the light of the purposes of the trust. *See* comment e to Restatement (Third) Trusts § 60.

214. **Answer (C) is correct.** Assuming the trust agreement did not contain a "spendthrift" or "forfeiture" provision and state law does not limit the beneficiary's power of alienation, the assignment of a beneficiary's future interest is valid. Restatement (Third) Trusts § 51. UTC § 501 has codified this generally accepted common law principle. At C's death, the trust estate should be delivered to Q, if G survives C. UPC 2-707.

     Answer (A) is incorrect. A beneficiary of a trust owns an interest in property that, as a general rule, is assignable.

     Answer (B) is incorrect. The assignee cannot acquire an interest greater than that owned by the beneficiary.

     Answer (D) is incorrect. As a general rule, the assignment is enforceable against the trustee.

215.   **Answer (D) is correct.** As a general rule, the beneficiaries of an express trust can assign their interests to assignee, including the person serving as the trustee. Restatement (Third) Trusts § 51. However, this particular assignment is problematic even in the absence of a "spendthrift" or "forfeiture" provision, or a statute limiting the beneficiary's power of alienation. Because of the fiduciary relationship existing between C, G, and T, the transaction is suspect, and if there was improper conduct by T, or if C and G were not aware of all of the material facts, the assignment may be set aside. Restatement (Third) Trusts § 51 and comment b.

   Answer (A) is incorrect. In most states, O is a "stranger" to the trust because the trust is irrevocable and O did not retain any interest in, or power over, the trust estate. However, in a state that has adopted UPC § 2-707, G's remainder interest is a contingent interest, and if G does not survive C, G's descendants, or O, may have an interest in the property. Does this interest give O standing to challenge the transaction?

   Answer (B) is incorrect. If the assignment is valid, legal title and equitable title merged, and the trust no longer exists, subject to the possible interests of G's descendants and O.

   Answer (C) is incorrect. Answer (C) would be correct if the assignment is valid.

216.   **Answer (A) is correct.** The terms of the trust include a "spendthrift" provision. Accordingly, G cannot assign G's interest in the trust estate to Q. Restatement (Third) Trusts § 58. UTC § 502 codifies the widely accepted principle of trust law. However, comment d(1) to UTC § 502 states that the trustee may choose to honor the assignment unless G revokes the assignment.

   Answer (B) is incorrect. In most jurisdictions, a beneficiary may not transfer an interest in a trust in violation of a valid "spendthrift" provision.

   Answer (C) is incorrect. Whether the assignee paid consideration for the assignment is irrelevant.

   Answer (D) is incorrect. The spendthrift provision made it impossible for G to make a legally binding transfer. However, G may be estopped to deny the assignment once the property is delivered to G.

217.   A trustee has the fiduciary duty to act impartially, giving due regard to interests of all of the beneficiaries. In addition, T has a fiduciary duty to exercise a discretionary power in good faith and in accordance with the terms and purposes of the trust and the interests of the beneficiaries. Accordingly, either beneficiary has standing to bring a cause of action to remedy a breach of trust. Bogert § 157. The Uniform Trust Code has codified these generally accepted principles of trust law. *See* UTC §§ 803, 814(a), 1001 and comment to UTC § 1001.

218. **Answer (D) is correct.** Because O granted T the discretionary power to make distributions, the burden of proof is typically on the beneficiary to plead and prove that the trustee "abused" the trustee's exercise or non-exercise of the discretionary power. Restatement (Third) Trusts § 50.

   Answers (A) and (C) are incorrect. The burden of proof is on the beneficiaries.

   Answer (B) is incorrect. The determinative issue is whether T "abused" the discretion granted by the settlor. The trier of fact is not to substitute its judgment, or even the judgment of a reasonably prudent trustee, for the decision of the trustee.

219. **Answer (D) is correct.** The Restatement treats "support" trusts as a category of discretionary trusts. Restatement (Third) Trusts § 60. Accordingly, the issue is whether the trustee abused its discretion. Restatement (Third) Trusts § 50. The Uniform Trust Code appears to have adopted the Restatement view. UTC § 504. *The burden of proof may differ in states that have not adopted the Restatement view.*

   Answer (C) is incorrect. In states that have not adopted the Restatement view, the burden is typically on the beneficiary to prove what amount was actually necessary for C's health, support, education, or maintenance.

   Answers (A) and (B) are incorrect. The burden of proof is on the beneficiaries.

220. S, B, and C are entitled to Blackacre. At common law, A, B, and C inherited fractional remainder interests in the trust estate, and when A died, A's vested one-third remainder interest passed to S because conditions of survivorship are not implied with respect to future interests. *See* comment to UTC § 2-707 and Restatement (Third) Trusts § 55. *The result is likely to differ in a state that has adopted UPC § 2-707. UPC § 2-707 converts A's remainder interest into one contingent on A surviving M, and because A did not survive M, A's interest reverted to O.* Averill § 11.05.

221. **Answer (C) is correct.** At common law, S would have succeeded to A's vested remainder interest because conditions of survivorship are not implied with respect to future interests. *See* comment to UPC 2-707 and Restatement (Third) Trusts § 55. *The result is likely to differ in a state that has adopted* UPC § 2-707.

      Answer (A) is incorrect. The gift of the remainder was a "fractional" gift, not a class gift.

      Answer (B) is incorrect. D is not a beneficiary of the trust.

      Answer (D) is incorrect. At common law, A's interest passed to S. *However, if applicable,* UPC § 2-707 *would convert A's remainder interest into one contingent on A surviving M, and because A did not survive M, G would be substituted for A.*

222. O created a class gift of the remainder interest. The class "opened" when the trust was created and "closed" at M's death. Restatement (Second) Donative Transfers § 26. At common law, A, B, and C owned vested remainder interests subject to partial divestment as soon as the trust was created, and D acquired the same interest when D was born. Restatement (Second) Donative Transfers § 26.2. When A died, A's interest passed to S. Thus, S, B, C, and D succeed to the trust estate. Restatement (Second) Donative Transfers § 27.3. *The result is likely to differ in a state that has adopted UPC § 2-707. UPC § 2-707 would convert A's interest into one contingent on A surviving M, and because A did not survive M, the other members of the class take.*

223. **Answer (C) is correct.** If born alive, the child in embryo becomes a "member of the class" and will acquire an interest in the trust estate, thereby partially divesting the other remainder beneficiaries. *See* Restatement (Second) Donative Transfers § 26.2. *The result is likely to be the same in a state that has adopted* UPC § 2-707.

      Answers (A), (B), and (D) are incorrect for the reasons given.

224. **Answer (B) is correct.** At common law, the settlor created remainder interests contingent on the remainder beneficiaries surviving M. In addition, the settlor created alternative future interests in the survivor or survivors of the remainder beneficiaries. Restatement, Property §§ 250, 277. *The result is likely to be the same in a state that has adopted* UPC § 2-707 *because the trust agreement created an alternative future interest. See* UPC § 2-707(b)(4).

Answer (A) is incorrect. D is not a beneficiary of the trust.

Answer (C) is incorrect. A's interest was expressly conditioned on surviving M.

Answer (D) is incorrect. O expressly provided for alternative future interests in the event A, B, or C died before M.

225. **Answer (D) is correct.** A and A's devisee, S, are excluded. Restatement (Second) Donative Transfers § 27.3. If the child in embryo is born alive, the child will be a member of the class of beneficiaries. Restatement (Second) Donative Transfers § 26.2. *The result is likely to be the same in a state that has adopted* UPC § 2-707.

Answer (A) is incorrect. The child will be entitled to an interest if born alive.

Answer (B) is incorrect. A's interest was expressly contingent on A surviving M, and the child may be entitled to an interest.

Answer (C) is incorrect. The child will be entitled to an interest, if born alive.

226. **Answer (A) is correct.** The class of remainder beneficiaries "closed" when M died because B, C, and D were entitled to possession at that time. A child of the sister conceived after that point in time is not a beneficiary. Restatement (Second) Donative Transfers § 26.2. *The result is likely to be the same in a state that has adopted* UPC § 2-707.

Answers (B), (C), and (D) are incorrect. The class has already closed.

227. A generally accepted common law rule creates a presumption that O must have intended to include all of the sister's children whenever born. Restatement (Second) Donative Transfers § 26.2. A's interest passed to O's sister, S, subject to partial divestment if S has any more children. Restatement (Second) Donative Transfers § 27.3. According to one source, the yet to be born children "own" equitable contingent remainder interests. Casner § 4.34. In any event, the class stays open until it biologically closes at the sister's death.

228. **Answer (A) is correct.** Notwithstanding the "spendthrift" provision, a vested remainder interest in trust is transferable by will or by intestacy. See comment (g), Restatement, (Third) Trusts § 58.

Answers (B), (C), and (D) are incorrect for the reasons given.

229. **Answer (A) is correct.** Notwithstanding the "spendthrift" provision, a vested remainder interest in trust is transferable by will or by intestacy. See comment (g), Restatement (Third) Trusts § 58.

    Answers (B), (C), and (D) are incorrect for the reasons given.

230. **Answer (C) is correct.** Conditions of survivorship are not implied with respect to future interests, like legal remainder interests. *See* Restatement, Property § 165. B's interest was devised to S.

    Answer (A) is incorrect. The remainder interest had been devised to B when O died and then passed to S when B died.

    Answer (B) is in correct. A only inherited a life estate.

    Answer (D) is incorrect. B's vested remainder was devised by B to S.

231. **Answer (C) is correct.** The remainder interest devised to B was contingent on B surviving A. At B's death, B's remainder interest ceased to exist, and the charity's alternative contingent remainder became a vested remainder. Restatement, Property §§ 157, 239.

    Answer (A) is incorrect. B's interest was contingent on B surviving A.

    Answer (B) is incorrect. A inherited a life estate.

    Answer (D) is incorrect. B's interest was contingent on B surviving A.

232. B1 and B2 inherit the remainder interest. At common law, the gift to B would have lapsed, and the remainder interest would have been devised to the charity. *See* comment to UPC § 2-603. However, most states have enacted "antilapse" statutes that create a substitute gift for the deceased devisee's descendants who survive the testator. UPC § 2-603 is a typical "antilapse" statute. At B's death, B did not own an interest in Blackacre that B could devise to S.

233. **Answer (A) is correct.** At common law, B's equitable vested remainder would have been devised by B to S. *See* Restatement (Third) Trusts § 55. *The result is likely to differ in a state that has adopted* UPC § 2-707. UPC § 2-707 *would convert B's interest into a remainder contingent on B surviving A.*

    Answer (C) is incorrect. B's interest passed to S.

    Answer (B) is incorrect. A only inherited a life estate.

    Answer (D) is incorrect. At common law, B's interest passed to S.

234. **Answer (A) is correct.** B's remainder interest was contingent on B attaining age 21. The charity's alternative contingent remainder interest became a vested remainder when B died. Restatement, Property §§ 156 (comment c), 157 (comment w).

   Answer (B) is incorrect. A inherited only a life estate.

   Answer (C) is incorrect. Because B's interest was contingent on B attaining age 21, B could not devise it to S.

   Answer (D) is incorrect. The antilapse statute is not applicable because B did not die before O.

235. **Answer (C) is correct.** B's interest became a vested remainder when B reached age 21. When B died, it was devised by B to S. Restatement, Property §§ 156, 157, 165.

   Answer (A) is incorrect. The charity's interest terminated when B reached age 21.

   Answer (B) is incorrect. A owned only a life estate.

   Answer (D) is incorrect. The antilapse statute is not applicable.

236. **Answer (B) is correct.** B's interest was not contingent on B attaining age 21. O's expressed intent was that only possession was to be delayed until B attained age 21. When B died, B's interest passed to S. *See* comment a to Restatement, Property § 157.

   Answers (A), (C), and (D) are incorrect. B's vested remainder was devised by B to S.

237. **Answer (D) is correct.** The generally accepted common law rule does not require B to reach age 21 prior to A's death. Accordingly, the charity's contingent interest became possessory at A's death pending the determination of whether B attains age 21. Restatement, Property §§ 156, 240.

   Answers (A), (B), and (C) are incorrect for the reasons given.

238. **Answer (C) is correct.** B inherited a vested remainder subject to divestment if B died without any children surviving him. That event did not occur so B's interest was devised by B to S. Restatement, Property § 165.

   Answers (A) and (B) are incorrect. The remainder interest was devised by B to S.

   Answer (D) is incorrect. The antilapse statute is not applicable.

239. **Answer (B) is correct.** O's will provides that B's vested remainder is divested if B is not survived by children. Because there is no evidence that C survived B, B's interest terminated. Restatement, Property § 157(d).

Answer (A) is incorrect. B's interest has been divested.

Answer (C) is incorrect. Charity No. 1 will take possession when A dies.

Answer (D) is incorrect. The antilapse statute is not applicable.

240. **Answer (D) is correct.** At O's death, C2 inherited from O a vested remainder subject to divestment if A is not survived by any children. When C2 died, C2 devised that interest to S. S now owns the interest that will be divested if neither C1, C3, nor any other child of A survives A. Restatement, Property §§ 157, 165.

Answer (A) is incorrect. C2's interest was not divested because C2 did not survive A.

Answer (B) is incorrect. S inherited C2's interest and C3 became a member of the class of remainder beneficiaries.

Answer (C) is incorrect. S's interest will be divested if A is not survived by children.

241. **Answer (B) is correct.** The remainder interests of C1, C2, and C3 were contingent on each of them surviving A. When C2 died, C2's interest terminated. Restatement, Property § 157.

Answer (A) is incorrect. C2's contingent interest terminated when C2 died before A.

Answer (C) is incorrect. C3 became a member of the class of contingent remainder beneficiaries when C3 was born.

Answer (D) is incorrect. The antilapse statute is not applicable.

242. G1 and G2 acquired fee simple title. A devise does not have to designate the beneficiary by name. The identity of the grandchildren is a fact of independent significance. Because the disposition of Blackacre was a present or immediate class gift, the class closed at O's death. Children conceived after B's death are not members of the "class" of beneficiaries, whether born during or following formal administration of O's estate. Restatement (Second) Donative Transfers § 26.1.

243. **Answer (B) is correct.** If the child in embryo is born alive, the class of beneficiaries closes, and that child acquires fee simple title. *See* comment c to Restatement (Second) Donative Transfers § 26.1.

Answer (A) is incorrect. The child must be born alive before the child can acquire title to the property.

Answer (C) is incorrect. If the child in embryo is born alive, the class closes and any other children A may in the future have are excluded.

Answer (D) is incorrect. If A has a child who is born alive, the charity will be divested.

244.	Because there were no members of the class of beneficiaries alive or "in embryo" at O's death, the class remains "open" until it biologically closes at A's death. The charity acquires title subject to divestment upon the birth or adoption of the first child of A. The birth or adoption of any other children A may have will partially divest any previous child or children. Restatement (Second) Donative Transfers § 26.1.

245.	**Answer (A) is correct.** Because the specific devise in O's will was a "per capita" gift, the class of beneficiaries "opens" and "closes" at O's death. The charity acquires fee simple title because A did not have any children at that time, and the land passed under the residuary clause. Restatement (Second) Donative Transfers § 26.1.

	Answers (B) and (C) are incorrect. The general "closing" rules for class gifts do not apply in a "per capita" gift situation.

	Answer (D) is incorrect. The specific devise failed and the land passes to the residuary beneficiary, not by intestate succession.

246.	**Answer (D) is correct.** O devised executory interests to O's grandchildren who are alive at the described event. The charity owns fee simple title subject to the grandchildren's executory interests. Restatement, Property §§ 25, 158.

	Answer (A) is incorrect. The grandchildren's executory interests can divest the charity.

	Answer (B) is incorrect. The executory interest has been devised to a "class" of beneficiaries and the class stays open until a member of the class is entitled to possession.

	Answer (C) is incorrect. The executory interest is contingent on grandchildren being alive on the twenty-first anniversary of O's death.

247.	**Answer (D) is correct.** Because A is alive, the executory interest devised to O's grandchildren is valid. The charity retains fee simple title until the charity is divested on the twenty-first anniversary of O's death, if grandchildren of O are then surviving. Restatement, Property §§ 25, 158.

	Answer (A) is incorrect. The grandchildren's executory interest can divest the charity.

	Answer (B) is incorrect. The executory interest has been devised to a "class" of beneficiaries and the class stays open until a member of the class is entitled to possession.

	Answer (C) is incorrect. The executory interest is contingent on grandchildren being alive on the twenty-first anniversary of O's death.

248.	**Answer (C) is correct.** The executory interest is valid. Because A is dead and cannot have any more children, the class has "closed." If G1 or G2 is alive on the one-hundredth anniversary of O's death, that event will occur during each child's own lifetime, and the rule against perpetuities is not violated. Restatement (Second) Donative Transfers, Chapter 1.

Answer (A) is incorrect. The rule against perpetuities was not violated.

Answer (B) is incorrect. If either G1 or G2 is alive on the one-hundredth anniversary of O's death, the charity is divested.

Answer (D) is incorrect. The class of beneficiaries is limited to A's children, G1 and G2.

249.   The charity owns fee simple title subject to an executory limitation. Restatement, Property § 158. At common law, the grandchildren's executory interests would have violated the rule against perpetuities and been invalid. As of the time of O's death, the possibility existed that the first child of A to reach age 25 would not do so until after the expiration of the period of the "Rule." Restatement (Second) Donative Transfers, Chapter 1. However, under UPC § 2-901(a)(2), it is likely that the executory interest will vest, if it ever does, within 90 years of O's death. If not, the interest can be reformed pursuant to UPC § 2-903. *Some states that have not adopted the Uniform Probate Code approach have modified the common law rule in other ways that may validate the grandchildren's interests.*

250.   **Answer (B) is correct.** G2 had satisfied the condition of the devise prior to O's death and acquired fee simple title at O's death. Restatement, Property § 156.

Answer (A) is incorrect. Because G2 reached age twenty-five prior to O's death, the charity never acquired an interest in Blackacre.

Answers (C) and (D) are incorrect. The devise was not a class gift. Because G2 reached age 25 prior to O's death and G2 survived O, no other child of A acquires an interest in Blackacre.

251.   **Answer (C) is correct.** There is no problem with the rule against perpetuities. All of A's children will attain age twenty-one, if they ever do, within twenty-one years of A's death. Restatement (Second) Donative Transfers, Chapter 1. When the first child attains that age, the charity is divested, and that child owns the fee simple title subject to partial divestment if any other children of A reach age twenty-one. Restatement, Property § 239.

Answer (A) is incorrect. The grandchildren's executory interests are valid.

Answer (B) is incorrect. The class of beneficiaries includes any grandchild who reaches the age of twenty-one.

Answer (D) is incorrect. O did not die intestate.

252.   **Answer (C) is correct.** There is not a perpetuities problem. Because A died before O, the class of potential beneficiaries was limited to G1, G2, and the child in embryo, and all three Restatement (Second), Second, Donative Transfers, Chapter 1.

Answer (A) is incorrect. The executory interests of the grandchildren are valid.

Answer (B) is incorrect. The child in embryo is a life in being for perpetuities purposes, if born alive.

Answer (D) is incorrect. The charity will be divested as soon as the first child attains age twenty-five.

253. The charity owns fee simple title subject to an executory limitation. Restatement, Property § 158. At common law, the executory interest conveyed to the grandchild would have violated the rule against perpetuities. Because the disposition is an inter vivos transfer by deed, at the time of the conveyance, there existed the possibility that O could have another child who would be the parent of the first grandchild to reach twenty-one and that grandchild may not reach twenty-one until after the perpetuities period. However, under UPC § 2-901 (A)(2), it is likely that a grandchild will reach age twenty-one within 90 years of the original conveyance. If not, the interest can be reformed pursuant to UPC § 2-903. *Some states that have not adopted the Uniform Probate Code approach have modified the common law rule in other ways that may validate the conveyance.*

254. **Answer (B) is correct.** The class of remainder beneficiaries includes any other children A may have, but does not violate the common law rule against perpetuities because the grandchildren's remainder interests will vest, if they do vest, at A's death. Restatement (Second) Donative Transfers § 26.2.

Answer (A) is incorrect. The remainder interest is devised to a class of beneficiaries that stays "open" until A's death. A is presumed to be capable of having more children. Of course, A could also adopt more children.

Answer (C) is incorrect. The specific devise is valid.

Answer (D) is incorrect. The remainder interest does not violate the common law rule against perpetuities.

255. A has a life estate, and G owns the remainder interest. However, G's interest is subject to partial divestment, if A has more children. Restatement (Second) Donative Transfers § 26.2. At common law, the remainder interest would have violated the rule against perpetuities, because, after the conveyance, O could have had more children whose lifetimes could extend beyond the perpetuities period, and their children would have been included within the class of remainder beneficiaries. Consequently, the contingent remainder interests of the unborn grandchildren may not vest in time. Restatement (Second) Donative Transfers, Chapter 1. However, under UPC § 2-901(a)(2), it is likely they will vest with 90 years of the conveyance. If not, the remainder interest could be reformed pursuant to UPC § 2-903. *Some states that have not adopted the Uniform Probate Code approach have modified the common law in other ways that may validate the grandchildren's remainder interest.*

256. At common law, the remainder interests devised to A's grandchildren would have violated the rule against perpetuities. At the time of O's death, there existed the possibility that A could have more children who could then have more children who would be included in the class of remainder beneficiaries. Consequently, the remainder interests of those grandchildren of A may not vest until the death of one of A's after-born children after the perpetuities period. The "all or nothing" rule would have invalidated even the vested interests of the other grandchildren. Restatement (Second) Donative Transfers, Chapter 1. However, under UPC § 2-901(a)(2), it is likely that the contingent interests will vest, if they ever do, within 90 years of O's death. If not, the remainder interests of the grandchildren can be reformed under UPC § 2-903. *Some states that have not adopted the Uniform Probate Code have modified the common law rule in other ways that may validate the grandchildren's interests.*

257. At common law, the remainder interest of A's children would have violated the rule against perpetuities. The identity of A's widow will not be known until A's death, and it is possible that she was not a "life in being" when O died. Consequently, her remaining lifetime may extend beyond the perpetuities period, and the children's interest would remain contingent until then. The interest of any children born after O's death would have violated the rule, and the "all or nothing" rule would have caused the interests of even G1, G2, and G3 to be invalid. Restatement (Second) Donative Transfers, Chapter 1. However, under UPC § 2-901(a)(2), it is likely that the contingent interests will vest, if they ever do, within 90 years of O's death. If not, the remainder interests of the grandchildren can be reformed under UPC § 2-903. *Some states that have not adopted the Uniform Probate Code have modified the common law rule in other ways that may validate the grandchildren's interests.*

258. **Answer (C) is correct.** A owns the equitable life estate and is the donee of a power of appointment, and the charity owns an equitable remainder interest that is subject to divestment, if A validly exercises the power of appointment in a will. It will not be known until A dies if the power is exercised and the charity is divested. Restatement (Second) Donative Transfers § 15.2. C1 and C2 are not beneficiaries. UTC § 103(2).

   Answer (A) is incorrect. A only owns an equitable life estate and is the donee of a testamentary non-general power of appointment.

   Answers (B) and (D) are incorrect. A's exercise of the power will not be effective until A's death. Until the power is exercised, the objects of the power have expectancies and are not beneficiaries.

259. **Answer (B) is correct.** A was the donee of a non-general testamentary power of appointment. Because such a power is presumed to be "exclusive," A can appoint to any one or more of the objects of the power or permissible appointees. When the will is admitted to probate, the charity is divested. *See* Restatement (Second) Donative Transfers § 21.1. *Statutes in a few states provide that a power may be deemed non-exclusive.*

   Answer (A) is incorrect. The charity's remainder interest has been divested.

   Answer (C) is incorrect. Because the power was "exclusive," A was not required to include C3. In addition, A was exercising a power of appointment and not devising A's own property. Consequently, the typical "pretermitted" or "omitted" child statute, like UPC § 2-302, is not applicable.

   Answer (D) is incorrect. Neither S nor C3 acquired an interest in the trust estate.

260. In order for the charity's remainder interest to be divested, A, as the donee of the power, must validly exercise the power. A testamentary power can only be exercised in a document that is formally sufficient to be admitted to probate. Comment b to Restatement (Second) Donative Transfers § 18.2. Thus, the charity was not divested. UPC § 2-503 *(or a similar statute in a non-UPC state)* may provide the opportunity to probate the defective will, if there is clear and convincing evidence that A intended the document to be A's will. If relief is not available under UPC § 2-503, C1 and C2 could argue that the appointment is still effective according to Restatement (Second) Donative Transfers § 18.3.

261.   **Answer (A) is correct.** It is widely accepted that a general disposition of a testator's property in a will does not, as a general rule, exercise a non-general power of appointment. *See* Restatement (Second) Donative Transfers § 17.3. The Uniform Probate Code has codified this principle. See UPC § 2-608.

        Answers (B), (C), and (D) are incorrect for the reasons given. There is, however, a minority viewpoint. *See* Will of Block, 157 Misc.2d 716, 598 N.Y.S.2d 668 (Surrogate's Court, New York County, 1993).

262.   **Answer (A) is correct.** A failed to exercise the power. Consequently, the charity was not divested. Restatement (Second) Donative Transfers § 18.2.

        Answers (B), (C), and (D) are incorrect. A was not under any legal obligation to exercise the power. The permissible appointees have no standing to complain about A's inaction.

263.   **Answer (B) is correct.** Although A did not expressly exercise the general testamentary power in A's will, a court is likely to find that the power was, in fact, exercised. It is generally accepted that a general power can be impliedly exercised, if the donee's intent is clearly expressed and/or the disposition would otherwise be ineffective. UPC § 2-608. *See also* Restatement (Second) Donative Transfers § 17.4.

        Answer (A) is incorrect. A court is likely to find that the power was impliedly exercised by A.

        Answers (C) and (D) are incorrect. The value of A's augmented estate in order to determine S's elective share amount does not include property over which A had a testamentary general power of appointment. *See* UPC § 2-205(1)(i). *The result may differ in a non-UPC state.*

264.   **Answer (C) is correct.** Because O's will contained a "gift over" in the event the power was not exercised, the charity's remainder interest was not divested. UPC § 2-608. A did not expressly or impliedly exercise the testamentary general power of appointment. *See* Restatement (Second) Donative Trusts § 17.3. *The result may differ in a state that has not adopted the Uniform Probate Code. Some states have created a presumption, by statute or case law, that A did exercise the power.*

        Answers (A) and (B) are incorrect. A did not have a legal obligation to exercise the power and did not manifest an intention to exercise the power.

        Answer (D) is incorrect. Because A did not hold an inter vivos general power, the trust estate is not included in A's augmented estate for S's elective share determination. *See* UPC § 2-205(1)(i). *The result may differ in a non-UPC state.*

265. Blackacre passes to C subject to S's marital share. UPC § 2-205(1)(i) appears to exclude the appointive property from the augmented estate. However, A's use of "blending clause" to exercise the general testamentary power may have the effect of "capturing" Blackacre for A's probate estate. *See* Restatement (Second) Donative Transfers § 22.1. If case law adopts the "doctrine of capture," Blackacre may be included in A's augmented estate in order to compute S's elective share amount, if any. *The result may differ in a non-UPC state.*

266. **Answer (A) is correct.** A appears to have exercised the power in favor of an object of the power who predeceased A. However, due to the "blending clause" and the "doctrine of capture," the antilapse provisions of UPC § 2-603 create a substitute gift in favor of CC even though CC was not an object of the power. See Restatement (Second) Donative Transfers § 22.1. *The result may differ in states that have not enacted the Uniform Probate Code.*

      Answer (B) is incorrect. C died before A and could not devise Blackacre to CS.

      Answer (C) is incorrect. S did not acquire any interest in Blackacre.

      Answer (D) is incorrect. The charity has been divested.

267. **Answer (A) is correct.** A attempted to exercise the power in favor of an object of the power who predeceased A. However, the antilapse provisions of UPC § 2-603(b)(5) create a substitute gift in favor of CC whether or not CC was an object of the power. *The result may differ in states that have not enacted the Uniform Probate Code. See* Restatement (Second) Donative Trusts § 18.6.

      Answer (B) is incorrect. C died before A and could not devise Blackacre to CS.

      Answer (C) is incorrect. S did not acquire any interest in Blackacre.

      Answer (D) is incorrect. The charity has been divested.

268. To the extent the probate estate is insufficient to satisfy O's debts, Blackacre can be subjected to the payment of claims against A's estate because A's power was a testamentary general power of appointment. Blackacre passed to C, but subject to possibly being reached by A's executor to pay A's debts. *See* Restatement (Second) Donative Transfers § 13.4. If A's executor does not pursue Blackacre, A's creditors can presumably pursue Blackacre under the rules relating to fraudulent transfers, if A's probate estate cannot satisfy the debts.

269. **Answer (D) is correct.** A's residuary clause "blends" Blackacre into A's probate estate and the blended property is abated ratably with other residuary assets to pay O's debts. Restatement (Second) Donative Transfers §§ 13.4, 22.1.

      Answers (A), (B), and (C) are incorrect. Blackacre is subject to the probate claims procedures.

270. **Answer (D) is correct.** It is generally accepted that, during the settlor's lifetime, the settlor's creditors may reach the maximum amount that can be distributed to, or for the benefit of, the settlor even if the initial creation and funding of the trust were not fraudulent transfers. Restatement (Second) Donative Trusts § 13.3; Restatement (Third) Trusts § 60. The Uniform Trust Code has codified these principles. *See* UTC § 505(a)(2).

Answers (A), (B), and (C) are incorrect. A settlor who is also a beneficiary cannot use a trust as a shield against the settlor's creditors.

271. Whether or not the terms of the trust contain a "spendthrift provision," the entire trust estate, under modern practice, may to be available to A's creditors if: (i) someone other than A created the trust and granted a presently exercisable general power of appointment or (ii) A is the settlor/beneficiary of the express trust. UTC § 505 supports this conclusion. Even if A is not the settlor, A's discretionary power to appoint to himself (even if limited by an ascertainable standard) allows the creditors to reach the maximum amount available to A. This result is "unaffected by a purported spendthrift restraint." See comment g, Restatement (Third) Trusts § 60. *The result may differ in a state that has not adopted the Restatement approach if someone other than A was the settlor.*

272. **Answer (D) is correct.** Any property over which the decedent possessed a general power of appointment (i.e., the authority to appoint to the donee, the donee's estate, the donee's creditors, or the creditors of the donee's estate), either immediately prior to or at the time of death, is included in the decedent's gross estate even if the decedent does not exercise the power. IRC § 2041. A only had a non-general power over Blackacre so it is not included in A's gross estate. However, A did possess a general testamentary power over the trust estate.

      Answers (A), (B), and (C) are incorrect. A did not have the power to appoint Blackacre to his estate or creditors, so Blackacre is not included in A's gross estate. Because A had the power to appoint the trust estate to A's probate estate, the power is a general power, and the trust estate is included in A's gross estate.

273. **Answer (D) is correct.** Any property over which the decedent possessed a general power of appointment (i.e., the authority to appoint to the donee, the donee's estate, the donee's creditors, or the creditors of the donee's estate), either immediately prior to or at the time of death, is included in the decedent's gross estate even if the decedent does not exercise the power. IRC § 2041. A only had a non-general power over Blackacre so it is not included in A's gross estate. However, A did possess a general testamentary power over the trust estate.

      Answers (A), (B), and (C) are incorrect. A did not have the power to appoint Blackacre to his estate or creditors, so Blackacre is not included in A's gross estate. Because A had the power to appoint the trust estate to A's probate estate, the power is a general power, and the trust estate is included in A's gross estate.

274. The trust estate, but not Blackacre, will be included in A's gross estate. Any property over which the decedent possessed a general power of appointment (i.e., the ability to appoint to the donee, the donee's estate, the donee's creditors, or the creditors of the donee's estate), either immediately prior to or at the time of death, is included in the decedent's gross estate. IRC § 2041. Because A did not have the power to appoint Blackacre to his estate or creditors, A only had a non-general power. Thus, Blackacre is not included in A's gross estate. However, A did possess a general testamentary power over the trust estate because A could have appointed it to A's probate estate.

275. **Answer (D) is correct.** If a decedent had the power immediately prior to the decedent's death to appoint the property to the decedent, the power was a general power, and the value of the appointive property is included in the decedent's gross estate unless the power was limited by an "ascertainable" standard. IRC § 2041(b)(1)(A). A's power over trust one was limited by an ascertainable standard, and the trust estate is excluded; but A's power over trust two

was not limited by an ascertainable standard. The value of trust two is included in A's gross estate. Treas. Reg. § 20.2041-1(c)(2).

Answers (A), (B), and (C) are incorrect. An "ascertainable" standard is one that limits distributions for the purposes of the "health, education, maintenance, or support" of the donee. A standard defined by the words "comfort or welfare" is not "ascertainable" and is likely to cause inclusion of trust two in A's gross estate.

276.   **Answer (B) is correct.** A's interests in both trusts terminated at A's death, and A did not possess any power (directly or indirectly) over either trust estate. The federal estate tax is an excise tax on a decedent's privilege to transfer property at death. IRC § 2033.

      Answers (A), (C), and (D) are incorrect. Because A was not the settlor, did not possess a power of appointment, and did not have the right to transfer any part of the trust estates when A died, neither trust estate is included in A's gross estate under IRC § 2033.

277.   All probate assets, whether real, personal, tangible or intangible, are included in the decedent's gross estate. Accordingly, the fair market value of any property of O passing by will or intestate succession by reason of O's death is included. IRC § 2033. The fact that a spouse may have a right to an elective share does not affect the makeup of the decedent's gross estate. See IRC § 2034. The fact that they were devised to S does not affect the makeup of the gross estate, but the net value of the assets devised to S will qualify for the marital deduction and be deducted from the value of the gross estate to determine the value of the taxable estate. IRC § 2056. *If any of the described assets were community property according to the law of X, only the decedent's half interest would generally be included in O's gross estate.*

278.   **Answer (A) is correct.** The gross estate includes the value of all property transferred by the decedent during life if the decedent retained for life the possession or enjoyment of, or the right to receive the income from, the property transferred. IRC § 2036.

      Answers (B), (C), and (D) are incorrect. IRC § 2036 causes inclusion. It does not matter whether O's retained interest is a life estate or a fee simple interest subject to an executory limitation.

279.   **Answer (A) is correct.** Nonprobate assets are also included in the decedent's gross estate. IRC §§ 2036, 2038, 2040.

      Answers (B) and (C) are incorrect. One cannot avoid inclusion in the gross estate by making this type of nonprobate disposition of the property.

      Answer (D) is incorrect. Even though the checking account is in the names of both O and A, 100% of the account is included in O's gross estate because O created and funded the account. IRC § 2040.

280. **Answer (A) is correct.** An insurance policy on the decedent's life is included in the decedent's gross estate if (i) the policy is payable to the decedent's probate estate or (ii) the decedent owned the policy immediately prior to death. IRC § 2040.

   Answers (B), (C), and (D) are incorrect. O owned both policies at the time of death. Accordingly, the proceeds of each are included in the gross estate.

281. O did not own either policy at the time of death, and neither policy was payable to O's estate. Accordingly, neither policy is included in the gross estate under IRC § 2042. However, the whole life policy is included in the gross estate under IRC § 2035, because O transferred the policy to A within three years of O's death. The proceeds of the term policy are excluded from the gross estate, but the value of the policy on the date of the assignment (in excess of any available annual exclusion for gift tax purposes) will be added to O's taxable estate to determine the tax base. IRC § 2001.

282. **Answer (B) is correct.** Because O did not own the stock at the time of death, the stock is not included in the gross estate. The estate tax is an excise tax on the transfer of property at death. IRC § 2033.

   Answers (A), (C), and (D) are incorrect. O did not own the stock at the time of death. However, the value of the stock on the dates of the gifts (in excess of any available annual exclusion for gift tax purposes) will be added to O's taxable estate to determine the tax base. IRC § 2001.

283. Notwithstanding claims to the contrary by some who promote the use of the revocable trust, rather than a will, as the key document in an estate plan, the creation and funding of a revocable trust are not taxable events. The remainder interests given to A and B are not taxable gifts because of the power of revocation. IRC § 2511. All items of income, deductions, and credits will be reported on O's income tax return during O's lifetime. IRC § 676. At O's death, the value of the trust estate is included in O's gross estate. IRC § 2038.

284. **Answer (A) is correct.** The two plans add $1,500,000 to O's gross estate even though A and B will have to report the $1,500,000 on their income tax returns when received. IRC § 2039.

   Answers (B), (C), and (D) are incorrect. Both plans are included in the gross estate. A and B will be entitled to an income tax deduction for any estate taxes attributable to the plans. IRC § 691.

285. **Answer (A) is correct.** The amount of any debt legally owed by O and payable out of assets included in O's gross estate is properly deducted from the gross estate to determine the taxable estate. IRC § 2053.

   Answers (B), (C), and (D) are incorrect. It does not matter whether the debts are secured or unsecured. However, if O is not personally liable for a secured debt, the debt is subtracted from the fair market value of the asset securing the debt to determine the amount to include in the gross estate. Treas. Reg. § 20.2053-1(a)(1)(iv).

286. **Answer (A) is correct.** In addition to the debts owning by O prior to O's death, expenses of last illness, funeral expenses, and administration expenses are also deductible. IRC § 2053. Administration expenses can be deducted on either the decedent's estate tax return or the fiduciary income tax return, but not both. Treas. Reg. §§ 1.642(g)-1 and 20.2053-1(a).

Answers (B), (C), and (D) are incorrect. The amounts actually paid for these types of expenses are generally deductible.

287. **Answer (C) is correct.** While the amount devised to O's children is not deductible, the devise to S qualifies for the "marital deduction," and the devise to the charity qualifies for the "charitable deduction." IRC §§ 2055, 2056.

Answers (A), (B), and (D) are incorrect. Congress, for public policy reasons, encourages testamentary gifts to decedents' spouses and to qualified charities.

288. **Answer (B) is correct.** The $1,000,000 devised to the first described trust would not qualify for the marital deduction because S was given a "non-deductible terminable" interest in the trust. IRC § 2056(b)(1). The second trust appears to meet the requirements of a "qualified terminable interest property" trust in that S is entitled to all of the trust's income for the remainder of her lifetime. IRC § 2056(b)(7).

Answer (A) is incorrect. However, if the second trust does not meet the requirements of a "QTIP" trust, or if O's executor does not make the "QTIP election," this answer would be correct.

Answer (C) is incorrect. The first trust does not qualify for the marital deduction.

Answer (D) is incorrect. In any event, whatever amount passes to the charity qualifies for the charitable deduction, assuming the devise to the charity meets the requirements of IRC § 2055.

289. The trust estate of the first trust will not be included in S's gross estate when she dies. At her death, her life estate simply terminates, and the children's remainder interest becomes possessory. IRC § 2033. Whether the trust estate of the second trust will be included in S's gross estate depends on two factors. First, did the trust meet the requirements of a "QTIP trust"? Second, did O's executor make the "QTIP election?" IRC § 2056(b)(7). If the answer is yes to both questions, the trust estate of the second trust is included in S's gross estate. IRC § 2044. Any estate taxes attributable to the inclusion of the trust estate in S's taxable estate are apportioned to O's children, A and B, as remainder beneficiaries of the trust. UPC § 3-916. *Absent a state statute like UPC § 3-916, the burden of the estate tax may fall on the decedent's residuary estate.*

290. **Answer (D) is correct.** Assuming the trust qualifies as a "QTIP Trust" and O's executor elected to treat it as a "QTIP Trust," the fair market value of the trust at S's death is included in S's gross estate. IRC § 2044.

Answer (A) is incorrect. If the trust does not qualify as a "QTIP trust" or if the executor did not elect to treat it as a "QTIP Trust," no part of the trust estate (other than any income accrued, but not paid, at date of death) would be included in S's gross estate.

Answers (B) and (C) are incorrect. The fair market value of the trust estate on S's date of death is included in the gross estate, if the trust is a "QTIP trust." IRC § 2044.

PRACTICE FINAL EXAM: ANSWERS

291. **Answer (B) is correct.** A creditor of a decedent has the option to pursue its claim in any jurisdiction where a property of the decedent is located. *See* Casner § 14.45; Restatement (Second) Conflict of Laws § 260, 263. However, once the debt has been satisfied in one jurisdiction, it cannot be collected in other jurisdictions.

Answers (A) and (C) are incorrect for the reasons given.

Answer (D) is incorrect. While a creditor of a decedent has the option to pursue its claim in any jurisdiction where a property of the decedent is located, the creditor will not likely pursue the claim in a federal court. Despite the apparent "complete diversity of citizenship" among the parties, federal courts typically decline to accept jurisdiction over proceedings that interfere with state probate proceedings. See *Markham v. Allen*, 326 U.S. 490, 494 (1946).

292. **Answer (D) is correct.** The value of H's inter vivos transfer to P in excess of $10,000 is included in the value of the augmented estate. UPC § 2-205(3)(iii). According to UPC § 2-210, P is liable to W for the amount of W's elective share amount.

Answer (A) is incorrect. UPC §§ 2-209 and 2-210 provide that the recipient of a nonprobate transfer described in UPC § 2-205(3) (iii) is liable to surviving spouse for the recipient's pro-rata share of the amount of the elective share. *If X is a non-community property state that has neither adopted the augmented estate concept followed in the Uniform Probate Code nor an elective system, Answer (A) would be correct. Answer (A) could also be the correct answer in a community property state if W did not seek to have all or part of the transfer avoided or to impose a constructive trust on W's half that had been assigned to P by H in order to prevent unjust enrichment by P. See* McGovern, *§3.8.*

Answers (B) and (C) are incorrect. C, as an heir of H, would be entitled to an intestate share of H's probate estate, but there is no probate estate.

293. **Answer (B) is correct.** If C3's paternity was established either prior to O's death or subsequent to O's death, G, as C3's child, would succeed to an interest in O's probate estate "by representation," if O dies intestate. UPC §§ 2-106, 2-114(a). *The result is likely to be the same in a non-UPC state.*

197

Answer (A) is incorrect. SP, in her individual capacity, is not an heir and does not have standing to contest the probate of the will. However, SP, acting in a fiduciary capacity on behalf of G, would have standing to contest the will, if C3's paternity is established.

Answer (C) is incorrect. Statutes typically allow paternity to be established before or after the death of the biological father or child.

Answer (D) is incorrect. The concept of representation gives G standing.

294. **Answer (C) is correct.** When a devisee disclaims, the property disclaimed passes as if the disclaimant had predeceased the testator. UPC § 2-1106(b). The "antilapse" provisions of UPC § 2-603 then provides for a "substitute gift" in favor of the disclaimant's descendants. *The same result is likely to occur in a state that has not enacted the Uniform Probate Code.*

Answers (A) and (B) are incorrect. A disclaimer is not an assignment. The property passes from O to GG.

Answer (D) is incorrect. There is a "substituted gift" to GG.

295. **Answer (D) is correct.** At A's death, A's life estate terminated, and B's remainder interest became fee simple title. Blackacre was not part of A's probate estate and could not be devised by A to C. However, the doctrine of "equitable election" is applicable, and if B wishes to share in A's residuary estate, A will have to convey Blackacre to C. *See* Atkinson § 138.

Answer (A) is incorrect. The will triggers the doctrine of equitable election.

Answers (B) and (C) are incorrect. A did not have testamentary power over Blackacre. At A's death, Blackacre is B's property.

296. **Answer (C) is correct.** UPC § 2-502 (a) (3) requires that the witnesses sign the will after the testator signed the will. However, the prevailing view is to uphold the execution of the will if the testator and the witnesses all signed as part of a single continuous transaction. McGovern § 4.3. Further, UPC § 2-503's harmless error rule allows the court to admit a will to probate that was not executed with the requisite formalities if the proponent can establish by clear and convincing evidence that the testator intended the document to be a will. *States that have not enacted the Uniform Probate Code may have a "substantial compliance" rule.*

Answers (A) and (B) are incorrect. Even though O did not strictly comply with UPC § 2-502, the will may be admitted to probate.

Answer (D) is incorrect. The Uniform Probate Code allows a probate court to excuse a "harmless error" in the execution of a will under certain circumstances. *In a state that has not enacted the Uniform Probate Code, or a statute similar to UPC § 2-503, research may indicate that the courts have relaxed that doctrine of "strict compliance" in favor of a doc-*

trine of "substantial compliance." Some courts have created specific exceptions that might apply in the situation (e.g. the signing of the will by the witnesses and the testator was one "continuous transaction").

297. **Answer (A) is correct.** It appears that the 1990 will was revoked by the execution of the 2000 will, but the 2000 will was not revoked because the nurse was not in O's presence when the 2000 will was destroyed. UPC § 2-507. While the will was destroyed at O's direction, it was not destroyed in O's "presence," so the estate is likely to pass to B. Atkinson § 86. Most courts have ruled that a will is not revoked under these circumstances because a will must be revoked in the prescribed statutory manner. *The result may be different in a state that has extended its "harmless error" rules to revocations by physical acts.*

    Answers (B) and (C) are incorrect. A constructive trust is not an appropriate remedy. O simply failed to comply with the prescribed statutory requirements of revoking a will.

    Answer (D) is incorrect. The testator failed to comply with UPC § 2-507. However, a few cases have held that a will was revoked due to the testator's subsequent ratification of intent after the will's destruction by the agent. Atkinson § 86. *See* Restatement (Third) Property (Wills and Other Donative Transfers) § 4.1.

298. **Answer (A) is correct.** Although a grandchild generally takes by representation if a decedent dies intestate and the grandchild's parent who was the child of the intestate dies before the intestate, the Uniform Probate Code limits the protection afforded by the "omitted children" provisions of UPC § 2-302 to omitted children and not to the issue of an omitted child who died before the intestate. Because O's will devised all of O's estate to their surviving parent, C1 and C2 will not receive an interest in O's probate estate even though they were omitted from the will. UPC § 2-302 (a) (1). The births of C1, C2, and C3 did not revoke the will. UPC § 2-508. *In almost every state that has not enacted the Uniform Probate Code, statutes grant "omitted" or "pretermitted" children limited protection from accidental disinheritance, and in some states, children of deceased children are afforded rights in their grandparent's estate under some circumstances; the details vary from state to state.* McGovern § 3.5.

    Answers (B) and (C) are incorrect. The birth of the children after the execution of the will did not revoke the will.

    Answer (D) is incorrect. C3 died before O, neither C3's heirs nor G3 is entitled to an interest in O's estate.

299. **Answer (A) is correct.** UPC § 2-607 provides that a specific devise passes subject to the mortgage, and UPC § 3-902 directs that the unsecured debt should be paid out of the residuary devise. *In those states that have not enacted the Uniform Probate Code, or a statute similar to UPC § 2-607, the common law rule of exoneration creates a presumption that O intended S to inherit the home, free of indebtedness.* McGovern § 8.2.

Answers (B) and (C) are incorrect. The Uniform Probate Code creates a presumption of "non-exoneration." Jurisdictions that still follow the common law rule of "exoneration of liens" grant S the right to receive the home free of debt.

Answer (D) is incorrect. In some jurisdictions the secured creditor can elect either to have the debt paid in due course of administration or pursuant to the terms of the creditor's contract with the decedent. This decision should not affect whether S or D bears the burden of the debt.

300. **Answer (C) is correct.** Had it not been for the disclaimer, S would have inherited from C the interest of C in O's probate estate. The disclaimer had the legal effect of transferring the interest C would have inherited from O to G. UPC § 2-801(d). If C had filed the disclaimer, S would appear to be without an effective remedy. However, if C's executor filed the disclaimer, S may have a breach of fiduciary duty claim against the executor. As the executor of C's estate, the fiduciary duties are generally owing to the beneficiary of C's estate, S. McGovern § 2.8.

Answer (A) is incorrect. The value of C's augmented estate for elective share computation purposes does not appear to include a disclaimed interest in another person's estate. *See* UPC § 2-205 and commentary that follows. *However, a particular state's law may bar or limit the right to disclaim if the surviving spouse did not inherit from the deceased spouse an amount equal to the elective share considering the value of the disclaimed property.*

Answer (B) is incorrect. If C filed the disclaimer prior to C's death, C had the right to do so.

Answer (D) is incorrect for the reasons given.

301. **Answer (C) is correct.** O and F had agreed that, if O devised Blackacre to F, F would hold it for G. Even though the document does not meet the technical requirements of a will, but assuming the proponents of the will can otherwise prove by clear and convincing evidence that O intended the document to be O's will, the document may still be admitted to probate. UPC § 2-503. However, because the will makes no reference to the intended trust, an express trust was not created in the will. Restatement (Third) Trusts § 17. If F does not volunteer to perform as agreed, the court will admit evidence of the oral agreement in order to impose a constructive trust on F to prevent F from being unjustly enriched. F will ordinarily be ordered to transfer the property to another who will carry out the intended purposes of the oral agreement. Restatement (Third) Trusts § 18.

Answer (A) is incorrect. However, if the will cannot be established pursuant to UPC § 2-503, O died intestate, and O's probate estate passes by intestate succession to C.

Answer (B) is incorrect. If the will is not admitted to probate, C inherits the property. G may argue for the imposition of a constructive trust on C to avoid C's unjust enrichment, but would probably fail in this effort in most jurisdictions.

Answer (D) is incorrect. In any event, F will not acquire or retain Blackacre.

302. **Answer (D) is correct.** A creditor of the settlor may reach the maximum amount that can be distributed by the trustee to or for the benefit of the settlor. The Uniform Trust Code has codified this generally accepted common law principle. *See* UTC § 505(a)(2) and comments.

Answers (A), (B), and (C) are incorrect. Because O retained an interest in the trust that allows T to distribute all or any part of the principal, the entire principal is available to the settlor's creditors.

303. **Answer (D) is correct.** The assignment of the legal title by the trustee to the beneficiaries would appear to merge the legal and equitable titles in C and G as the owners of the trust estate, causing the trust to go out of existence. No one else would appear to have standing to question the transaction. O did not expressly retain an interest in, or power over, the trust estate; C owns the equitable life estate; and G appears to own the vested remainder interest. McGovern § 9.6. However, in a state that has adopted the approach of UPC § 2-707, G's interest is a contingent reminder. If G would predecease C, a substitute gift is created in G's descendants, if any. G's descendants may have a cause of action for breach of fiduciary duty against T, if G does not survive C. If G does not have any descendants, the trust estate would revert to O or O's heirs. Does UPC § 2-707 give standing to O to object to the transaction?

Answers (A), (B), and (C) are incorrect for the reasons given.

304. At common law, the grandchildren's executory interest would be invalid because it violated the "rule against perpetuities." Even though G1 and G2 were alive when O died, there existed the possibility that the class of beneficiaries would include children of A born after O's death whose interests would not vest until after the period of the "Rule." However, the Uniform Probate Code has modified the common law rule. *See* UPC § 2-901. Accordingly, despite the uncertainty of whether the interests will vest within 21 years of the death of someone alive when O died, the interest will vest or terminate within 90 years of O's death. *Some states that have not adopted the Uniform Probate Code approach have modified the common law rule against perpetuities in other ways that may validate the grandchildren's executory interest.*

305. At common law, the grandchildren's remainder interest violates the rule against perpetuities, because, even at age 85, A is presumed to be capable of having more children whose lifetimes could extend beyond the perpetuities period. Because children of these afterborn children may be members of the class of remainder beneficiaries, under the "all or nothing" rule, if the interest of any member of the class violates the rule, the gift to the entire class

is void. However, under UPC § 2-901(a)(2), it is likely the survivor of A's children will die within 90 years of O's death so that the interests of all of the grandchildren are valid. Although the terms of the trust do not require it, UPC § 2-707 requires that the grandchildren survive A. If not, a substituted gift is created in their children. If not, the remainder interest can be reformed under UPC § 2-903. *Some states that have not adopted the Uniform Probate Code have modified the common law in other ways that may validate the grandchildren's remainder interest.*

306. The commentary to Restatement, Third, Trusts § 56 takes the position that trust property subject to a presently exercisable general power is treated as the property of the donee and subject to the claims of the donee's creditors. On the other hand, creditors of the donee of a nongeneral power cannot reach the appointive property. Here, A's power to appoint to himself is limited by an ascertainable standard, and A can only appoint to himself pursuant to a prescribed standard. Notwithstanding A's power being limited by the standard, the Restatement takes the position that the creditor can reach the maximum amount A can properly distribute to himself. *See* comment c. Restatement (Third) Trusts § 60. The Uniform Trust Code appears to have adopted the view that the described trust is a discretionary trust, even though A's general power is limited to an ascertainable standing the same. *See* UTC § 504(b)-(d). *The result may differ in a state that has not adopted the UTC approach.*

307. **Answer (D) is correct.** Any property over which the decedent possessed a general power of appointment (i.e., the authority to appoint to the donee, the donee's estate, the donee's creditors, or the creditors of the donee's estate), either immediately prior to or at the time of death, is included in the decedent's gross estate. IRC § 2041. A only had a non-general power over Blackacre so it is not included in A's gross estate. However, A did possess a general testamentary power over the trust estate. The value of the trust estate is included in A's gross estate, but is also deducted from the gross estate to determine the value of the taxable estate due to the marital deduction.

    Answers (A), (B), and (C) are incorrect. A did not have the power to appoint Blackacre to his estate or creditors, so Blackacre is not included in A's gross estate. Because A had the power to appoint the trust estate to A's probate estate, the power is a general power, and the trust estate is included in A's gross estate.

308. The law varies from state to state. However, the lawyer representing E may in some circumstances be liable to G, the only beneficiary of the estate, for failure to use care to protect G's interests. The lawyer's duty to G arises from the fact that E has fiduciary obligations to G. Certainly, if the lawyer knowingly assists E in violating E's fiduciary duties to G, or represents both E and G, the lawyer is liable to G for a breach of the lawyer's duties. However, the lawyer who represents only E and makes it clear to G that the lawyer does not represent G minimizes exposure to liability. In this situation, the lawyer's duty to E should arise in most situations only when the lawyer knows that appropriate action by the lawyer

is necessary to prevent or mitigate a breach of E's duty to G. Restatement (Third) of The Law Governing Lawyers § 51. (Restatement (Third) The Law Governing Lawyers § _____).

309. The law varies from state to state. At common law, a lawyer owed a duty of care only to the client and not to a third party who may have been damaged by the lawyer's negligent misrepresentation of the client. In other words, the "privity barrier" insulated the lawyer from liability to the third party. However, a majority of jurisdictions have relaxed the "privity banner" in the estate planning context. Other states retain the "privity barrier." Restatement (Third) The Law Governing Lawyers § 51. See *Barcelo v. Elliott*, 923 S.W.2d 575 (Tex. 1996).

INDEX

INDEX